The Forces

Between Molecules

Maurice Rigby

Department of Chemistry, King's College, London

E. Brian Smith

Physical Chemistry Laboratory, South Parks Road, Oxford.

William A. Wakeham

Department of Chemical Engineering and Chemical Technology, Imperial College, London.

Geoffrey C. Maitland

Schlumberger Cambridge Research, Cambridge.

CLARENDON PRESS · OXFORD
1986

Oxford University Press, Walton Street, Oxford OX2 6DP

Oxford New York Toronto
Delhi Bombay Calcutta Madras Karachi
Petaling Jaya Singapore Hong Kong Tokyo
Nairobi Dar es Salaam Cape Town
Melbourne Auckland

and associated companies in
Beirut Berlin Ibadan Nicosia

Oxford is a trade mark for Oxford University Press

Published in the United States
by Oxford University Press, New York

British Library Cataloguing in Publication Data
The Forces between Molecules
1. Intermolecular forces
I. Rigby, Maurice
541.2'26 QD461
ISBN 0–19–855207–6
ISBN 0–19–855206–8 Pbk

Library of Congress Cataloging in Publication Data
The Forces between Molecules
Bibliography: p.
Includes index.
1. Intermolecular forces I. Rigby, Maurice
QD461.167 1986 541.2'26 86–5190
ISBN 0–19–855207–6
ISBN 0–19–855206–8 (pbk.)

Set by Macmillan India Ltd.
Printed in Great Britain by
St Edmundsbury Press,
Bury St Edmunds,
Suffolk

Preface

A knowledge of the forces between molecules is fundamental to an understanding of the structure and properties of physical and biological materials. Although there are a number of elementary books concerned with the properties of gases, liquids, and solids, these rarely give more than superficial attention to a consideration of molecular interactions. This book aims to fill this gap in the literature by providing an account of the nature of intermolecular forces at an introductory level, suitable for final year undergraduates or beginning graduate students in a wide range of disciplines. With this in mind, we have sought to give a broad and balanced view of the subject with particular emphasis on physical insight. We have excluded much of the mathematical detail which for many has proved a barrier to understanding the subject at this level. This approach is particularly appropriate in view of the availability of the recent advanced treatise by the same authors, *Intermolecular forces—their origin and determination*, (referred to hereafter as **MRSW**). The present book is designed to complement this monograph and we have taken the opportunity to direct readers to specific sections of **MRSW** where more information may be required.

In recent years, considerable advances have taken place in the field of intermolecular forces and it is now possible to give a definitive account of the interactions between many of the simplest molecules. At the same time the routes to understanding more complex systems have become clearer. In view of these developments, it is now possible to give a coherent account of the subject suitable for those approaching it for the first time. At this level, a far wider range of systems may be described than have been dealt with in more advanced texts, including **MRSW**. Whilst the recent rapid advances for simple molecules are given due attention here, we also describe the current state of knowledge for interactions involving polar systems, ions, large polyatomic molecules, synthetic and biological polymers, surfaces, and colloidal systems. Although the intention is to provide physical understanding rather than quantitative detail, many readers requiring information on specific systems may well find this book to be an adequate source.

The first part of the book is concerned with methods for characterizing molecular interactions. Particular emphasis has been placed on the newer methods which have led to such rapid recent progress in our knowledge of intermolecular forces involving spectroscopic and molecular beam scattering techniques. Each chapter is followed by a number of problems which readers may use to test their understanding of the material presented. The remainder of the book is concerned with our current knowledge of intermolecular forces for a number of representative systems of increasing complexity. Here we give both the essential features of these interactions and selected references to guide the interested reader to the current literature.

We are grateful to our colleagues, families, and friends who have given us encouragement and support during the preparation of the book. Several people read the manuscript in detail and we are particularly grateful to Professors David Buckingham, John Murrell, and John Rowlinson for their many useful comments. We also thank Miranda Lubbock for her sterling efforts in typing the bulk of the manuscript. Any errors or omissions are entirely the responsibility of the authors; we should be pleased to hear of any which have escaped our attention.

January 1986

M.R.
E.B.S.
W.A.W.
G.C.M.

Acknowledgements for figures

We are grateful to the publishers and authors for permission to reproduce the following figures: The Royal Society of Chemistry (Figs 8.3 and 8.4 (1982)); Taylor and Francis Ltd. (Fig 8.5 (1984)); Macmillan Journals Ltd. (Fig. 8.14 (1982)). A number of figures from other sources have been reprinted from *Intermolecular forces—their origin and determination*, by G. C. Maitland, M. Rigby, E. B. Smith, and W. A. Wakeham (Clarendon Press, Oxford, 1981). These are: Figs 2.2, 2.16–2.18, 3.4–3.12, 4.7, and 8.1. Full journal references are given in the figure captions.

Contents

1 The nature of intermolecular forces

1.1.	Introduction	1
1.2.	Electrostatic energy	4
1.3.	Induction energy	8
1.4.	Dispersion energy	10
1.5.	Long-range energy: summary	11
1.6.	Short-range energies	12
1.7.	The hydrogen bond	16
1.8.	Representation of intermolecular interactions	17
	Monatomic systems	19
	Polyatomic systems	21
	Unlike interactions	25
1.9.	Non-pairwise additivity	25
1.10.	Experimental sources of information	28
	Gas imperfection	28
	Gas transport properties	28
	Molecular beams	29
	Spectra of van der Waals molecules	29
	Solid and liquid properties	29
	Appendix 1A. Electrostatic interaction energy	30
	Appendix 1B. The dispersion energy according to the Drude model	32
	Suggested further reading	34
	Exercises	34

2 Molecular beams

2.1.	Introduction	36
2.2.	Molecular beam experiments	37
2.3.	The scattering of atoms	41
	The classical mechanical theory of binary collisions	41
	Scattering cross-sections	45
	The behaviour of the classical cross-sections	47
	The quantum-mechanical theory	48

2.4. The use of molecular beam scattering data for the
      determination of intermolecular pair potentials   53
2.5. The scattering of polyatomic molecules   54
Suggested further reading   60
Exercises   60

3   Spectroscopic measurements

3.1. van der Waals molecules   62
3.2. Experimental studies   64
      Non-polar molecules   64
      Polar molecules   65
3.3. The interpretation of the spectra of van der Waals dimers 66
3.4. Experimental results for the inert gases   70
3.5. The interpretation of spectra for non-spherical systems 72
      Weakly anisotropic systems   76
      Strongly anisotropic systems   78
Suggested further reading   80
Exercises   80

4   Gas imperfection

4.1. Introduction   81
4.2. Joule–Thomson effect   82
4.3. van der Waals equation of state   84
4.4. The virial equation of state   86
4.5. Intermolecular forces and virial coefficients   87
4.6. The determination of intermolecular forces from second virial
      coefficients   93
4.7. Principle of corresponding states   96
4.8. Mixtures   100
4.9. Experimental methods   101
4.10. Conclusions   103
Appendix 4A. Intermolecular forces and virial coefficients   103
Suggested further reading   106
Exercises   106

5   The transport properties of gases

5.1. Introduction   107
5.2. Viscosity   110
5.3. Thermal conductivity   112
5.4. Diffusion   113
5.5. Application to real gases   114
5.6. Polyatomic gases   118
5.7. Transport properties and intermolecular forces   119

5.8.   Experimental measurements   121
    Viscosity   121
    Thermal conductivity   124
    Binary diffusion coefficient   124
    Thermal diffusion factor   125
Suggested further reading   125
Exercises   125

6   The solid state

6.1.   Introduction   127
6.2.   Experimental measurements   129
6.3.   Theory: static lattice properties   130
6.4.   Lattice vibrations   132
6.5.   Molecular interactions from solid state data   137
Suggested further reading   140
Exercises   140

7   The liquid state

7.1.   Introduction   141
7.2.   Liquid structure   142
7.3.   Computer simulation   147
7.4.   Perturbation theories   150
7.5.   Molecular liquids   154
7.6.   Liquid crystals   156
7.7.   Mixtures and solutions   157
    Liquid mixtures of non-electrolytes   158
    Solutions of solids in non-aqueous liquids   160
    Electrolyte solutions   161
    Aqueous solutions of non-electrolytes   162
Suggested further reading   163
Exercises   163

8   Potential functions—the state of the art

8.1.   The development of intermolecular potentials   165
8.2.   The basis of recent advances   165
8.3.   Potential functions for monatomic systems   168
    The inert gases   168
    Open-shell atoms   170
    Group II closed-shell atoms   172
    Ion–atom interactions   172
8.4.   Potential functions for simple polyatomic systems 172
    Review   172
    H_2–He and H_2–H_2 173
    H_2–inert gas systems   174

	Atom–linear molecule systems	177
	Diatomic molecules	177
	Polar molecules	179
	Water	181
	Ionic systems	184
	Benzene	185
	Potentials for atomic and molecular systems	185
8.5.	Potential energy functions for large polyatomic molecules	185
	Site–site point charge models	186
	Applications of site–site functions	189
	Potential functions based on convex cores	190
8.6.	Interactions in the liquid phase	192
	General solvent effects	192
	The hydrogen bond and related interactions	193
	Liquid crystals	195
8.7.	Interactions involving solid surfaces	197
	Molecule–surface (gas–solid) interactions	198
	Surface–surface interactions	201
	The hydrophobic interaction	207
	Hydration forces	208
8.8.	Summary	209
	Suggested further reading	209
	Appendix 8A. References to potential functions for selected systems	211
Appendix 1.	Characteristic properties of some simple substances	215
Appendix 2.	Molecular parameters	216
Appendix 3.	Corresponding states correlation of thermophysical properties	217
Appendix 4.	Collision integrals and second virial coefficients for a realistic potential	219
Appendix 5.	Inversion functions for gas phase properties	221
	Answers to exercises	225
	Index	227

1
The nature of intermolecular forces

1.1. Introduction

For as long as the idea of atoms and molecules has existed man has speculated as to the nature of the forces between them. The Greek and Roman atomist philosophers saw the forces in concrete terms and regarded strongly interacting molecules as 'hooked and intertangled'. In the nineteenth century our present ideas of the molecular structure of matter began to emerge, and it became apparent that the interactions between molecules played a major part in determining the properties of matter. The derivation of the perfect gas equation of state, using a model of non-interacting point molecules, suggested strongly that the existence of solids, liquids, and imperfect gases implied the occurrence of forces between molecules. However, it was not until the late nineteenth century that the modern view of these forces, that molecules repel each other at short range and attract at long range, became established, though it was clearly stated by Clausius in 1857. This concept, and the systematic study by Andrews of carbon dioxide near to its critical point, enabled van der Waals in 1873 to develop his important equation of state, in which molecules were assumed to be hard spheres which attracted each other at long range. The van der Waals equation,

$$\left(P + \frac{a}{\bar{V}^2}\right)(\bar{V} - b) = RT \tag{1.1}$$

contains a parameter, a, which reflects the strength of molecular attraction, and b, a parameter proportional to the volume of the molecules. R is the gas constant, P the pressure and $\bar{V}$ the molar volume of the fluid. Although approximate, the van der Waals equation shows qualitatively the chief features of imperfect gas behaviour, and illuminates the factors which determine the position of the gas–liquid critical point, and define the range of existence of liquids.

In the early part of the twentieth century there was much speculation concerning the origin and form of intermolecular interactions, but it was not until after the establishment of the principles of quantum mechanics that a

1

satisfactory understanding of the nature of intermolecular forces could be developed in 1930. A further 40 years was then to elapse before a precise description of the forces between even the simplest molecules, the inert gases, was achieved.

Although it is customary to speak of intermolecular forces, it proves generally to be more convenient to express the interaction of two molecules in terms of the intermolecular potential energy, $U(r)$, which results from their interaction at a separation r. Since the interactions are short-ranged, it is convenient to take as the zero of U the value corresponding to infinite separation of the molecules. The intermolecular force, $F(r)$, is related to the energy through the expression

$$F(r) = -\frac{dU(r)}{dr} \qquad (1.2)$$

Equivalently the intermolecular energy, $U(r)$, is equal to the work done in bringing the molecules together from infinite separation to a separation r.

$$U(r) = \int_r^\infty F(r)\,dr$$

In general, the intermolecular energy and force will depend on the relative orientations of the molecules, as well as their separation, but for spherical molecules it depends only on r. The general form of the intermolecular potential energy function for such molecules is shown in Fig. 1.1. It often proves convenient to characterize some of the principal features of the potential function in terms of a small number of parameters. These are usually the collision diameter, σ, the separation at which $U(r) = 0$, and the separation, r_m, at which the energy has a minimum value, $-\varepsilon$. On relating the form of $U(r)$ to eqn (1.2), we see that the intermolecular force is attractive ($F(r)$ is negative) when r has values greater than r_m, and is repulsive for $r < r_m$. We note that for $\sigma < r < r_m$, the intermolecular force is repulsive, but the energy is negative, and the common practice of regarding all negative intermolecular energies as attractive is imprecise.

As we have indicated above, for non-spherical molecules the intermolecular energy may depend on the relative orientation of the molecules and may also be affected by their internal states. This evidently makes the representation and characterization of these interactions a much more difficult problem. Further complications arise when groups of three of more molecules must be considered, as in liquids, solids or compressed gases. To a first approximation, the total intermolecular energy of a group of more than two molecules may be calculated by summing the energies for all the pairs of molecules in the group. However, more precise studies show that the interaction of any two molecules may be perturbed by the presence of neighbouring molecules so that the total

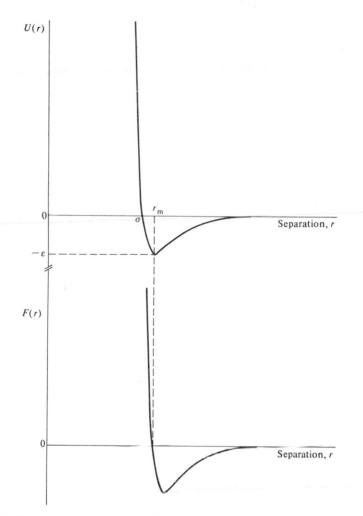

Fig. 1.1 The intermolecular potential energy function.

energy of the group may not be exactly equal to the sum of the pair energies. These points will be discussed in more detail later.

Before considering the origins of molecular interaction energies, it is helpful to have some idea of their approximate magnitude. The enthalpy of vaporization of a liquid at its boiling point, T_b, may be roughly estimated using Trouton's rule, $\Delta H_{vap} \simeq 10\,RT_b$. We may associate this value of ΔH_{vap} with the energy needed to separate the molecules from their neighbours, which are about 10 in number, at a separation near to r_m. Then we see that for one mole,

$\Delta H_{vap} \simeq 10 N_A \varepsilon / 2$, where the factor of two prevents us from counting each pair interaction twice. Thus we find that $\varepsilon \simeq 2kT_b$. For low boiling substances such as Ar or N_2, the value of ε is thus about 1.2 kJ mol^{-1}, while for compounds such as benzene, which are liquid at room temperature, the intermolecular forces are much stronger, and ε is much larger, perhaps 5 kJ mol^{-1}.

We must now attempt to determine the origin of these interactions. It might be thought that gravitational interactions were the source of intermolecular forces. A simple calculation reveals that the typical magnitude of such energies is around 10^{30} times smaller than the values which we have just estimated. It is clear then that we must look elsewhere for the source of the forces between molecules, and we find that their origin is electromagnetic, arising from the charges on the electrons and nuclei of the atoms and molecules.

Several different types of electromagnetic interaction may be conveniently distinguished. When atoms or molecules with closed shells of electrons approach each other so that substantial *overlap* of the charge clouds occurs, the energy increases. This repulsive interaction has a similar origin, but is of the opposite sign, to the attraction which may arise in valence interactions when open shell atoms come together with the formation of a chemical bond. At larger separations, when there is negligible overlap, further electrostatic interactions may occur. If the species involved carry a net electrical charge then clearly there is a (long-range) Coulombic interaction. Even if there is no net charge, the symmetry of the distributions of positive and negative charge on each molecule may often still lead to a direct *electrostatic energy*. Furthermore, the electrical field resulting from the charge distribution of one molecule may induce small changes in the electronic distribution of a nearby molecule. This also leads to an interaction energy, generally called an *induction energy*. Finally, there remains a rather subtle source of attractive forces due to the *dispersion effect*, in which instantaneous dipoles associated with the rapid movements of electrons in one molecule are correlated with those in a neighbour. This interaction is often the major source of attractive forces and is present for all types of molecule.

For some classes of molecules, other types of interaction energy may arise, which can be of considerable importance. These may resemble more nearly the valence interactions characteristic of atoms with partially filled electron shells, and include hydrogen bonding and charge transfer interactions, both of which may contribute strong attractive forces, with dramatic effects on physical and chemical properties. Such interactions will be considered later.

1.2. Electrostatic energy

Direct electrostatic contributions to the interaction energy of a pair of uncharged molecules occur when they have charge distributions that are not spherically symmetrical. Then the Coulombic interactions between the positively charged nuclei and negatively charged electrons of one molecule with the corresponding charges of the other molecule will sum to give a total energy that is generally non-zero, and that depends strongly on the separation and relative orientation of the molecules. The distribution of charges within a molecule is generally described in terms of the multipole moments of the molecule. Some of the lower moments are illustrated in Fig. 1.2, where we see that the lowest order moment is the total net charge of a particle, which is of course zero for neutral molecules. The first-order moment, the dipole, arises when the centres of positive and negative charge of the molecule do not coincide. It may be represented in terms of fractional charges, $\delta\pm$, separated by a distance, r, and the magnitude of the dipole moment is given by the product, $r\delta$. In many cases molecules have zero dipole moments, by virtue of their symmetry. Thus, for example, the linear molecule carbon dioxide has no dipole moment, since it is symmetrical about the carbon atom, but the polarity of the C–O bonds gives rise to a charge distribution (shown in the fig. 1.2) that corresponds to the next highest moment, the quadrupole. Still higher moments, of orders 2^n, with $n > 2$, may be generated by suitable distribution of 2^n charges. An arrangement in which the octopole ($n = 3$) is the lowest non-zero multipole is illustrated. In general a molecule may possesses a series of multipole moments, and although there is a tendency to emphasize the importance of the lowest non-zero moment, the complete representation of the charge distribution requires the inclusion of all the moments.

For pairs of molecules separated by a distance that is great compared with the molecular dimensions, the direct electrostatic energy may be expressed in terms of the separation, relative orientation and the multipole moments. Since we wish to concentrate here on the form of the results, the derivation of the energy expression is summarized in Appendix 1A. Let us consider two linear

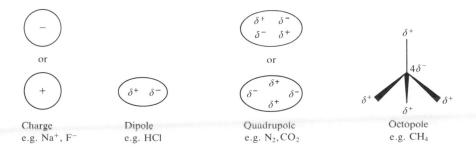

Fig. 1.2 Schematic representation of electric multipoles. The examples show only the lowest non-zero moment for each species.

molecules, A and B, which have dipole and quadrupole moments μ_A, Θ_A, and μ_B, Θ_B, at a separation r, and with relative orientations defined by the angles θ_A, θ_B and ϕ illustrated in Fig. 1.3. (For non-linear molecules, more angles will be needed to define the orientation, and the definition of the quadrupole moment may become cumbersome.) The interaction energy may then be written

$$U_{AB} = \frac{\mu_A \mu_B}{(4\pi\varepsilon_0)r^3} f_1(\theta_A, \theta_B, \phi) + \frac{\mu_A \Theta_B}{(4\pi\varepsilon_0)r^4} f_2(\theta_A, \theta_B, \phi)$$

$$- \frac{\mu_B \Theta_A}{(4\pi\varepsilon_0)r^4} f_2(\theta_B, \theta_A, \phi) + \frac{\Theta_A \Theta_B}{(4\pi\varepsilon_0)r^5} f_3(\theta_A, \theta_B, \phi). \quad (1.3)$$

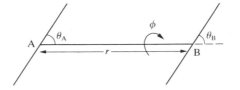
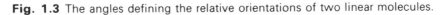

Fig. 1.3 The angles defining the relative orientations of two linear molecules.

We see that various terms arise that are associated with the interactions between different pairs of multipoles. The first of these, the dipole–dipole energy, falls off as r^{-3} for a given orientation, while the dipole–quadrupole term decreases more rapidly, as r^{-4}, and the quadrupole–quadrupole energy faster still, as r^{-5}.†

The orientation dependence of the energy is contained in the functions f_1, f_2 and f_3, which have the forms

$$f_1(\theta_A, \theta_B, \phi) = \sin\theta_A \sin\theta_B \cos\phi - 2\cos\theta_A \cos\theta_B \quad (1.4)$$

$$f_2(\theta_A, \theta_B, \phi) = \tfrac{3}{2}[\cos\theta_A(3\cos^2\theta_B - 1) - 2\sin\theta_A \sin\theta_B \cos\theta_B \cos\phi] \quad (1.5)$$

$$f_3(\theta_A, \theta_B, \phi) = \tfrac{3}{4}[1 - 5\cos^2\theta_A - 5\cos^2\theta_B - 15\cos^2\theta_A \cos^2\theta_B$$

$$+ 2(4\cos\theta_A \cos\theta_B - \sin\theta_A \sin\theta_3 \cos\phi)^2]. \quad (1.6)$$

If we focus our attention first on the dipole–dipole energy, and consider the relative orientation shown in Fig. 1.4(a), for which $\theta_A = \theta_B = 0$, then we see that

$$U_{\mu\mu} = -\frac{2\mu_A \mu_B}{(4\pi\varepsilon_0)r^3}$$

† In general, the interaction energy between multipoles of orders n_1 and n_2 drops off as $r^{-(n_1 + n_2 + 1)}$.

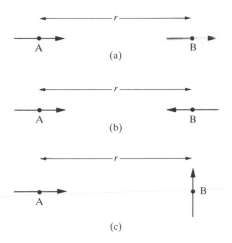

Fig. 1.4 Orientations for some specific dipole–dipole interactions.

while for the orientation in Fig. 1 4(b), in which one dipole has been reversed, we find

$$U_{\mu\mu} = + \frac{2\mu_A\mu_B}{(4\pi\varepsilon_0)r^3}$$

and for orientation 1.4(c), for which $\theta_A = 0$, $\theta_B = \pi/2$, we have

$$U_{\mu\mu} = 0.$$

The size and sign of the dipole–dipole energy thus depends very strongly on the orientation and if the energy is averaged over all possible orientations, treating them all as equally probable, the net result for the dipole–dipole energy, and for all the other direct electrostatic interactions between uncharged species, is zero. However, such an averaging process is not realistic, since not all relative orientations are equally probable. If we ignore quantum mechanical effects, each configuration occurs with a probability that is proportional to the associated Boltzmann factor, $\exp(-U(\omega)/kT)$, where ω represents the orientation. This factor favours configurations with negative energy, relative to those with positive energy, and the overall Boltzmann weighted energy, $\langle U \rangle$, reflects this:

$$\langle U \rangle = \frac{\int U(\omega) \exp[-U(\omega)/kT] \, d\omega}{\int \exp[-U(\omega)/kT] \, d\omega}. \tag{1.7}$$

For high temperatures the exponentials in eqn (1.7) may be expanded to give

$$\langle U \rangle = \frac{\int U(\omega)[1 - U(\omega)/kT + \ldots] \, d\omega}{\int [1 - U(\omega)/kT + \ldots] \, d\omega}$$

The first term in the numerator is simply $\int U(\omega) \, d\omega$ which, as mentioned above, is zero. The first non-zero term in the result for the dipole–dipole energy is then found to be

$$\langle U \rangle_{\mu\mu} = -\frac{2\mu_A^2 \mu_B^2}{3r^6 kT (4\pi\varepsilon_0)^2} \tag{1.8}$$

and we see that the Boltzmann-weighted average of the dipole–dipole energy is negative, inversely proportional to the temperature and the product of the squares of the two dipole moments, and decreases as r^{-6}. Similar expressions may be obtained for the Boltzmann-weighted angle averages of the dipole–quadrupole and quadrupole–quadrupole energies

$$\langle U \rangle_{\mu\theta} = \frac{-1}{r^8 kT (4\pi\varepsilon_0)^2} [\mu_A^2 \Theta_B^2 + \mu_B^2 \Theta_A^2] \tag{1.9}$$

$$\langle U \rangle_{\theta\theta} = \frac{-14\Theta_A^2 \Theta_B^2}{5r^{10} kT (4\pi\varepsilon_0)^2}. \tag{1.10}$$

In all cases we see that the energies are negative, inversely proportional to temperature, and fall off with a distance dependence, which is the square of that for the corresponding fixed orientation case.

1.3. Induction energy

In the direct electrostatic case considered above the charge distributions of the molecules are assumed to be those that characterize the isolated molecules. However, under the influence of the fields that result from the presence of neighbouring molecules, some modification of the charge distribution will occur, and this effect gives rise to a further type of interaction, the induction energy.

When a molecule is placed in a uniform electric field, $\mathscr{E}$, there is a redistribution of its charge, known as polarization. This is shown schematically in Fig. 1.5. A dipole moment is induced in the molecule; this moment is proportional to the field,

$$\mu_{\text{ind}} = \alpha\mathscr{E}$$

Electric field $\mathscr{E}$

Fig. 1.5 The process of induction.

where α is the static polarizability of the molecule. In this equation the molecule is presumed to be isotropic, and the direction of the induced dipole coincides with that of the field, $\mathscr{E}$. In general, for non-spherical molecules, the polarizability $\boldsymbol{a}$ is a tensor quantity, and the directions of μ_{ind} and $\mathscr{E}$ may differ. The energy of the induced dipole in the field $\mathscr{E}$ is

$$U = -\int_0^{\mathscr{E}} \mu_{ind} \cdot d\mathscr{E} = -\int_0^{\mathscr{E}} \alpha \mathscr{E} \cdot d\mathscr{E} = -\frac{1}{2} \alpha \mathscr{E}^2.$$

The field produced by a dipolar molecule at a position P shown in Fig. 1.6 is of a magnitude

$$\mathscr{E}(r, \theta) = \mu[1 + 3\cos^2 \theta]^{1/2}/[4\pi\varepsilon_0 r^3]$$

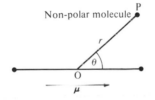

Non-polar molecule

Fig. 1.6 Interaction of a dipolar molecule with a polarizable non-polar molecule.

and hence the interaction energy due to the induced dipole may be written

$$U = -\alpha\mu^2 (3\cos^2 \theta + 1)/[2r^6 (4\pi\varepsilon_0)^2].$$

This energy is attractive for all orientations and falls off as r^{-6}. If it is averaged over all orientations, giving each orientation the appropriate Boltzmann weighting, the leading term in the induction energy is found to be

$$\langle U \rangle_{ind} = \frac{-\mu^2 \alpha}{(4\pi\varepsilon_0)^2 r^6}. \tag{1.11}$$

We note that in this case, in contrast to the direct electrostatic terms, the energy is not temperature dependent, since, for the induction energy, the first term in the expansion of the exponential does not average to zero. For two identical molecules, each of dipole moment μ and polarizability α, the total induction energy becomes

$$\langle U \rangle_{\text{ind}} = \frac{-2\mu^2\alpha}{(4\pi\varepsilon_0)^2 r^6}. \tag{1.12}$$

In addition to the induction of dipoles, higher order moments may also be induced, and should be included in a more complete treatment of induction. Furthermore, for non-spherical molecules the anisotropy of the polarizability must be considered, and the induction energy will also depend on the orientation of the polarizable molecule.

1.4. Dispersion energy

The two contributions to long-range energy discussed so far arise from classical electrostatics. For molecules with no permanent dipole or higher order moments these electrostatic and induction contributions are absent and the molecular interactions arise from a different source. Even for the small polar molecule HCl, the electrostatic and induction contributions account for only about 20 per cent of the long-range attractive energy. The most important source of attractive intermolecular energy is the dispersion energy first identified by London in 1930. Dispersion energy cannot be completely described in classical terms, as its origins are quantum mechanical, but we may gain some insight into its nature from the following analysis.

We mentioned earlier that dispersion forces arise from the interaction of instantaneous dipoles in the molecules. The electrons in an atom or molecule are in continual motion, even when in their ground state. Thus, though on average the dipole moment of a spherically symmetric atom is zero, at any instant a temporary dipole moment can occur. This dipole can induce a dipole moment in a neighbouring atom and, as in classical induction forces, the net effect will be attraction. Such a force, arising as it does from correlation between the charge fluctuations, might be expected to be very small. However, the calculations of London showed that its magnitude was sufficiently large for it to be the origin of the attraction between spherically symmetric atoms and molecules, and to be the major attractive contribution for most polar molecules. An investigation of the dispersion energy based on a simple model of a molecule due to Drude is described in Appendix 1B.

The expression for the leading term in the dispersion energy that results from this calculation may be represented as:

$$U_{\text{dis}} = \frac{-3\alpha^2 E_1}{4(4\pi\varepsilon_0)^2 r^6} = \frac{C_6}{r^6} \tag{1.13}$$

where the polarizability of the molecule and its ionization energy are α and E_I, respectively. The dispersion energy is seen to be attractive, and to fall off as r^{-6}. The coefficient C_6 in eqn (1.13) is approximate, being based on a simplified model, but a precise expression for C_6 can be obtained. In favourable cases, it can be evaluated quite accurately, using a combination of experimental and theoretical results characterizing electronic transitions within the interacting molecules. The origin of this first term in the dispersion energy lies in the interaction between an instantaneous dipole on one molecule and the induced dipole in another. We note that the r dependence is the same as that for the classical dipole-induced dipole term described above.

In addition to this first term there are further dispersion contributions, and the series may be written

$$U_{dis} = \frac{C_6}{r^6} + \frac{C_8}{r^8} + \frac{C_{10}}{r^{10}} + \cdots \tag{1.14}$$

where the additional terms represent contributions arising from the interactions of higher order instantaneous multipoles, such as quadrupoles and octopoles. Although at large separations only the leading term makes a substantial contribution to the attractive energy, at shorter separations, near to r_m, it is found that the higher order terms may contribute as much as 20 per cent of the total dispersion energy. At still smaller separations, these higher order terms might be expected to become even more important. However, when overlap of the electron clouds begins to occur, the procedures used in the calculation of the long range energy become inappropriate, and new and important effects arise, which result from the distortion of the charge clouds when overlap occurs.

1.5. Long-range energy: summary

Table 1.1 compares the values of the various long range energy contributions for several simple molecules at separations approximating to r_m. These intermolecular energies may be compared with the much larger bond energies of the various species, and with the energies of sublimation of the solids. For the dipole–dipole term the calculation is for 300 K, at which temperature the kinetic energy of one mole of gas molecules is 3.7 kJ. It is apparent that the intermolecular energies are much smaller than the bond energies, but may be comparable with the kinetic energy, especially for the larger molecules. With the exception of small, highly polar molecules like water, the dispersion energy is the major contribution to the long-range energy. The induction energy is almost always small, unless one or both of the interacting species is charged.

Table 1.1

		Interaction energies ($kJ\ mol^{-1}$)				
		Intermolecular attractive terms			Single bond	
Molecule	r_m(nm)	U_{el}	U_{ind}	U_{disp}	energies	ΔU^0_{sub}
Ar	0.37	—	—	−1.1	—	7.6
Xe	0.43	—	—	−1.9	—	16
CO	0.40	-4×10^{-5}	-8×10^{-4}	−1.3	343	6.9
HCl	0.42	−0.2	−0.07	−1.8	431	18
NH_3	0.29	−6.2	−0.9	−12.9	389	29
H_2O	0.30	−16.1	−0.9	−5.3	464	47

The intermolecular energies are quoted for 1 mole of pairs at separation r_m.

1.6. Short-range energies

When two molecules approach so closely that their electron clouds overlap the Pauli exclusion principle restricts the extent to which the electrons may occupy the overlap region and so reduces the electron density there. The positively charged nuclei are thus incompletely shielded from each other and are therefore mutually repelled. These forces are not easy to treat theoretically in non-bonding systems but a description of the repulsive forces that arise in the case of two hydrogen atoms in their ground state is provided by the Heitler–London or valence bond model and can be used to give some insight into the origins of these forces. In addition it has been found in recent years that detailed studies of the H_2 system have given results which, with suitable modification, have provided a very useful basis for developing intermolecular potential energy functions for larger molecules.

The wave function, ψ, of two hydrogen atoms A and B when they are far apart may be written

$$\psi = \psi_A(1)\psi_B(2)$$

where $\psi_A(1)$ is the wave function of electron 1, which is located near nucleus A. However, as the two atoms approach this wave function becomes inadequate in that it contains no provision for electron 1 to be associated with nucleus B and vice versa, and also as it does not satisfy the symmetry conditions of the Pauli principle. Heitler and London suggested that two wave functions for the interacting atoms could be written

$$\psi_\pm = \psi_A(1)\psi_B(2) \pm \psi_A(2)\psi_B(1)$$

thus allowing for the exchange of electrons between the atomic wave functions and meeting the requirements of the Pauli principle.

The Heitler–London theory then leads to an expression for the interaction energy, which can be represented as

$$U_{\pm} = \frac{Q \pm J}{1 \pm S^2}.$$ (1.15)

The integrals Q, J, and S are known respectively as the coulomb, exchange, and overlap integrals, and are defined as follows.

$$Q = \int \psi_A(1) \psi_B(2) V_e \, d\tau$$

$$J = \int \psi_A(1) \psi_B(1) \psi_A(2) \psi_B(2) V_e \, d\tau$$

$$S = \int \psi_A(1) \psi_B(1) \, d\tau,$$

where V_e is the electrostatic interaction energy of the two atoms:

$$V_e = \frac{-e^2}{4\pi\varepsilon_0} \left[\frac{1}{r_{a2}} + \frac{1}{r_{b1}} - \frac{1}{r_{12}} - \frac{1}{r} \right]$$

r_{a2} represents the distance between nucleus A and electron 2, the separation of the two electrons is r_{12}, and that of the nuclei is r (See Fig. 1.7). e is the charge of the proton. The contributing integrals and the resultant energy curves when 1s atomic orbitals are used for ψ_A and ψ_B are shown in Fig. 1.8. The positive signs in the wave function lead to positive signs in the energy equation (1.15) and as J is large and negative, to a negative interaction energy. This wave function then corresponds to that of the bonding ground state molecule, in which the spins of the electrons are antiparallel. Such a state, in which the electron spins are paired, is called a singlet state. The negative signs in the wave function and energy correspond to the non-bonding, repulsive state and in this state, a triplet state, represented $^3H_2$, the electron spins are parallel. It is this repulsive interaction that is analogous to that which occurs when two closed shell atoms interact.

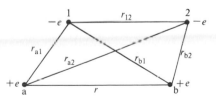

Fig. 1.7 The interaction of two hydrogen atoms.

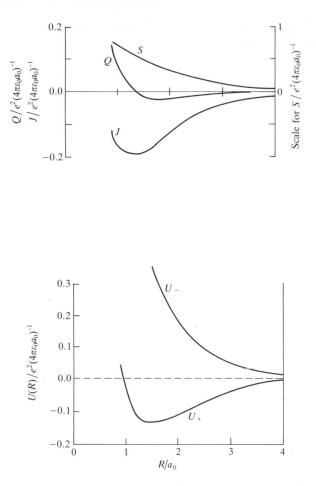

Fig. 1.8 The contributing integrals and resultant energy curves for the interaction of two hydrogen atoms.

The dominant contribution to this energy comes from the exchange integral—the short-range repulsive forces between closed shell atoms and molecules are often termed 'exchange forces'. It should be noted however that the 'exchange' is not a physical process. It arises purely from the attempt to express the molecular wave function in terms of the atomic wave functions. The Hellmann–Feynman theorem of quantum mechanics states that if exact wave functions are used, the total energy may be exactly calculated by the direct evaluation of the classical coulombic electrostatic contributions. No explicit exchange term arises in such an approach, and it seems preferable to refer to the short range repulsive interactions as *overlap forces*.

The Hellmann–Feynman theorem permits us to interpret the interactions between two hydrogen atoms in terms of the electron densities that result from the bonding and non-bonding wave functions. These are illustrated in Fig. 1.9. The bonding function is found to lead to an increase in electron density in the region between the nuclei, compared with that which would result from a superposition of the densities of two (non-interacting) atoms. The two positively charged protons are then attracted to the negatively charged region and so there is an attractive force between them. The non-bonding wave function leads to a decreased electron density between the nuclei, as shown in Fig 1.9(b). The nuclei are consequently incompletely shielded from each other, and electrostatic repulsion results. At very short separations the interaction energy for the repulsive wave function varies as $1/r$, owing to the nuclear repulsion. At larger separations, the energy decays as e^{-2r/a_0} where a_0 is a constant, the Bohr radius. Similar results are also obtained when more accurate calculations are carried out, using more flexible wave functions. A generalized exponential form,

$$U_{rep} = A e^{-Br},$$

for the repulsive energy has been frequently used in representations of short-range intermolecular energy. It has generally been found capable of giving an accurate description of the results of several alternative calculations of the short-range energies of a variety of molecules, and probably represents the most satisfactory concise way of representing the energy in this region.

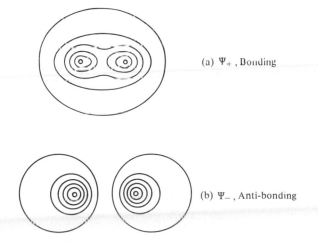

(a) Ψ_+ , Bonding

(b) Ψ_- , Anti-bonding

Fig. 1.9 Contours of equal electron density for H_2, in a plane containing the nuclei.

We have now described methods by which estimates of both the short-range repulsive and long-range attractive interactions may be separately obtained using theoretical approaches. However, these methods cannot be used directly to study the intermediate region of separations, by the addition of the two contributions. The procedures used to derive the two sets of results are inconsistent, and cannot be used when both give rise to energies of comparable magnitude. The long-range energy is expressed in terms of the properties of the isolated molecules. When overlap of the electron clouds becomes significant, as the molecules come together, distortion of the charge distribution occurs, and the isolated molecule properties are no longer appropriate. For small molecules with few electrons the well region can be studied, using more advanced quantum mechanical techniques than those we have described. Such 'ab initio' calculations can give reasonably reliable results, but their use is restricted to small molecules, and in general the characterization of the vitally important well region of the potential must be carried out through the analysis of experimental results for a number of different properties. These procedures are summarized in section 1.10, and are described in more detail in Chapters 2 to 7.

1.7. The hydrogen bond

Although the dispersion energy, the electrostatic interactions of multipoles, and induction energies form the principal sources of attractive forces between molecules, other types of attractive interactions are also observed in certain instances, and these are often of great importance. Foremost and most widespread of these interactions is the hydrogen bond, whose occurrence in simple liquids such as water has profound effects on the observed physical properties, and whose structural role in biological macromolecules is of enormous importance.

Hydrogen bonding is observed in circumstances where a hydrogen atom covalently bonded to an electronegative atom, A, such as oxygen, nitrogen or a halogen, is able to approach another electronegative atom, B, which may be in the same or a different molecule. A relatively strong attractive interaction energy is then observed in the A–H $\cdots$ B system, typically having a magnitude between 12 and 30 kJ mol^{-1}, and a bond angle AĤB most commonly near to 180°. Structural investigations usually indicate that the A–H bond becomes slightly longer than in a non-H-bonded system, while the H $\cdots$ B distance greatly exceeds that of a normal HB covalent bond.

In view of the widespread nature of H-bonding and its importance in many areas, there have been numerous theoretical investigations into the origin of the interaction, and *ab initio* studies have been successfully used to elucidate its nature. Current thinking favours the view that the major part of the interaction is derived from sources which we have considered earlier, and that the main component, perhaps as much as 80 per cent of the energy, is electrostatic in origin, though some covalent contribution may also be significant. The A–H bond is polar, owing to the large electronegativity of A, and this leaves the proton of the H atom relatively exposed. The small size of the H atom, resulting from the absence of inner electron shells, permits atom B to approach closely to the A–H system before repulsive interaction terms become large. The electrons of B can then interact relatively strongly with the partially exposed H nucleus, especially if B has lone pairs of electrons. This fairly simple picture of the origin of the H bond appears to account reasonably well for its principal features, though a small number of H-bonded systems are known, such as the ion HF_2^-, in which the bond is extremely strong and cannot be described in this way.

When H-bonding occurs, the structural consequences may be profound. For example, in ice (Fig. 1.10(a)) and to a substantial extent also in liquid water, there is a three-dimensional network structure in which each O atom is surrounded by four H atoms, tetrahedrally arranged, of which two are covalently bonded and two are H-bonded. In other liquids, chains of molecules or small rings may be formed. Hydrogen fluoride, HF (Fig. 1.10(b)) provides an example of the former occurrence, while rings of various sizes have been postulated in alcohols. In some classes of molecules, notably carboxylic acids (Fig. 1.10(c)) the geometry of the interacting groups is such as to favour the production of dimers of molecules, which then have no further capacity for H-bonding. When H-bonds form between molecules of different types that do not H-bond in the pure state, dramatic consequences are seen in the properties of the mixture and in the thermodynamic changes which accompany the mixing process. The strongly exothermic mixing of trichloromethane (chloroform) and propanone (acetone) provides a well-documented example (Fig. 1.10(d)).

Generally speaking, owing to the relatively large interaction energy, the experimental characterization of H bonds in the liquid and solid states has followed the procedures used in the study of covalent chemical bonds, rather than those that are usually adopted when studying intermolecular interactions. Spectroscopic investigations, particularly using infra-red and nuclear magnetic resonance techniques, have probably provided the bulk of the available information. In recent years hydrogen bonding systems have been increasingly studied in the gas phase, often using microwave and radio-frequency spectroscopic techniques. Supporting studies of other properties, such as gas imperfections, have also been used.

1.8. Representation of intermolecular interactions

Although the theoretical investigation of intermolecular interactions can give valuable insight into the nature and origins of the forces between molecules, we

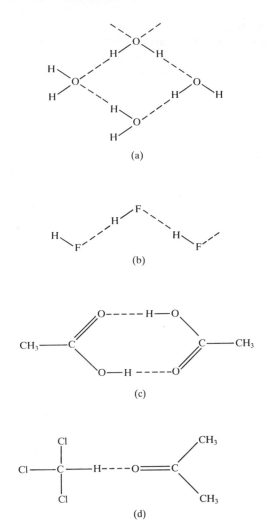

Fig. 1.10 Some examples of hydrogen bonding.

have seen that it is not possible at the present time to obtain detailed information about the intermolecular potential at all separations directly from quantum mechanical studies. In the important region of the potential well it is particularly difficult to obtain accurate results, although these can be established in favourable cases at large and at small separations. Information about the well region has in consequence generally been obtained by the analysis of experimental results for a wide range of properties which depend on the molecular interactions. Such an analysis may proceed in two essentially different ways.

For a small number of the properties of systems of monatomic molecules it is possible to proceed directly from a set of measured data points of one property as a function of temperature to a series of points on the potential energy curve. Such an *inversion procedure*, if available, gives the most desirable route to the potential, and should make it possible to assess the consequences of experimental uncertainty on the derived potential function. Unfortunately, inversion has only been successfully applied to a small number of properties, and has sometimes required the introduction of additional data, such as the asymptotic behaviour of the potential at long or short range.

Where such an inversion is not possible, some algebraic representation of the potential has to be assumed, containing several adjustable parameters. Calculations of the properties are made using the assumed potential, and parameter values adjusted to give optimum agreement with the experimental results. In many cases simultaneous fits have been made to results for a number of different properties. Such broad-ranging fitting procedures have been found to be necessary if reliable results are to be obtained, and it is important also that, where possible, complementary properties are studied, which are sensitive to different aspects of the potential. When a potential has been found that is able to reproduce the measured properties within experimental error, it has often been assumed that it represents the true intermolecular potential. Provided that the data fitted are sensitive to the detailed form of the interaction and cover a wide range of conditions, it is likely that this procedure will give a fairly reliable potential function, but it must not be assumed that fitting an inflexible model function to a limited range of data points will give more than a rough indication of the magnitude of the energy. If possible it is desirable to incorporate into trial potential functions any reliable information that may be available from theoretical studies, and it is clear that any acceptable function must be compatible with such results. The successful application of this approach relies on the choice of suitable trial potential functions, and we consider here a few of the vast number of intermolecular potentials that have been used in this way. It is convenient to consider first the interactions of monatomic systems, and then to proceed to more complex molecules.

1.8.1. Monatomic systems

For these systems the interaction energy depends only on the separation of the atomic nuclei, and it is possible, and fairly convenient, to represent the intermolecular energy either graphically or in the form of a table of interaction energies for different separations. However, such an approach does not lend itself conveniently to the calculation of properties, which generally involve integration of functions of $U(r)$ over a large range of separations, r. Analytical functions are much more convenient for such calculations, even when, as is common, the integrations must be performed numerically.

The best-known potential function for monatomic systems is the Lennard-Jones 12–6 function, which may be written

$$U(r) = 4\varepsilon [(\sigma/r)^{12} - (\sigma/r)^{6}]. \qquad (1.16)$$

In this potential there are two adjustable parameters only, the collision diameter, σ, and the well depth, ε. Once these are fixed the potential is completely defined, and no adjustment to the shape of the potential is possible. We note that at large r, the energy falls off as r^{-6}, as suggested by theoretical analysis of the dispersion energy, though no provision is made for the higher order terms, in r^{-8}, r^{-10} etc. The short-range energy has the form A/r^{12}, in contrast to the exponential form, $\exp(-Br)$, suggested by theory. It is not too surprising then that the 12–6 potential does not give a reliable representation of the interaction potential of any known molecules, whatever values of the parameters are chosen. Nevertheless, it has the considerable advantage of relative simplicity, whilst showing broadly the characteristics of real inter-molecular potentials, and it has been very widely used in statistical mechanical studies of many kinds. Indeed the behaviour of systems of Lennard–Jones molecules is now quite well known. A more general form of this function, the n-6 potential, where the repulsive exponent takes a value other than 12, has also been used.

An improved form of potential might be expected when the r^{-12} repulsive term is replaced by a theoretically based exponential term, and such a potential, the exp–6 model

$$U(r) = [A \exp(-Br) - C/r^{6}] \qquad (1.17)$$

$$= \frac{\varepsilon}{(1 - 6/\alpha)} \left[\exp\alpha [(1 - r/r_{m})] - (r/r_{m})^{6} \right]$$

has also been extensively used. This potential has three disposable parameters, the well depth, ε, the separation r_{m} (or σ), and a further parameter α, which determines the steepness of the repulsive interaction. The inclusion of this third parameter allows a little more flexibility in the shape of this potential, but recent accurate investigations have concentrated largely on functions with very many more parameters. One that has been the basis of much important work is due to Barker and co-workers. It contains up to nine terms, and is written

$$U(r) = \exp[\alpha(1 - r/r_{m})] \sum_{i=0}^{n} A_{i}(r/r_{m} - 1)^{i}$$

$$+ \frac{C_{6}}{[\delta + (r/r_{m})^{6}]} + \frac{C_{8}}{[\delta + (r/r_{m})^{8}]} + \frac{C_{10}}{[\delta + (r/r_{m})^{10}]} . \qquad (1.18)$$

Most potentials that have been found able to give accurate descriptions of the

interactions of monatomic systems have large numbers of adjustable parameters. An exception to this rule is the $n(\bar{r})$–6 potential, which has just one
parameter, γ, in addition to ε and r_m ($\bar{r} \equiv r/r_m$).

$$U(r) = \varepsilon \left[\frac{m}{n-m} \left(\frac{r_m}{r}\right)^n - \frac{n}{n-m} \left(\frac{r_m}{r}\right)^6 \right] \tag{1.19}$$

where $n = 13.0 + \gamma(r/r_m - 1)$.

This simple three-parameter potential gives a remarkably accurate representation of the potential functions of the inert gases. Another widely used and
successful function, which is a reasonable compromise between flexibility,
mathematical complexity, and physical realism, is the seven-parameter
Hartree–Fock dispersion (HFD) function

$$U(r) = A \exp(-\alpha r/r_m) + \left(\frac{C_6}{r^6} + \frac{C_8}{r^8} + \frac{C_{10}}{r^{10}}\right) F(r/r_m)$$

where the *damping function* F is given by

$$F(r/r_m) = \exp\left[-(Dr_m/r - 1)^2\right] \quad r \lesssim Dr_m$$
$$= 1 \qquad\qquad\qquad\qquad r > Dr_m. \tag{1.20}$$

Despite the complexity of many of the above representations, they can all be
expressed in terms of a shape function $\mathcal{F}$ and two *parameters of scale*, such as ε
and σ, so that

$$U(r) = \varepsilon \mathcal{F}(r/\sigma). \tag{1.21}$$

Comparing the form of eqn (1.21) with the models introduced above, we
note that they all contain two scale parameters, usually ε and either σ or r_m, and
that the shape function is determined by the algebraic form of the potential
and by any further disposable parameters, which we term *shape parameters*.
Thus we see that the Lennard–Jones 12–6 potential has no shape parameters.
The exp-6 and $n(r)$-6 potentials each have one, α and γ, whereas the HFD
potential has six such parameters and the Barker model has eight or more.
Different molecules that have potential functions with the same shape function
$\mathcal{F}$ but different values of the scale parameters are said to have *conformal
potentials*. We can make an important generalization for such molecules. For
that class of substances for which $\mathcal{F}(r/\sigma)$ is the same, as long as they behave
classically and their intermolecular energy is pairwise additive, we can express
their thermophysical properties in terms of just two parameters (which are
related to, but need not be equal to ε and σ). Their behaviour is then said to
follow the Principle of Corresponding States. This topic will be discussed
again in Chapter 2.

1.8.2. Polyatomic systems

When the interactions of molecular systems are considered, the energy now
depends on the relative orientation of the molecules, as well as their separation.

In the simplest case, the interaction of a spherical atom with a linear molecule, a single angular variable, θ, is sufficient to define the orientation (Fig. 1.6). However, for two linear molecules, three angles are required (Fig 1.3), while in general up to five angular variables may be needed, in addition to the separation. In such cases it is evidently impracticable to represent the energy conveniently in a tabular form, since so many variables are involved, and graphical representation of the whole potential surface is also very difficult. It is possible to display the energy as a function of separation for fixed relative orientations. However, such a procedure focuses attention on specific configurations, which are easily visualized but which will generally be of no special importance in determining the properties of the system.

It is evident, then, that the representation of the interaction energy of polyatomic systems presents problems, and the best solution is not clear at the present time. In the simplest cases, such as atom–diatom interactions, a pictorial representation of the three-dimensional surface may give useful insight (Fig 1.11), while contour diagrams (Fig 1.12) provide an alternative approach.

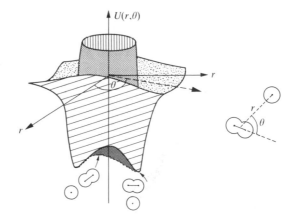

Fig. 1.11 A three-dimensional representation of the potential surface for the interaction of an atom and a diatomic molecule.

Several methods have been used to represent such surfaces using *analytical functions*. At the crudest level, the angular variation of the potential (its 'anisotropy') is neglected completely and one of the simple spherical functions described earlier for atoms is used. Such 'effective spherical potentials' may have a limited usefulness in data interpolation exercises, but bear little relation

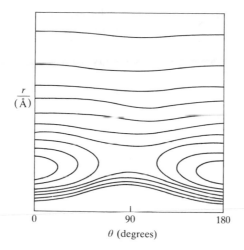

r
(Å)

0   90   180

θ (degrees)

Fig. 1.12 Contour diagram of the surface in Fig. 1.11.

to physical reality. A considerable amount of work has been carried out using potentials consisting of a spherical part, most often of the Lennard–Jones 12–6 form, together with appropriate multipole–multipole terms, and sometimes also with induction energy terms. Such potentials have given some useful insight into the effects of permanent multipoles on the properties of systems, but are unrealistic in that they neglect totally the anisotropy of the dispersion and short-range repulsive interactions.

A relatively easy way to generalize atom–atom potential function representations to molecules is to regard the latter as being composed of a number of independent sites, which interact with similar sites in neighbouring molecules (See Fig 1.13). A simple function, like the Lennard–Jones 12–6, is usually chosen for the site–site interactions, although in principle a function of any complexity can be used. This type of potential function is known variously as a *site–site potential* or a *multi-centre potential*. Specifically for the 12–6 case, applied to two diatomic molecules, the potential has the form

$$U_{ij} = \sum_{\alpha=1}^{2} \sum_{\beta=1}^{2} 4\varepsilon_{\alpha\beta} \left[(\sigma_{\alpha\beta}/r_{\alpha\beta})^{12} - (\sigma_{\alpha\beta}/r_{\alpha\beta})^{6} \right]$$

The interaction sites may or may not coincide with the atomic sites in the molecules; sometimes additional sites are added at intermediate positions along the bonds. Although these potentials are convenient to evaluate, the physical basis of breaking down the total interaction in this way is not entirely clear (see Chapter 8). If such a separation of the function into site–site interactions is not used, alternative approaches may be considered. The full

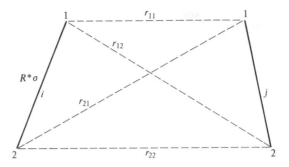

Fig. 1.13 A site–site model for the interaction of two diatomic molecules.

potential energy function may be written $U(r, \omega)$, where ω represents the angular variables needed in a given case. One approach that has been quite widely used expands the full potential in a form using a series of distance-dependent terms multiplied by appropriate angle-dependent quantities:

$$U(r, \omega) = \sum_i \sum_j \sum_k U_{jk}(r) A_{ijk}(\omega)$$

where the angular factors, $A_{ijk}(\omega)$, are known functions. For instance for atom–diatom interactions, where there is only one angular variable, $i = j = k$ and the $A_{ijk} = A_i$ are the Legendre polynomials, $P_i(\cos\theta)$:

$$P_0(x) = 1; \quad P_1(x) = x; \quad P_2(x) = (3x^2 - 1)/2; \text{ etc.}$$

whereas for molecule–molecule interactions, where three angles are required to specify relative orientation, they take the form of spherical harmonics. For some molecules, certain terms disappear as a result of symmetry constraints, e.g. for homonuclear diatomics only terms of even i appear. This *potential expansion* (or *POTEX*) approach is in principle capable of reproducing exactly any potential surface, provided that sufficient terms are retained in the expansion. Its practical value is governed by the rapidity with which the expansion converges, and the ease with which the 'coefficients' $U_i(r)$ may be determined. Several variations on this general approach have been investigated, and will be considered further in Chapter 8.

An alternative to this angular expansion of the whole potential is to represent the potential parameters by similar kinds of polynomial expansions. Usually it is just the scale parameters ε and σ that are treated in this way, e.g.

$$U(r, \omega) = \varepsilon(\omega)U^*(r/\sigma(\omega))$$

$$\varepsilon(\omega) = \sum_i \varepsilon_i A_i(\omega)$$

$$\sigma(\omega) = \sum_i \sigma_i A_i(\omega).$$

In this case the *shape* of the radial potential does not vary with angle; this is a feature that may limit its application in some cases but which appears to be an adequate approximation for a wide range of systems. This constraint may be relaxed simply by expanding shape parameters in a similar fashion. The major advantage of this *parameter expansion* (or *PAREX*) representation over the potential expansion procedure is one of economy, as relatively few terms are required to represent highly anisotropic potentials.

1.8.3. Unlike interactions

The expressions so far presented are applicable to pairs of molecules whether they are identical or different in nature. When the properties of mixtures are under investigation the interactions between unlike molecules are of particular importance. Although in general the potential energy function for a pair of unlike molecules A . . B need not be related to those for the like pairs, A . . A and B . . B, it is often helpful to have an approximate expression for the interactions of the unlike molecules based on those of the like molecules. It is commonly assumed that the potential energy functions for all these interactions are conformal, and hence that the unlike interaction is determined if the values of the parameters σ_{AB} and ε_{AB} are known. Expressions for σ_{AB} and ε_{AB} in terms of the corresponding quantities for the pure substances are known as *combining rules*. The most widely used rules are the Lorentz–Berthelot rules, in which the collision diameter is taken to be the arithmetic mean, and the well depth to be the geometric mean, of those for the pure species:

$$\sigma_{AB} = \tfrac{1}{2}(\sigma_{AA} + \sigma_{BB})$$
$$\varepsilon_{AB} = (\varepsilon_{AA}\,\varepsilon_{BB})^{1/2}.$$

For the rather few cases in which the assumption of conformality seems to be reasonably well founded, and for which the unlike interactions have been well characterized, it appears that the geometric mean rule often overestimates ε_{AB}, especially when the well depths of the pure species are very different. Several other forms of combining rule have been suggested, some of moderate complexity. Of simple rules, the harmonic mean rule for ε_{AB} appears to be the most successful:

$$\frac{1}{\varepsilon_{AB}} = \frac{1}{2}\left[\frac{1}{\varepsilon_{AA}} + \frac{1}{\varepsilon_{BB}}\right].$$

The arithmetic mean rule for σ_{AB} appears to be reasonably accurate, though it tends to underestimate its value slightly.

1.9. Non-pairwise additivity

Thus far we have been concerned only with the interactions of pairs of molecules. However, when more than two molecules simultaneously interact, as in Fig 1.14, the total energy of interaction is not generally exactly equal to

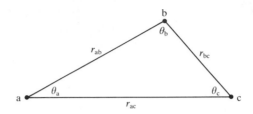

Fig. 1.14 The angles and separations that define a three-molecule system.

the sum of the pair interaction energies

$$U_{abc} \neq (U_{ab} + U_{ac} + U_{bc})$$

We can regard this inequality as arising from the manner in which the presence of a third molecule perturbs the interaction of the other two. An obvious example of non-additivity is seen in the induction energy. The induced moments of a polarizable molecule are governed by the field experienced by that molecule. If this results from the nearby presence of two or more polar molecules, it is evident that substantial cancellation of the field may occur, so reducing the total induction energy. This is illustrated in Fig. 1.15. This effect would only be expected to be large in cases where the two-body induction energy was substantial. It is consequently important in the interaction of charged or highly polar species with polarizable molecules, but is usually unimportant for small non-polar molecules. In these cases the major contribution to the non-additivity appears to arise in the long-range dispersion energy. We have seen earlier that dispersion forces can be regarded as arising from the electronic motions getting into phase. If a third molecule approaches a pair so that the resulting triplet is linear we can see that correlation of the

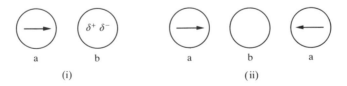

Fig. 1.15 (i) Polarization of a molecule, b, resulting from the presence of a polar molecule, a. (ii) Cancellation of the fields from two polar molecules, a, resulting in no polarization of b.

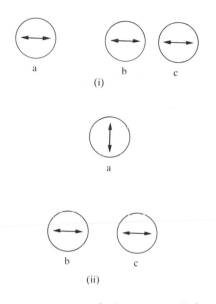

Fig. 1.16 Schematic representation of electron correlation for three-molecule systems in two geometries

electrons in molecules b and c can be enhanced by both correlating with a. (Fig 1.16(i)). Thus the dispersion forces are increased for this geometry. However if a forms an approximately equilateral triangle with b and c (Fig 1.16(ii)) then we see that the coupling of their electronic motion will be reduced when both try to interact with a. This then leads to a weakening of the dispersion interaction. The leading correction term arising from this behaviour was first evaluated by Axilrod and Teller and is called the triple-dipole contribution, U_{DDD}. It may be expressed in terms of the coordinates defined in Fig 1.14:

$$U_{abc} = \frac{C_6}{r_{ab}^6} + \frac{C_6}{r_{bc}^6} + \frac{C_6}{r_{ac}^6} + v_{abc}\frac{(3\cos\theta_a\cos\theta_b\cos\theta_c + 1)}{(r_{ab}\,r_{bc}\,r_{ac})^3}$$

If the molecules a, b and c are identical, v_{abc} may be approximately related to the coefficient C_6 and the polarizability α by the equation

$$v_{abc} = \frac{-3\alpha C_6}{4\,(4\pi\,\varepsilon_0)}$$

For non-spherical molecules the triple-dipole energy depends on the relative orientation of the molecules, as well as their positions. Short-range repulsive interactions would also be expected to be non-additive, but *ab initio* calculations for small molecules suggest that these effects are only important at rather small separations.

Non-additive contributions may alter the calculated lattice energies of solids by around 10 per cent. All properties that involve the simultaneous interaction of more than two molecules must be analysed with special care if information regarding the pair potential is sought.

1.10. Experimental sources of information

As mentioned earlier, the complete determination of intermolecular potentials for the whole separation range is not generally possible without using experimental results for suitable properties, some of which are described below. The properties that depend on intermolecular interactions may be divided into two groups, those which arise from the interactions of pairs of molecules, and those in which groups of three or more molecules interact simultaneously. The complications resulting from the failure of the assumption of pairwise additivity of intermolecular energy complicates the analysis of the latter properties in terms of the intermolecular pair potential function, and ideally such properties would be used in the study of many-body interactions, after the pair potential had already been established. This desirable state of affairs has not generally been achieved, and properties from both groups have been widely used in studies of the pair potential, after making reasonable assumptions about the non-additive energies.

1.10.1. Gas imperfection

The deviations of gases from perfect behaviour can be expressed in the form of a *virial equation*

$$\frac{P\bar{V}}{RT} = 1 + \frac{B(T)}{\bar{V}} + \frac{C(T)}{\bar{V}^2} + \dots$$

where $\bar{V}$ is the molar volume of the gas. $B(T)$ and $C(T)$ are called the second and third virial coefficients. The second virial coefficient may be shown to depend on the interactions of pairs of molecules and so can provide valuable information about the pair potential $U(r, \omega)$. The third virial coefficient involves the interactions of molecules in groups of three, and so is less directly useful in the study of $U(r, \omega)$. It is also usually subject to rather large experimental errors.

1.10.2. Gas transport properties

The transport of momentum, energy or mass through a gas under the influence of gradients of velocity, temperature or concentration is dependent on intermolecular forces, since these determine the nature of the collisions between molecules that result in the transport. The coefficients that relate the transport to the gradients involved—shear viscosity, thermal conductivity and diffusion—are directly related to the pair potential for a dilute gas. For hard sphere molecules the coefficients can be simply expressed in terms of the molecular diameter, σ, but for real molecules they depend on the detailed nature of $U(r, \omega)$.

1.10.3. Molecular beams

In studying the transport properties of dilute gases many types of collision between molecules must be considered. The molecules approach each other with a wide range of kinetic energies, whose distribution depends on the temperature of the experiment. In molecular beam studies, more restricted classes of collision can be investigated, in which the relative kinetic energies may be controlled within close limits. A beam of mono-energetic molecules is produced, and is allowed to collide either with molecules at a low pressure in a small scattering chamber, or with a similar beam travelling at right angles to the initial beam. Two general types of measurement are commonly made. The extent to which the intensity of the incident beam is reduced by scattering of molecules out of the beam may be measured, and used to determine the 'integral collision cross-section'. This depends on the energy of the molecules in the beam, and its variation with energy can provide a useful test of a pair potential. Alternatively, the number of molecules scattered into a particular solid angle from the initial direction may be analysed to give the 'differential cross-section', which is a function both of relative energy and of scattering angle. Accurate and extensive measurements of this cross-section for spherical molecules may in favourable circumstances be inverted to give the pair potential. More generally, such measurements may be used to determine the parameters of some assumed analytical form for $U(r, \omega)$.

1.10.4. Spectra of van der Waals molecules

Despite the fact that pairs of atoms such as the inert gases or pairs of molecules such as nitrogen do not combine to form chemically bound molecules, they can form small quantities of physically bound dimers under appropriate conditions. Such a system is called a van der Waals dimer and has some similarities to a chemically bound molecule. In particular the electronic and vibration–rotation spectra of the dimers exhibit similar features to those of normal small molecules. Analysis of these spectra can lead to structural parameters for the dimers, which in turn give detailed information about the well region of the intermolecular potential. van der Waals molecules may also be observed in molecular beams and their spectra studied by microwave and radiofrequency techniques.

1.10.5. Solid and liquid properties

The lattice energy, nearest-neighbour spacing and properties such as the compressibility and heat capacity of molecular solids can be related to intermolecular forces. As mentioned above, when studying the pair potential, allowance must be made for non-pairwise additive contributions to the many-body energy.

The same problem occurs in liquids, where the calculation of even the pairwise additive energy is much more difficult. The absence of a regular structure in liquids means that sophisticated computer simulation calculations have to be performed in order to calculate liquid properties, such as the equation of state, for an assumed intermolecular potential.

A general conclusion from studies of the solid and liquid properties of the inert gases has been that by using the Axilrod–Teller triple dipole correction for non-pairwise additivity, pair potentials may be obtained that are consistent with those obtained from other sources. It is not yet known whether a similar simplification will be successful for more complex molecules.

In the chapters that follow we examine in more detail how the properties introduced above can be used to obtain information about intermolecular potentials. The final chapter summarizes our current knowledge of inter-molecular interactions for a wide range of systems.

Appendix 1A. Electrostatic interaction energy

Consider the simple case in which a molecule may be represented by a linear charge distribution, as shown in Fig. A1.1. This consists of two charges about an axis, O, taken to be the centre of gravity of the molecule. Charge Q_1 is located on the z axis at $-z_1$, and Q_2 is at z_2. First let us evaluate the electrostatic potential, ϕ, due to the molecule at the point P shown in the figure. This may be expressed in terms of the separations of P from Q_1 and Q_2,

$$\phi = \frac{1}{4\pi\varepsilon_0}\left[\frac{Q_1}{r_1} + \frac{Q_2}{r_2}\right]$$

where ε_0 is the permittivity of free space. An alternative representation in terms of the coordinates r, θ of point P and the axial separations of the charges from the origin may be written

$$(4\pi\varepsilon_0)\phi = \frac{Q_1}{[r^2 + z^2 + 2z_1 r\cos\theta]^{1/2}} + \frac{Q_2}{[r^2 + z^2 - 2z_2 r\cos\theta]^{1/2}}.$$

Fig. A1.1 A linear charge distribution.

In cases where $r \gg z_1$ and $r \gg z_2$, the denominator may conveniently be expanded in powers of z_1/r and z_2/r, using the binomial theorem, to give

$$(4\pi\varepsilon_0)\phi = \frac{Q_1 + Q_2}{r} + \frac{(Q_2 z_2 - Q_1 z_1)\cos\theta}{r^2} + \frac{(Q_1 z_1^2 + Q_2 z_2^2)}{2r^3}(3\cos^2\theta - 1) + \dots$$

which may be written in the alternative form

$$(4\pi\varepsilon_0)\phi = \frac{Q}{r} + \frac{\mu\cos\theta}{r^2} + \frac{\Theta}{2}\frac{(3\cos^2\theta - 1)}{r^3} + \dots$$

We have written $Q = Q_1 + Q_2$ for the total charge of the molecule. $\mu = Q_2 z_2 - Q_1 z_1$ and is the dipole moment of the molecule, or the first moment of the charge distribution. $\Theta = Q_1 z_1^2 + Q_2 z_2^2$, and is the quadrupole moment of the linear charge distribution. (It should be noted that the value of the first non-zero moment is independent of the origin of the coordinates used.) This multipole expansion is appropriate only for $r \gg z_1, z_2$, and is thus suitable only for the study of long-range intermolecular interactions.

Let us consider the interaction of two such polar molecules, A and B, placing a second similar charge distribution, $Q_1' Q_2'$ with its centre of mass at P, as shown in Fig. A1.2. The distance r is now the separation of the centres of mass of the two distributions, and their relative orientation is defined by the three angles θ_A, θ_B, and ϕ shown in the figure. The electrostatic interaction energy, U_{el}, of these two distributions may be represented

$$U_{el} = Q_1' \phi(r_1) + Q_2' \phi(r_2)$$

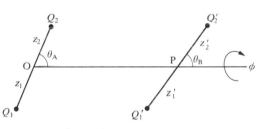

Fig. A1.2 The interaction of two linear polar molecules.

where $\phi(r_1)$ and $\phi(r_2)$ are the electrostatic potentials due to the first distribution, $Q_1 Q_2$, at the charges Q_1' and Q_2', respectively. By the application of simple (but rather tedious) trigonometry, the distances r_1 and r_2, and their orientations relative to $Q_1 Q_2$ may be expressed in terms of r, z_1, z_2, and the angles θ_A, θ_B, ϕ. The potentials $\phi(r_1)$ and $\phi(r_2)$ may be expanded in terms of z_1/r and z_2/r, provided r is large, to give

$$(4\pi\varepsilon_0)U_{el} = \frac{QQ'}{r} + \frac{1}{r^2}(Q'\mu\cos\theta_A - Q\mu'\cos\theta_B)$$

$$- \frac{\mu\mu'}{r^3}\left(2\cos\theta_A\cos\theta_B - \sin\theta_A\sin\theta_B\cos\phi\right)$$

$$+ \frac{1}{2r^3}\left(Q\Theta'(3\cos^2\theta_B - 1) + Q'\Theta_A(3\cos^2\theta_A - 1)\right) + \dots$$

If the total charge of each molecule is zero, $Q = Q' = 0$, and the leading term is seen to be the dipole–dipole energy,

$$U_{\mu\mu} = \frac{1}{4\pi\varepsilon_0}\left[-\frac{\mu\mu'}{r^3}(2\cos\theta_A\cos\theta_B - \sin\theta_A\sin\theta_B\cos\phi)\right]$$

where μ' is the dipole moment of the second charge distribution. The terms resulting from some of the higher multipoles, which result when the expansion is carried further, have been given earlier. We note that these low-order terms in the multipole expansion merely represent the lowest non-zero contributions to the electrostatic energy, and also that they are valid only when the dimensions of the molecules are small compared to their separation.

Appendix 1B. The dispersion energy according to the Drude model

In section 1.4 the dispersion energy was attributed to the interaction of instantaneous dipoles in the molecules. A very simple model of a molecule that permits such interactions was proposed by Drude. In a simple version of this approach, we represent each molecule by two charges, $+Q$ and $-Q$, and assume that the positive charge is stationary, while the negative charge performs simple harmonic oscillations about it with a frequency v in the z-direction, which is along the line joining two such molecules, a and b (see Fig. A1.3). If the instantaneous displacements of the two charges on molecules a and b are z_a and z_b, then at any time t the molecules have instantaneous dipole moments $\mu_a = Qz_a(t)$ and $\mu_b = Qz_b(t)$, though the average dipole moment is zero. If the force constant of the simple harmonic oscillator is k, and the mass of the oscillating charge is m, we have

$$v = \frac{1}{2\pi}\sqrt{\frac{k}{m}}.$$

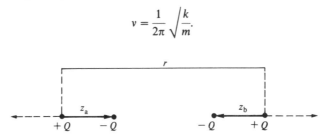

Fig. A1.3 The one-dimensional Drude model of the dispersion interaction.

When the molecules are separated by a great distance, the Schrödinger wave equation for molecule a may be written

$$\frac{1}{m}\frac{\partial^2\psi}{\partial z_a^2} + \frac{8\pi^2}{h^2}[E_a - \tfrac{1}{2}kz_a^2]\psi = 0.$$

This is the Schrödinger equation for a simple harmonic oscillator, in which $\tfrac{1}{2}kz_a^2$ is the potential energy of the oscillator. The eigenvalues of molecules a and b in this case are

$$E_a = (n_a + \tfrac{1}{2})hv; \quad E_b = (n_b + \tfrac{1}{2})hv.$$

The lowest permitted state corresponds to both molecules in their zero point, $n = 0$, levels, and thus has a total energy

$$E(\infty) = E_a + E_b = h\nu.$$

For smaller separations, r, which are still large compared with molecular dimensions, and the amplitude of the vibrations, there is an additional term in the Schrödinger equation, resulting from the electrostatic interaction of the two dipoles. The Schrödinger equation for the two-molecule system then reads

$$\frac{1}{m}\frac{\partial^2\psi}{\partial z_a^2} + \frac{1}{m}\frac{\partial^2\psi}{\partial z_b^2} + \frac{8\pi^2}{h^2}\left[E - \tfrac{1}{2}kz_a^2 - \tfrac{1}{2}kz_b^2 - \frac{2z_a z_b Q^2}{(4\pi\varepsilon_0)r^3}\right]\psi = 0.$$

The effect of the additional term is to change the vibration frequencies, and hence the energy, by an amount which depends on the separation, r. A change of variables permits the equation to be rewritten in a manner that reveals the form of the solutions. If we introduce the new variables

$$Z_1 = \frac{z_a + z_b}{\sqrt{2}}, \; Z_2 = \frac{z_a - z_b}{\sqrt{2}}$$

we may then write

$$\frac{1}{m}\frac{\partial^2\psi}{\partial Z_1^2} + \frac{1}{m}\frac{\partial^2\psi}{\partial Z_2^2} + \frac{8\pi^2}{h^2}[E - \tfrac{1}{2}k_1 Z_1^2 - \tfrac{1}{2}k_2 Z_2^2]\psi = 0$$

where $k_1 = k - \dfrac{2Q^2}{4\pi\varepsilon_0 r^3}$ and $k_2 = k + \dfrac{2Q^2}{4\pi\varepsilon_0 r^3}$.

This modified equation has the form appropriate to two *non-interacting* simple harmonic oscillators, with changed force constants. The corresponding frequencies are

$$\nu_1 = \nu\sqrt{\left(1 - \frac{2Q^2/4\pi\varepsilon_0 r^3}{k}\right)},$$

$$\nu_2 = \nu\sqrt{\left(1 + \frac{2Q^2/4\pi\varepsilon_0 r^3}{k}\right)}.$$

The lowest energy is now the sum of the zero-point energies for each of these oscillators

$$E(r) = \tfrac{1}{2}h(\nu_1 + \nu_2)$$

and on expanding the expressions for the modified frequencies using the binomial theorem, and retaining only the first significant term we find

$$E(r) = h\nu - \frac{Q^4 h\nu}{2(4\pi\varepsilon_0)^2 r^6 k^2}.$$

The interaction energy U is thus

$$U = E(r) - E(\infty) = \frac{-Q^4 h\nu}{2(4\pi\varepsilon_0)^2 r^6 k^2}.$$

The force constant, k, may be related to the polarisability of the molecules, α, which represents the displacement of charge which arises when a molecule is placed in a static field. We find

$$\alpha = Q^2/k$$

and hence

$$U = \frac{-\alpha^2 h\nu}{2(4\pi\varepsilon_0)^2 r^6}.$$

In an improvement of the model, the oscillation of the charge in three dimensions can be resolved into components in the x, y, and z directions, to give for the dispersion energy

$$U_{\text{disp}} = \frac{-3\alpha^2 h\nu}{4(4\pi\varepsilon_0)^2 r^6}.$$

In order to estimate the magnitude of U_{disp} according to this model, we must introduce a value for the energy, $h\nu$. London assumed that $h\nu$ could be equated with the ionisation energy of the molecule, E_{I}, and so wrote

$$U_{\text{disp}} = \frac{-3\alpha^2 E_{\text{I}}}{4(4\pi\varepsilon_0)^2 r^6}.$$

The value obtained in this way for this, the leading coefficient, C_6, in the complete dispersion energy expansion

$$U_{\text{disp}} = C_6/r^6 + C_8/r^8 + C_{10}/r^{10} + \ldots$$

is only about 25 per cent smaller for Ar than the results subsequently obtained from the most refined and extensive calculations.

Suggested further reading

Maitland, G. C., Rigby, M., Smith, E. B., and Wakeham, W. A. (1981). *Intermolecular forces: their origin and determination.* Chapters 1 and 2. Clarendon Press, Oxford. (Referred to in text as MRSW.)
Maitland, G. C. and Smith, E. B. (1973) *Chem. Soc. Rev.* **2**, 181.
Murrell, J. N. and Boucher, E. A. (1982) *Properties of liquids and solutions.* Chapter 2. Wiley, New York.
Reed, T. M. and Gubbins, K. E. (1973) *Applied statistical mechanics.* Chapters 4 and 5. McGraw-Hill, New York.

Exercises

E1.1. The dipole moment of hydrogen chloride is $3.4 \times 10^{-30}\,\text{C m}$, and its (mean) polarizability $\alpha/(4\pi\varepsilon_0) = 2.63 \times 10^{-30}\,\text{m}^3$. Calculate the contributions to the inter-molecular energy from dipole-dipole and dipole-induced dipole interactions, for the two relative orientations $\rightarrow \rightarrow$, $\rightarrow \uparrow$, and a centre of mass separation of $5.00 \times 10^{-10}\,\text{m}$.

$[4\pi\varepsilon_0 = 1.113 \times 10^{-10}\,\text{C}^2\text{J}^{-1}\text{m}^{-1}]$

E1.2. The dispersion interaction coefficients, C_6, C_8, and C_{10} for two argon atoms have values -67.2, -1708 and -53000 atomic units, respectively. Use these values to calculate the relative contributions to the energy, U_8/U_6 and U_{10}/U_6, at $4r_m$ and at $1.5r_m$, given that $r_m = 3.76\text{Å} = 7.11$ atomic units (a_0).

E1.3. A general n–m pair potential function may be written

$$U(r) = \varepsilon \left[\left(\frac{m}{n-m} \right) \left(\frac{r_m}{r} \right)^n - \left(\frac{n}{n-m} \right) \left(\frac{r_m}{r} \right)^m \right]$$

where $U(r_m) = -\varepsilon$. For the case of an 18–6 potential, show that the ratio r_m/σ is $3^{1/12}$ (where $U(\sigma) = 0$), and hence that the potential may be written in the alternative form

$$U(r) = A\varepsilon \left[(\sigma/r)^{18} - (\sigma/r)^6 \right].$$

What is the value of A?

2
Molecular beams

2.1. Introduction

The relative motion of two bodies under the influence of a force acting between them has long been the subject of intensive scientific study. Perhaps the most familiar example is the motion of a planet around the sun under the influence of gravitational attraction. Indeed, this particular study provided confirmation that the force of attraction was proportional to the inverse square of the distance between the bodies. It might be expected, therefore, that the study of the relative motion of two interacting molecules (a collision) would provide information about the forces between them. However, the study of molecular collisions is much more complicated than that of the orbits of the planets. First, as we have seen, the intermolecular forces possess both attractive and repulsive contributions, which enhance the variety of possible behaviour. Secondly, the theoretical analysis of the molecular motion cannot properly be carried out with classical mechanics because the small molecular mass ($m \sim 5 \times 10^{-26}$ kg) means that at thermal energies the de Broglie wavelength of a molecule ($\lambda = h/mv$) is sufficiently large that a quantum mechanical description of the process is essential. Quantum mechanics does not allow us to predict exactly the outcome of a single specific encounter of two molecules, but restricts us to the probable outcome of the collision. We are thus able to predict only the overall result of a large number of initially similar encounters.

Of course, it is also impossible to direct just two molecules towards each other and to observe their motion. However, it is possible to direct a beam of molecules with essentially the same energy, E, towards a second beam of 'target' molecules. This situation is equivalent to a large number of two-molecule collisions in each of which a molecule in the primary beam is deflected from its original course by the forces exerted by a target molecule. Consequently, at any angle, Θ, to the initial direction of the beam, a stream of molecules can be observed as shown in Fig. 2.1. The molecules in this scattered beam may not all have undergone identical collisions with a target molecule because, as we shall see, several types of encounter can lead to deflection through the same angle Θ. Nevertheless, if the flux of scattered molecules is measured at the detector as a function of the angle Θ a pattern of the intensity

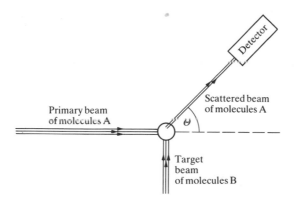

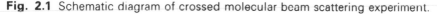

Fig. 2.1 Schematic diagram of crossed molecular beam scattering experiment.

$I(E,\Theta)$ is produced of the type shown in Fig. 2.2. This pattern is characteristic of the relative kinetic energy of the colliding molecules, E, and, most importantly, of the intermolecular pair potential through which they interact. It is this quite structured 'fingerprint' of the scattering experiment that may be used to derive information about the intermolecular pair potential.

It will be noticed that the scattering experiment yields very nearly what a quantum-mechanical analysis of the collision between just two molecules provides. That is, they both give the overall result of a large number of two-molecule collisions. The difference lies in the fact that in the theoretical analysis all of the encounters take place from an identical initial situation whereas, in the experiment, it is impossible to ensure this. However, the theoretical analysis is readily extended to take account of this difference.

2.2. Molecular beam experiments

The general features of an instrument for the observation of molecular scattering processes are illustrated schematically in Fig. 2.3. Fig. 2.3(a) shows the simplest kind of arrangement. Here, a beam of molecules is produced in a source and directed at a small volume of target gas. The selector, placed between the source and the target, ensures that only molecules possessing kinetic energies (or velocities) within a certain range of a prescribed value E (or v) may pass through it. When the molecular beam impinges on the target, collisions with the molecules of the target gas cause some of the beam molecules to be scattered out of the original direction of the beam, and the molecular flux in the forward direction is consequently reduced below its incident value. The molecular flux is observed by the detector (which may also have a further energy selector in front of it) as an intensity, I, which lies below that observed in the absence of the target gas, I_0. The loss of molecules from

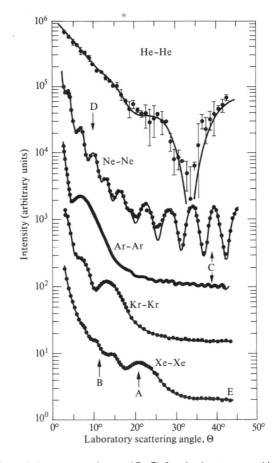

Fig. 2.2 Differential cross-sections $\sigma(\Theta, E)$ for the inert gases. He, Ne, Ar, Kr, and Xe, showing fine structure. Principal features: A, rainbow maximum; B, super-numary rainbow peaks; C, symmetry (identical particle) oscillations; D, high-frequency quantum oscillations; E, monotonic large-angle scattering. (Farrar, J. M., Schafer, T. P., and Lee, Y. T. (1973). AIP Conference Proceedings, Vol. 11, p. 279.)

the beam represents those molecules scattered at *all* angles (other than $\Theta = 0$) from the direction of the original beam.

The reduction in intensity is characterized by an 'integral cross-section', $Q(E)$, which depends upon the relative kinetic energy, g, of the colliding molecules; it is defined by the equation

$$\frac{I}{I_0} = \exp\left[-nlQ(E)\right] \tag{2.1}$$

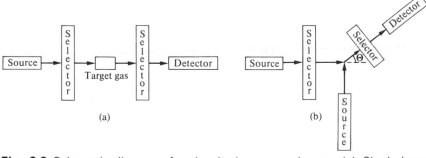

Fig. 2.3 Schematic diagram of molecular beam experiments. (a) Single-beam technique; (b) cross-beam technique. The selectors can be used to select particular velocities or internal states if required.

where n is the number of target gas molecules per unit volume and l is the length of the target gas sample cell in the direction of the beam. Figure 2.4 shows schematically the typical behaviour of the integral cross-section as a function of energy. The overall shape of this curve indicates that many more molecules are scattered out of the incident beam at low energy than at high energy. However, the curve also possesses some detailed structure, which we shall consider later.

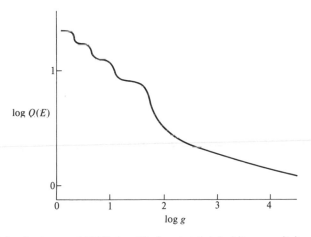

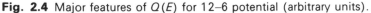

Fig. 2.4 Major features of $Q(E)$ for 12–6 potential (arbitrary units).

The description of the simplest kind of molecular beam scattering experiment belies the complexity of the equipment necessary to conduct the work. Indeed, the key to the dramatic advances in the study of molecular collisions that has taken place in the last twenty years was the development of supersonic nozzle sources, which produce beams of molecules of uniform velocity. In these devices a high-intensity supersonic beam of molecules is produced by adiabatic expansion of a gas, initially at a low temperature and a pressure of around 1 bar, through a suitably shaped nozzle into a high vacuum region maintained at about 10^{-9} bar. Further collimation and energy selection of the beam then allows a narrow beam of monoenergetic molecules to be obtained and directed at a target.

The target gas is maintained at a relatively low pressure ($\sim 10^{-4}$ bar) and at a low temperature, in a chamber which is traversed by the primary beam through entrance and exit slits. The low temperature of the target gas serves to reduce the spread of velocities of the target molecules, and the low pressure ensures that each molecule of the beam collides with only one target molecule. Upon leaving the target gas chamber the unscattered molecules in the beam proceed to a detector, which may be a mass spectrometer or a bolometer; this measures the total flux of particles. Measurements of $Q(E)$ are made by determining the molecular flux at the detector with and without the target gas in place according to eqn (2.1).

Figure 2.3 (b) shows the arrangement used to observe the scattered beam intensity as a function of angle, Θ, which results from collisions between the molecules of two intersecting beams. In this system the detector is able to rotate in the plane of the figure about the zone of interaction of the two beams. As indicated earlier, measurements of this type yield angular distributions of intensity such as those contained in Fig. 2.2 for each relative kinetic energy. The complicated fine structure of the angle-dependent intensity pattern proves to be a more sensitive characteristic of the intermolecular pair potential for the interaction of the molecules of the two beams than does the integral cross-section. The practical realization of the schematic arrangement shown in Fig. 2.3(b) involves a high degree of experimental sophistication. First, it is necessary to employ two supersonic-nozzle beams of the type described above, one for each of the interacting species, which intersect in a high vacuum region. Secondly, a detector sensitive to just one of the species, located within the high vacuum region, must be capable of rotation about the centre of intersection of the two beams to observe the scattered beam of one type of particle at any angle Θ. Obviously, the number of particles scattered at any one particular angle is a small fraction of the flux observed in the integral cross-section measurements. Consequently the problem of sensitivity of detection is exacerbated and, although the difficulty may be mitigated by increasing the area of the detector, there is an upper limit to this increase set by the need to retain good angular resolution in the measurements. For these reasons, instruments that satisfy all of these conditions have been developed only in the last fifteen years and make use of sophisticated electronic methods for beam intensity measurements.

2.3. The scattering of atoms

2.3.1. The classical mechanical theory of binary collisions

In this section we consider the classical mechanical theory of the scattering of atoms that interact through a spherically symmetric pair potential $U(r)$. Encounters between such systems represent the simplest kind of collision because the atoms possess no internal energy. Moreover, the use of classical mechanics, although not adequate for a complete description of the observed phenomena, does illustrate the general features of the process, and provides a framework with which to illustrate the ways in which quantum-mechanical effects influence the scattering.

In the molecular beam experiments described in the previous section, the frame of reference for the description of the scattering process was fixed relative to the laboratory. However, the theoretical analysis of the collision between two molecules is most easily carried out in a frame of reference that is fixed relative to the centre of mass of the colliding pair of molecules. We consider the encounter of two structureless particles of masses m_a and m_b, which interact through a spherically symmetrical pair potential $U(r)$ so that they exert an equal and opposite force of magnitude $F = \dfrac{-dU(r)}{dr}$ upon each other. The position vectors of the two particles relative to the laboratory frame of reference are $\mathbf{r}_a$ and $\mathbf{r}_b$, and their velocities in this frame of reference are $\mathbf{c}_a$ and $\mathbf{c}_b$, as shown in Fig. 2.5. The position of the centre of mass in the laboratory reference frame, $\mathbf{r}_c$, is then defined by the equation

$$\mathbf{r}_c = \frac{m_a \mathbf{r}_a + m_b \mathbf{r}_b}{m_a + m_b}, \tag{2.2}$$

whereas the vector corresponding to the separation of the two particles $\mathbf{r}$ is

$$\mathbf{r} = \mathbf{r}_a - \mathbf{r}_b. \tag{2.3}$$

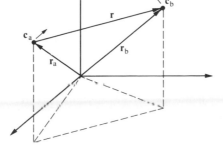

Fig. 2.5 Coordinate vectors of two colliding molecules.

Application of Newton's Law of motion

$$F = m_a \frac{d\mathbf{c}_a}{dt} = -m_b \frac{d\mathbf{c}_b}{dt}$$

to these particles reveals through eqn (2.2) that the centre of mass of the system moves with a constant velocity in the laboratory frame of reference (see Exercise E2.2). Furthermore, differentiation of eqn (2.3) with respect to time shows that the *relative* motion of the particles may be represented by the equation

$$\frac{d}{dt}\left(\frac{d\mathbf{r}}{dt}\right) = \frac{d\mathbf{c}}{dt} = \frac{d\mathbf{c}_a}{dt} - \frac{d\mathbf{c}_b}{dt} = \left(\frac{1}{m_a} + \frac{1}{m_b}\right)F = \mu^{-1}F$$

where μ is the reduced mass of the two-particle system ($\mu = m_a m_b/(m_a + m_b)$).

This result shows that the relative motion may be described by the equation of just one particle, which has the reduced mass of the original pair under the influence of the force field F. This equivalent one-body collision is sketched in Fig. 2.6 and serves to define the important physical parameters of the collision. The vector $\mathbf{r}$, which makes an angle θ with the initial direction of motion, now joins the centre of mass O to the particle of reduced mass μ which follows the trajectory T in the centre of mass frame of reference. The distance b is called the *impact parameter* and represents the closest distance of approach of the particle to the origin that would have occurred in the absence of $U(r)$. The vector $\mathbf{r}_0$ represents the position of closest approach of the two molecules and is known as the *classical turning point* for the encounter. The overall angle through which the direction of motion of the incoming body is rotated during the collison, χ, is known as the *angle of deflection*. It is related to the polar angle θ_0 by the equation

$$\chi = \pi - 2\theta_0.$$

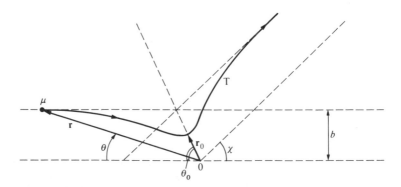

Fig. 2.6 One-body trajectory equivalent to a binary collision. b is the impact parameter, r_0 the classical turning point, χ the scattering angle, and μ the reduced mass of the colliding pair.

In order to describe the trajectory T of Fig. 2.6 classically, it is only necessary to consider the conservation of energy, E, and angular momentum L about the centre of mass O. This leads to differential equations for the angle θ and position r of the single particle with respect to the centre of mass, whose solution yields the trajectory T in parametric form. The particular quantity of interest in the encounter is the final deflection angle χ, which may be obtained in the form

$$\chi(b, g) = \pi - 2b \int_{r_0}^{\infty} \frac{dr/r^2}{\{1 - b^2/r^2 - U(r)/(\tfrac{1}{2}\mu g^2)\}^{1/2}} \tag{2.4}$$

where r_0 is given by the largest real solution of the equation

$$1 - b^2/r^2 - U(r)/(\tfrac{1}{2}\mu g^2) = 0$$

and g is the initial relative velocity.

For a constant initial relative velocity g the variation of the deflection angle with impact parameter b is called the *classical deflection function*. For a realistic intermolecular pair potential containing repulsive and attractive regions, the behaviour of the deflection function resembles that sketched in Fig. 2.7 for several initial relative velocities. Figure 2.8 illustrates some of the corresponding trajectories.

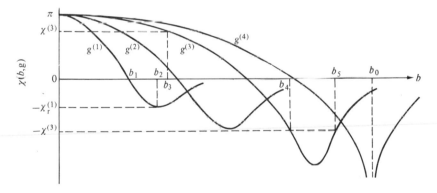

Fig. 2.7 Typical deflection functions for central force scattering, corresponding to the trajectories of Fig. 2.8. Relative initial speeds: $g^{(1)} > g^{(2)} > g^{(3)} > (2E_4/\mu)^{1/2} = g^{(4)}$. ($E_4$ refers to the critical orbiting energy.)

Let us first consider a fixed incident relative velocity $g^{(1)}$. Collisions in which the deflection angle is large and positive can be seen to arise at small values of the impact parameter b and correspond to nearly head-on collisions, at very small angular momentum, as illustrated in Fig. 2.8(a). The direction of approach of the particle is almost exactly reversed following the encounter,

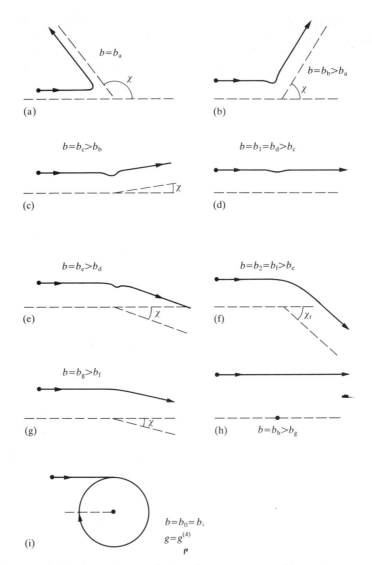

Fig. 2.8 Typical trajectories of collisions having a range of impact parameters, all at the same energy, $g^{(1)}$, except for (i) where $g = g^{(4)} < g^{(1)}$.

which involves essentially the repulsive wall of the intermolecular pair potential. As the value of b is increased, keeping g constant, the incoming particle is less affected by the short-range repulsive part of the potential and the deflection angle is reduced as in Fig. 2.8(b). As the impact parameter is increased still further, the attractive part of the intermolecular pair potential becomes more important and the incoming particle is first attracted towards the origin until the increasing repulsion from the potential at short range causes it to be deflected outwards again. In this case, the trajectory will resemble that in Fig. 2.8(c). At some value of the impact parameter for the energy $g^{(1)}$, the overall effects of attraction and repulsion will cancel exactly and the particle will suffer no net deflection ($\chi = 0$) which corresponds to the impact parameter b_1 of Fig. 2.7 and the trajectory in Fig. 2.8(d). This particular trajectory is known as the *glory trajectory*. As b is increased beyond b_1 the long-range attractive part of the potential becomes most significant and the trajectories resemble those of Fig. 2.8(e), in which the deflection angle is negative. Increasing b still further increases the deflection angle negatively (Fig. 2.8(e)) until a point is reached at which the magnitude of the attractive part of the intermolecular pair potential at long range diminishes so that it can no longer continue to increase the negative deflection of the particle. The maximum angle of the negative deflection corresponds to the impact parameter b_2 of Fig. 2.7 and is denoted by $\chi_r^{(1)}$. It is known as the *rainbow angle*—a name derived from the analogous extremum in the internal refraction of light by a water droplet, which is associated with the formation of an optical rainbow. The rainbow trajectory is sketched in Fig. 2.8(f). As b is increased beyond b_2 the negative deflection of the particle decreases as the inter-molecular attraction decays at long distances (Fig. 2.8(g)) until eventually the deflection becomes zero again when the impact parameter is so large that the intermolecular pair potential has no influence on the trajectory (Fig. 2.8(h)).

As the relative velocity is decreased to $g^{(2)}$ and $g^{(3)}$ the behaviour of the classical deflection function remains qualitatively the same, although the depth of the negative minimum in χ becomes greater and occurs at larger values of b. However, at or below a certain critical relative velocity $g^{(4)}$, the deflection angle becomes infinite at its extremum, which occurs at a characteristic value of $b = b_0$. This phenomenon is known as *orbiting* and the corresponding trajectory is sketched in Fig. 2.8(i). In this trajectory the attractive and repulsive forces on the particle are equal and opposite and the result is a closed orbit. The impact parameter for orbiting (b_0) and, consequently, the radius of the orbit, both increase as the relative velocity is decreased below $g^{(4)}$.

2.3.2. Scattering cross-sections

Our description of the experimental arrangements employed for the observation of molecular scattering indicates that it is not possible to ensure that all collisions take place with a single impact parameter, b. For this reason, it is not possible to determine the classical deflection function itself directly from experiment. Nevertheless, the flux of molecules scattered at a particular angle, which can be measured, may be related to a quantity derived from the classical deflection function. Let us consider the situation shown in Fig. 2.9, in which a beam of particles of flux I_0 impinges on a single scattering centre. Then all of

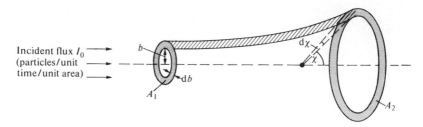

Fig. 2.9 Three-dimensional scattering: incident particles within the annular area A_1 are shown scattered through an angle χ into the annulus, area A_2.

those incoming particles whose impact parameters line in a small range $b \to b + db$ will pass through the annular ring of area $A_1 = 2\pi b\, db$. In turn, all of these particles will be scattered into a solid angle $d\Omega$ about the deflection angle χ subtended by the annular ring of area A_2 through which they will pass. If we define a quantity, called the *differential scattering cross-section* $\sigma\,(\chi, E)$, by the equation

$$\sigma\,(\chi, E) = \frac{\text{Number of scattered particles with energy } E/\text{unit time}/\text{unit solid angle about } \chi}{\text{Number of incident particles with energy } E/\text{unit time}/\text{unit area}}$$

then it follows that

$$\sigma\,(\chi, E) = \left| \frac{2\pi b\, db\, I_0/d\Omega}{I_0} \right|,$$

or, because $d\Omega = 2\pi \sin \chi d\chi$,

$$\sigma\,(\chi, E) = \left| \frac{b}{\sin \chi\, (d\chi/db)} \right|. \tag{2.5}$$

Now, in the laboratory frame of reference all the scattering into the annular ring at the angle χ of the centre of mass system, irrespective of the sign of χ, is detected at the same laboratory angle, Θ. Consequently, it is not possible to distinguish experimentally between positive and negative values of the deflection angle χ. This means that for a meaningful comparison with experiment, we should consider $\sigma\,(|\chi|, E)$ rather than $\sigma\,(\chi, E)$. Figure 2.7 illustrates that there are often two, and sometimes three, different impact parameters that lead to scattering through the same absolute deflection angle $|\chi|$. Consequently, we must write

$$\sigma\,(|\chi|, E) = \sum \left| \frac{b}{\sin \chi\, (d\chi/db)} \right|$$

where the summation extends over the contributing trajectories. The differential scattering cross-section $\sigma(|\chi|, E)$ may be related to the two experimentally accessible quantities in molecular beam experiments. First, the integral scattering cross-section, $Q(E)$, is just a measure of the total scattering irrespective of angle, so that

$$Q(E) = \int \sigma(|\chi|, E) \, d\Omega = 2\pi \int_0^\pi \sigma(|\chi|, E) \sin \chi \, d\chi. \qquad (2.6)$$

Second, the differential scattering cross-section may be related to the measured scattered particle flux $S(\Theta)$ at the laboratory scattering angle Θ. In this case it is necessary to transform from the centre-of-mass coordinate system used to describe $\sigma(|\chi|, E)$ to the frame of reference fixed in the laboratory, and to incorporate several characteristic parameters of the instrument.

2.3.3. The behaviour of the classical cross-sections

It is instructive to consider first the behaviour of the classical cross-section for molecules that behave as rigid spheres of diameter d. In this case if the impact parameter b is greater than d then $r_0 = b$ and there is no deflection, $\chi = 0$. On the other hand, when $b < d$, $r_0 = d$, and using eqn (2.4) we find

$$b = d \cos(\chi/2) \quad (b < d)$$

It then follows that the scattering cross-sections are given by

$$\sigma_{rs}(\chi, E) = d^2/4$$

and

$$Q_{rs}(E) = \pi d^2.$$

Hence, the scattering angle, the differential cross-section and the integral cross-section are all independent of energy for hard-sphere collisions and are determined by the diameter of the spheres, as would be expected intuitively.

For a realistic intermolecular pair potential containing attractive and repulsive branches the situation is rather different. In general, the classical deflection function and the differential scattering cross-section must be evaluated numerically and a sketch of the typical behaviour for just one energy is shown in Fig. 2.10. It can be seen that the cross-section becomes infinite at two different angles, $\chi = 0$ and $\chi = \chi_r$. The origin of this behaviour may be seen in eqn (2.5). Whenever $\sin \chi = 0$, the denominator of eqn (2.5) becomes zero, so that the scattering cross-section becomes infinite. The most obvious case for which $\sin \chi = 0$ corresponds to that of no deflection, when $\chi = 0$, which arises from trajectories such as that of Fig. 2.8 (h), in which the impact parameter is very large. However, there are other contributions to the scattering at $\chi = 0$ from trajectories such as the glory trajectory of Fig. 2.8 (d)

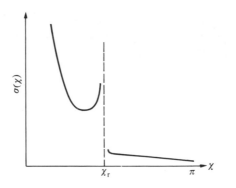

Fig. 2.10 Classical differential cross-section for a potential of the 12–6 type, showing the singularities at the rainbow angle, χ_r and as $\chi \rightarrow 0$.

in which the impact parameter is smaller and the particle is first attracted towards and then repelled from the scattering centre. In any event, because the total density of trajectories at $\chi = 0$ is just the sum of the number of particles arriving at $\chi = 0$ divided by the vanishing solid angle $d\Omega$, the classical differential scattering cross-section becomes infinite at $\chi = 0$.

At the rainbow angle, inspection of eqn (2.5) reveals that the differential scattering cross-section becomes infinite because $d\chi/db = 0$ there (see Fig. 2.7). Physically this corresponds to the fact that there is an infinite density of trajectories with slightly different impact parameters which converge on the angle χ_r.

One consequence of this classical behaviour of $\sigma(\chi, E)$ is that $Q(E)$, obtained by integrating over all angles, is predicted to be infinite, in contrast to the finite values observed experimentally. A comparison of the classical differential scattering cross-section of Fig. 2.10 with its experimental counterpart, the scattering intensity as a function of angle shown in Fig. 2.2, also reveals considerable differences. First, the experimental scattering intensity does not show the singularities predicted by the classical theory either at small angles or around the rainbow angle. Second, a number of oscillations can be discerned in the experimental scattering pattern that do not arise in our classical description. The origin of these differences must be attributed to the fact that classical mechanics provides an inadequate description of the scattering of atoms and that a quantum-mechanical treatment is necessary.

2.3.4. The quantum-mechanical theory

The detailed treatment of the quantum-mechanical theory of the scattering of atoms is beyond the scope of this book and the reader is referred to more specialized texts (e.g. MRSW, Chapter 4). Here, we concentrate upon a description of the physical processes that modify the classical behaviour of the scattering without considering the mathematical details.

Quantum mechanically, the behaviour of the system of two colliding particles under the influence of an intermolecular pair potential, $U(r)$, is described by the solution of the Schrödinger wave equation which, for the one-particle problem we have considered classically is

$$\left(-\frac{h^2}{2\mu}\nabla^2 + U(r)\right)\Psi(\mathbf{r}) = E\Psi(\mathbf{r}). \tag{2.7}$$

According to the usual Born interpretation of the wave function, $\Psi(\mathbf{r})$, its square yields the probability of finding two particles separated by the vectorial distance $\mathbf{r}$. Consequently, if we can obtain the solution of eqn. (2.7) for large separation, $r \to \infty$, beyond the range of the intermolecular pair potential, the angular distribution of the probability function about the scattering centre yields essentially the differential scattering cross-section defined earlier. The quantum-mechanical treatment of elastic scattering therefore reduces to the solution of the Schrödinger equation for the energy and intermolecular pair potential of interest. This process can, in practice, only be carried through numerically, but the qualitative consequences of quantum-mechanical effects, which have their origin in the wave-like description of the scattering, can be established without performing such calculations.

We first consider the classical deflection function $\chi(b, g)$ whose modulus, $|\chi|$, is sketched in Fig. 2.11. The modulus is used in this case to emphasize that the sign of χ cannot be determined experimentally. Three distinct branches of the deflection function have been labelled. The first, branch, (a), contains the positive values of χ; the second region containing the values from its zero crossing to the rainbow angle is labelled (b), and the final region beyond the rainbow angle is labelled (c). It can be seen that because it is not possible to distinguish experimentally between positive and negative values of χ, as many as three different impact parameters can lead to scattering at the same absolute deflection angle $|\chi|$. In a classical treatment the contributions to the scattered flux at $|\chi|$ are simply additive, as argued earlier. However, the wave description of the scattering process required by quantum mechanics implies that there may be interference between the wave functions for particles that arrive at the

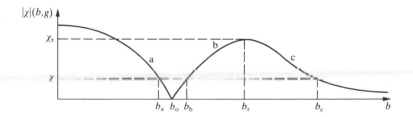

Fig. 2.11 The modulus of the classical deflection function.

same angle having traversed different paths. In this case, the simple addition of the fluxes from contributing trajectories will be incorrect.

To see this, let us first consider the glory effect discussed earlier, which provided a contribution to the singularity in the classical differential scattering at $\chi = 0$. The two trajectories that contribute to the forward glory are sketched in Fig. 2.12. One of these trajectories arises from scattering at a large impact parameter on the c-branch of the classical deflection function; the other arises from the zero crossing between the a and b branches at smaller impact parameters. From the sketches of the two trajectories it can be seen that their path lengths are different. The effect is analogous to the passage of two light beams through media of different refractive indices, in that the phases of the wave functions for each trajectory are shifted relative to each other. Consequently the wave functions interfere with each other, yielding a resultant amplitude that depends upon the relative phase difference. This in turn depends upon the exact difference in the path lengths of the two trajectories. One result of this interference is that the contribution to the particle flux at $\chi = 0$ from trajectories of this type remains finite, so that the glory effect no longer contributes to a divergence in the differential scattering cross-section as it did in the classical treatment.

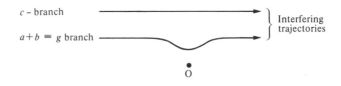

Fig. 2.12 Typical trajectories giving rise to the glory effect.

A second result of the interference which affects the integral cross-section arises because the relative phase shift of the two trajectories sketched in Fig. 2.12 depends upon the kinetic energy of the collision. This means that at some energies there is constructive interference between the two trajectories, whereas at others there is completely destructive interference. This change in the nature of the interference will repeat each time the relative phase shift changes by π. When the interference is constructive the differential scattering cross-section will attain a high value, but when the interference is destructive, it acquires a low value. This implies that when the integral scattering cross-section is calculated from the angle dependence of the differential scattering cross-section according to eqn (2.6), the contribution to the integral from $\chi \simeq 0$ oscillates between large and small values as the energy is changed, and gives rise to oscillations in the integral cross-section superimposed on the classical behaviour. This is illustrated in Fig. 2.13 for the case of a 12–6 potential, where

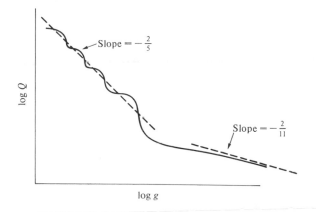

Fig. 2.13 Integral cross-section for 12–6 potential as a function of relative kinetic energy (schematic).

the so-called *glory oscillations* at low energies are shown superimposed on a background that reflects the behaviour of the potential at long range.

The form of the trajectories that contribute to these glory oscillations indicates that they involve both the attractive and repulsive regions of the potential and are therefore probing the intermolecular potential well. Indeed, a method has recently been developed whereby the spacing of the peaks of the glory oscillations in the integral cross section, as well as their amplitude and the spacing of the intersections of the oscillations with the mean asymptotic behaviour, may be used to determine the area of the potential well. In favourable circumstances the full form of the potential may be obtained by a direct inversion method. At high energies the repulsive part of the inter-molecular potential dominates the scattering and only the a-branch of the classical deflection function contributes to the scattering. Consequently, there are no glory interference effects and the oscillations in the integral cross-section die away as shown in Fig. 2.13. The limiting slope at high energies is determined by the steepness of the repulsive region of $U(r)$.

A further singularity in the classical differential scattering cross-section occurred at the so-called *rainbow angle*. Figure 2.14 contains sketches of three trajectories that lead to scattering at the same absolute deflection angle close to the classical rainbow angle. One trajectory arises from the a-branch, another from the b-branch and a final one from the c-branch. For angles slightly below the rainbow angle, the wave functions for the trajectories b and c have different phases owing to their different path lengths. Consequently the two wave functions will interfere with each other, the resultant amplitude and therefore the scattered flux depending upon the relative phase shift. As the scattering angle changes, the path length difference and the relative phase shift of the two

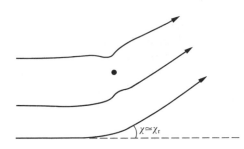

Fig. 2.14 Classical trajectories giving rise to the rainbow effect.

wave functions will be altered in a way reflected in the scattered flux. Once again, these changes in the scattered flux will oscillate as the relative phase shift passes through integer multiples of π. Consequently, near the rainbow angle it is to be expected that the differential scattering cross-section passes through a series of maxima and minima corresponding to constructive and destructive interference of trajectories from the b- and c-branches of the classical deflection function. These features of the scattering pattern, known as rainbows, can be observed as the relatively slow oscillations in the experimental results contained in Fig. 2.2. The maximum nearest to the classical rainbow angle is known as the *rainbow maximum*, and those at smaller angles as *supernumary rainbows*. It should also be noted that this same quantum-mechanical interference effect causes the classical singularity in the cross-section to be removed, although the effect is still a dominant feature of the scattering pattern, and a maximum is observed here in the differential cross-section.

In addition to the interference effects associated with trajectories b and c, the wave function for the trajectory from the a-branch of the classical deflection function can interfere with both of them. As before, the extent of the interference varies periodically as the relative phase shift of the a-trajectory is altered by movement to smaller deflection angles. These interference effects oscillate more rapidly with deflection angle and give rise to the *high-frequency quantum oscillations* in the scattering pattern seen at D in Fig. 2.2. In cases where supernumary rainbow peaks are observed, the rapid quantum oscillations will be superimposed upon them owing to the simultaneous interference of all three trajectories of Fig. 2.14. The high-frequency quantum oscillations persist at angles other than the rainbow angle as long as three trajectories can lead to the same deflection angle.

A further quantum-mechanical interference effect can be observed when the scattering of identical particles is considered. This arises because when two beams of identical particles are colliding, particles from either beam may leave the scattering centre and enter the detector and they are, of course, indistinguishable. In the centre of mass frame of reference, particles from one beam which reach the detector will have been deflected through an angle χ whereas particles from the other beam will have been deflected through an angle $(\pi - \chi)$. Because the particles from the two beams will have traversed a different path, there is a relative phase shift of the wave functions of the two particles, which will interfere in a way that depends upon the angle χ. As χ is changed the phase shift will move through integral multiples of π, leading to a further series of oscillations in the observed scattering pattern for identical particles. These oscillations, known as *symmetry oscillations*, are most marked when $\chi \sim \pi/2$ and the wave functions for the two interfering trajectories have a similar magnitude. The oscillations can be clearly seen in Fig. 2.2 for the Ne–Ne and Ar–Ar systems (C).

2.4. The use of molecular beam scattering data for the determination of intermolecular pair potentials

The modern advances in the experimental techniques of molecular beam scattering have enabled many of the detailed features of the differential and integral scattering cross-sections to be observed. However, for most systems not all of the features discussed above can be resolved in the experimental data and for this reason molecular beam data alone are seldom sufficient to determine the intermolecular pair potential of the species uniquely. One way in which molecular scattering cross-sections may be used to elucidate the form of the intermolecular potential takes the form of a trial-and-error procedure. Calculations of the differential and integral cross-sections are carried out for an assumed intermolecular pair potential and the results compared with the experimental data. Failure of the two sets of values to agree indicates that the assumed intermolecular pair potential is incorrect and so its parameters are adjusted or its form modified and the process repeated. It is quite clear from this description that such an approach does serve to disqualify intermolecular potentials from further consideration. On the other hand, it is by no means clear that an intermolecular pair potential, which does reproduce the experimental scattering data adequately, is unique and is the 'true' inter-molecular pair potential for the system. In view of this difficulty, attention has been concentrated upon methods whereby the beam scattering data may be inverted to yield $U(r)$ directly.

A number of schemes for the determination of intermolecular pair potentials from beam scattering data have been proposed. We have already mentioned one devised for the integral cross-section. For the differential cross-section there are two possible circumstances: either $\sigma(\chi)$ is known as a function of E at fixed angle, or, more commonly σ is known as a function of χ at a fixed energy. A variety of methods for the inversion of such data have been developed. Here we describe briefly just one example of the inversion of $\sigma(\chi)$ data for a fixed energy.

The inversion method proceeds in two stages; first the classical deflection function $\chi(b)$ is constructed in a piecemeal fashion using various characteristics of the experimental differential cross-section. This procedure is based upon the premise that the classical deflection function for a realistic pair potential will always have the form shown in Fig. 2.11, comprising a repulsive a-branch and an inner attractive b-branch, joined by a single extremum to an outer, attractive c-branch. We have already seen that the behaviour of the classical deflection function in each of these regions determines the behaviour of the differential scattering cross-section around a particular angle such as $\chi \simeq 0$ and $\chi = \chi_r$. It is, therefore, possible to employ measurements of the differential scattering cross-section around these angles to determine $\chi(b)$ within the corresponding branch of the classical deflection function. The segments of the deflection function obtained in this way may then be joined smoothly given the known constraints on its shape. The determination of $\chi(b)$ from $\sigma(\chi)$ at a given energy E is summarized in Figure 2.15, which demonstrates the physical relation of the various regions of the deflection function (and implicitly of $U(r)$) to the fine structure of the cross-sections. Once the classical deflection function has been constructed in this way a formal mathematical inversion of eqn (2.4) for $\chi(b, E)$ may be employed to determine $U(r)$.

As an example of the results attainable with this method, Fig. 2.16 contains the experimental differential scattering cross-section for Na–Hg at several energies, together with the derived intermolecular pair potential. In many cases the inversion method has not been applied in its full form because the resolution of the experimental data is insufficient. Molecular beam cross-sections in such cases then serve as just one element in a series of properties used to determine the potential.

2.5. The scattering of polyatomic molecules

When one or both of the molecules involved in a binary collision contains more than one atom there are two important effects that make the observed behaviour and its interpretation much more complex than in the atomic case.

1. The intermolecular pair potential energy for polyatomic systems is not simply a function of the separation of the centres of mass of the two molecules, but also depends upon the relative orientation of the two molecules and their internal coordinates. This means that, in contrast to the atomic case, the intermolecular pair potential is anisotropic and that the scattering can lead to motion out of the plane of the incoming trajectory.

2. Polyatomic molecules may possess energy in the internal modes of motion of the molecule, such as vibration and rotation. Owing to the fact that the intermolecular pair potential is anisotropic, some of this internal energy may be transferred from one molecule to another during the collision. Furthermore, some of the internal energy may be transferred from the internal

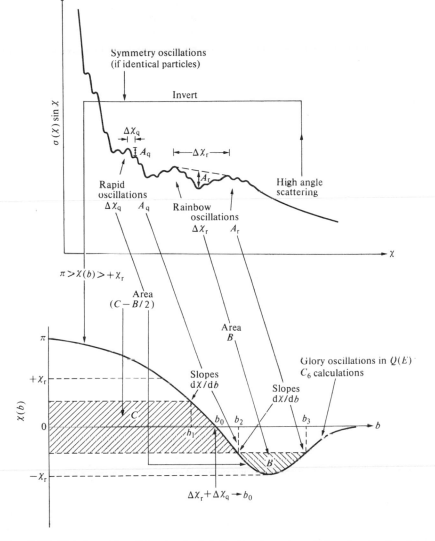

Fig. 2.15 Relationship of the classical deflection function $\chi(b)$ to the details of the differential scattering cross-section.

motion to translational kinetic energy of one or both molecules. These processes are known as inelastic collisions because translational kinetic energy is not, in general, conserved when they occur.

The study of these inelastic collision processes might be expected to yield information about the anisotropic intermolecular pair potential for the interaction. However, the experimental and theoretical difficulties associated

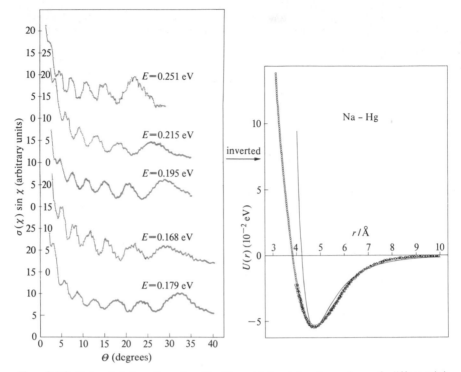

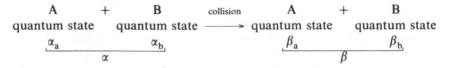

Fig. 2.16 Potential function for Na–Hg obtained by inversion of differential scattering cross-section. (Buck, U., and Pauly, H. (1971). *J. chem. Phys.* **51,** 1929.) Points are obtained by inversion of $\sigma(\Theta)$ at $E = 0.18$ eV ($\bigcirc$): $E = 0.19$ eV ($\Diamond$): $E = 0.20$ eV ($+$); $E = 0.22$ eV ($\triangle$); and $E = 0.25$ eV ($\square$); the solid line is a 12–6 potential having the same r_m and ε values as the inverted potential.

with such a study are much greater than for atomic systems, and it is only in the last few years that significant progress has been made. Here we merely illustrate the sources of the difficulties and mention the techniques that are currently being employed to overcome them.

Polyatomic molecules may exist in any one of a number of discrete quantum states characterized by a set of quantum numbers associated with each possible rotational and vibrational mode. We denote this entire set of quantum numbers by the symbol α or β. Consequently, in order to obtain a complete description of the collision of two such molecules, it is necessary to prescribe the internal quantum states of both molecules before and after collision. Thus, we must consider the collision between two molecules A and B as the process

$$
\begin{array}{ccccccc}
\text{A} & + & \text{B} & \xrightarrow{\text{collision}} & \text{A} & + & \text{B} \\
\text{quantum state} & & \text{quantum state} & & \text{quantum state} & & \text{quantum state} \\
\underline{\alpha_a} & & \underline{\alpha_b} & & \underline{\beta_a} & & \underline{\beta_b} \\
& \alpha & & & & \beta &
\end{array}
$$

Here the symbols α and β represent the quantum state of the entire two-molecule system before and after collision. In turn, this idea means that we must consider a more general definition of a differential scattering cross-section. At the most detailed level, we may consider the scattering of two molecules that, prior to collision, are in the state α and approach each other with a relative kinetic energy E. After collision the molecules are in the state β and in the centre of mass frame have been deflected through the polar angle χ and the corresponding azimuthal angle ψ. The so-called *individual differential cross-section is denoted by* $_i I_\alpha^\beta$ (E, χ, ψ) and is a measure of the flux of molecules that would be observed at the angles specified when two beams of molecules in the prescribed state collide. Experimentally, it is not often possible to define the quantum states of the two beams of molecules exactly either before or after collision. For example, each rotational energy level of a polyatomic molecule is degenerate and particular values of the magnetic quantum number associated with the degeneracy cannot always be distinguished. In such a case, the observed scattering is the sum over the appropriate quantum numbers of the cross-sections for the individual, but unresolved, cross-sections.

From the experimental point of view these new factors for polyatomic molecules mean that every effort must be made to define the quantum state of each of the colliding molecular beams as precisely as possible, both before and after collision. One way in which this state selection can be achieved for rotational levels is by passing the molecular beam through an electric or magnetic field, where it is deflected by an amount depending on its rotational quantum state. In combination with velocity selection and suitably positioned slits, a unique quantum state may be selected from the beam. An obvious immediate consequence of such a procedure is the reduction of the incident flux of molecules, because only a small fraction of the initial beam will be selected. This means that the problems of detection become much more severe. There have been, as yet, relatively few measurements of this type, and these have usually been performed on simple systems involving atoms and diatomic molecules. An example of the behaviour of such systems is shown in Fig. 2.17 for HD scattered by D_2. The elastic cross-section shows a similar oscillatory structure to that observed for spherical systems. The state-to-state inelastic differential cross-sections also show interference structure and prove to be a sensitive probe of the angular dependence of the interaction potential. The diffraction oscillations for different transitions are usually partly out of phase, so that when they are summed to give the total differential cross section, which is the quantity observed experimentally in the absence of state selection, the fine structure is damped compared to the spherical case. This tendency of anisotropic interactions to quench the interference structure of cross-sections is a general feature of the scattering of polyatomic molecules.

Where detailed state-to-state cross-sections are available, it is possible in certain favourable cases (e.g. inert gas $+ H_2$ or D_2) to obtain the major features

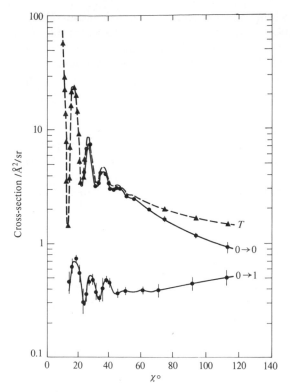

Fig. 2.17 Resolved differential scattering cross-sections for $j' \rightarrow j$, $0 \leftarrow 0$, and $1 \leftarrow 0$ transitions for HD scattered by D_2. T is the total differential cross-section. Energy $E_{tr} = 454$ meV. (Buck, U., Huisken, F., and Schleusener, J. (1978). *J. chem. Phys.* **68,** 5654.)

of the potential by direct inversion of the data. However, in general a multi-parameter fitting procedure must be used.

An alternative approach to the study of inelastic collision processes is simply to study the exchange of internal energy and translational energy. In a collision in which an energy $\Delta\varepsilon$ is transferred between internal and translational energy, the initial relative kinetic energy, E, may be increased or decreased to $E \pm \Delta\varepsilon$. In a molecular beam experiment this will be revealed as an increase or decrease in the relative velocity of the two molecules. If the flux of molecules that take a certain time to reach the detector from the scattering centre is observed, then a peak will be observed corresponding to the molecules whose velocity g_i is unaltered (at time t_i), and another peak will occur at a time t_f corresponding to the molecules whose velocities have been changed to g_f, because

$$\left(\frac{E}{E + \Delta\varepsilon} \right)^{1/2} = \frac{t_f}{t_i} = \frac{g_i}{g_f}.$$

This *time-of-flight spectrum* leads to a measure of the relative probability of elastic and inelastic collisions. Once again the detection problems in this type of experiment are severe, but as an example of the results that can be obtained after painstaking effort, Fig. 2.18 shows the time-of-flight spectrum recorded in studies of the vibrational inelastic scattering in the Li^+–H_2 system. The peaks in this system correspond to increasingly large vibrational quantum number increases in the hydrogen as the time of flight increases. In the case of rotationally inelastic scattering, intensity peaks can be observed in the energy loss spectra called *rotational rainbows*. These arise because particular rotational transitions are especially favoured by certain relative molecular orientations, by virtue of the potential anisotropy. These features are therefore of special value in the determination of non-spherical potentials. They also manifest themselves as maxima at high scattering angles in the differential cross-section.

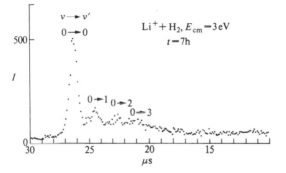

Fig. 2.18 Time-of-flight spectrum for vibrationally inelastic collisions of Li^+ with H_2.

From the theoretical point of view the introduction of the internal quantum states of the molecules implies that a quantum-mechanical treatment of the scattering process is necessary. As before, the Schrödinger equation for the wave function of the system may be written down, but its exact numerical solution for all but the simplest cases has so far proved beyond the capabilities of even the fastest computer. For this reason, a number of methods have been proposed in which the full Schrödinger equation is replaced by an approximate version resulting from various simplifications of the collision dynamics (Details are given in MRSW, Chapter 4). The most easily understood of these is the so-called *energy-sudden approximation*, in which it is assumed that the internal energy transferred in an inelastic collision is only a small fraction of the initial relative kinetic energy of the collision. This approximation is particularly suitable for collisions at high kinetic energies. A second approximation scheme is known as the *centrifugal-sudden approximation*. In this approach it is assumed that the initial angular momentum of the two colliding molecules is essentially unaltered throughout the collision. Each of these two approximations lead to a substantial simplification of the mathematical problem of treating a binary collision. When both of these approximations are made together, in the *infinite-order-sudden approximation*, even greater simplifications result and calculations of differential scattering cross-sections for specific internal transitions may be performed on a routine basis. As yet, because the exact solution for cases of interest is not available, the value of these approximation schemes has not been fully established.

In view of these difficulties it is perhaps not surprising that only a small amount has yet been learned about the interactions of polyatomic molecules from molecular beam scattering. However, the wealth of detail that scattering studies can be expected to yield encourage the belief that they will contribute substantially to progress in this area in the future. Indeed, molecular beams have already been employed with considerable success in the investigation of the interactions of molecules with surfaces. The results of these studies are discussed in Chapter 8.

Suggested further reading

Maitland, G. C., Rigby, M., Smith, E. B., and Wakeham, W. A. (1981). *Intermolecular forces: their origin and determination*. Chapter 4. Clarendon Press, Oxford. (Referred to in text as MRSW.)

Bernstein, R. B. ed. (1979). Atom–Molecule collision theory. Plenum, New York.

Child, M. S. (1974). Molecular collision theory. Academic Press, London.

Fluendy, M. A. D. and Lawley, K. P. (1973). Chemical applications of molecular beam scattering. Chapman and Hall, London.

Exercises

E2.1. For approximately what relative kinetic energy would you expect a quantum mechanical treatment of the scattering of two argon atoms to become necessary? The diameter of an argon atom is approximately 0.33 nm.

E2.2. Show that in a collision between two atoms the centre of mass of the system moves with a constant velocity in the laboratory frame of reference.

E2.3. If the interaction of two neon atoms is represented by a hard sphere potential, the differential scattering cross-section is approximately 1.7×10^{-20} m^2. Deduce the fractional reduction in the intensity of a beam of neon atoms passing through a 1 mm thick sample of neon gas at a pressure of 1 Pa and a temperature of 70 K. What is the hard sphere diameter of a neon atom?

3

Spectroscopic measurements

3.1. van der Waals molecules

In Chapter 2 we considered the collision of two molecules and saw that, under certain conditions, the encounter led to a situation in which the molecules orbit one another. This system of orbiting molecules is generally unstable and breaks up after a very short time. However, if the two molecules orbiting each other collide with a third molecule, then that molecule may remove some of the kinetic energy from the pair and lead to the formation of a more stable system that has a much longer lifetime. Pairs of molecules formed in this way are known as *van der Waals dimers or molecules*. Let us consider again the simplest case of the interaction of two atoms, discussed in Chapter 2, interacting through the spherically symmetric pair potential $U(r)$. The total energy of the pair of molecules is

$$\left. \begin{aligned} E &= \tfrac{1}{2}\mu g^2 + \tfrac{1}{2}\frac{L^2}{\mu r^2} + U(r) \\[2mm] &= \tfrac{1}{2}\mu g^2 + V(L, r). \end{aligned} \right\} \tag{3.1}$$

In these equations μ is the reduced mass of the pair of molecules, g the relative velocity of the two molecules in the centre of mass frame of reference, and L the initial angular momentum. Here, we have also defined the *effective potential energy* $V(L, r)$, which is the sum of a centrifugal term, $L^2/2\mu r^2$, and the intermolecular pair potential. Figure 3.1 contains plots of the effective potential energy for the case of zero angular momentum, $L = 0$, and a case when L is sufficiently large that $V(L, r)$ exhibits a positive outer maximum. For the case $L = 0$, if the energy of the system is greater than zero, then the two molecules constitute a collision pair in the continuum of states considered in Chapter 2. However, if a third molecule is present that removes kinetic energy from the pair, then they may fall into one of the discrete vibration–rotation energy levels in the potential well which, of course, resemble those of a chemically bound molecule. A pair of molecules in one of these states is termed a *bound dimer*.

In the case when the molecules approach each other with a non-zero angular

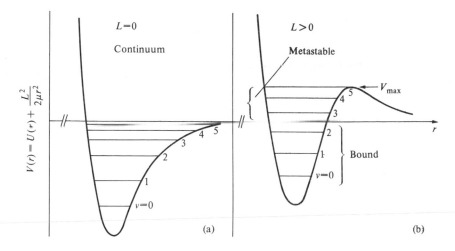

Fig. 3.1 Vibrational energy levels for a typical X_2 molecule having (a) no angular momentum ($L = 0$); (b) $L > 0$.

momentum and the effective potential exhibits an outer maximum, a third body may again remove energy from the rotating pair. If sufficient energy is removed the pair may again form a bound dimer in the discrete states within the well of the effective potential below $V(L, r) = 0$. However, if less energy is removed the pair may end up in one of the discrete states above $V(L, r) = 0$ but below the outer maximum in it. Pairs in these states are known as *metastable* (or *quasibound*) *dimers* because they can dissociate by quantum-mechanical tunnelling through the outer potential barrier.

As for any potential energy well, the allowed vibrational and rotational energies can be obtained from a solution of the Schrödinger equation. Such calculations have been performed for a number of model intermolecular pair potentials. It has been estimated on the basis of such calculations that Ne_2 possesses two bound states, Ar_2 170 and CsXe 2×10^5.

It should be clear from the preceding description of van der Waals dimers that they have many features in common with chemically bound diatomic molecules. However, there are a number of important differences that make the study of the dimers much more difficult than the study of chemically bound species. First, the potential well-depths (the dissociation energies) of dimers are typically 1 kJ mol^{-1}, which is several orders of magnitude smaller than that for a chemical bond. Consequently, only a small number of the atoms in a gas will be present in the form of dimers even at low temperatures, where $kT \sim \varepsilon$, the dissociation energy. For example, for argon at 120 K and 1 bar, only about 0.4 per cent of the atoms are present as bound dimers and 0.2 per cent as metastable dimers. Secondly, because the dimers are formed by collisions involving a third body, they may be dissociated in the same way. In addition, they may dissociate without collision by quantum-mechanical tunnelling through the centrifugal energy barrier. Although the latter mechanism is important for metastable dimers near the top of the barrier, most dimers dissociate by collision. Consequently, though increasing the density of a gas increases the number of dimers present, it also decreases their lifetime.

By analogy with chemically bound molecules it might be expected that considerable information about the intermolecular potential well can be obtained by studying the electromagnetic absorption spectrum of the dimers, which involves transitions between the various energy levels of the system. However, because of the small concentrations of dimers and because many van der Waals dimers of interest have no permanent dipole moment, it was not until recently that such studies became possible. In the last decade or so measurements of the absorption spectra of inert gas dimers, as well as dimers of like and unlike polyatomic molecules, have been performed.

3.2. Experimental studies

3.2.1. Non-polar molecules

The principles of the equipment used to carry out the first studies of the absorption spectra of van der Waals' dimers are the same as those employed in conventional spectroscopic studies of chemically bound molecules. That is, the gas under study is confined in an optical cell illuminated by a light source providing light of the appropriate frequency, and the light emerging from the cell is analyzed by a spectrograph to reveal the absorption lines. However, owing to the low concentrations of dimers present in the gas, the optical path length in the cell must be very large, and values as high as 13 m have been employed. Often the gas under study is maintained at liquid nitrogen temperatures to increase the dimer concentrations and at low pressures (1.3 $\times 10^{-6}$–0.1 bar) to increase their lifetime. For studies of inert gas dimers such as Ne_2, Ar_2, Kr_2, and Xe_2 the absence of a permanent dipole necessitated an indirect study of the transitions between the vibration–rotation energy states of the dimer. Tanaka and his co-workers carried out the first successful study of this type when they observed a series of absorption bands in the vacuum ultra-violet region of the spectrum arising from simultaneous electronic and vibration–rotation excitation of the dimer. In the original experiments the resolution was sufficient only to permit the identification of discrete lines arising from the vibrational transitions, but later work enabled the rotational fine structure to be resolved for one band.

Homonuclear molecules such as H_2, N_2 and O_2 do not themselves absorb in the infra-red region of the spectrum owing to the absence of a permanent dipole moment. However, when such molecules approach others their quadrupole moments can induce dipole moments in other species (Chapter 1). Furthermore, owing to the distortion of the electron distributions of the molecules, a dipole moment can exist in the interacting pair. These dipoles are modulated as the pair of molecules vibrates and rotates so that absorption in the infra-red is possible. The absorption can be of two types:

1. Where the transition occurs in the continuum region, that is, *collision pairs* exist. In this case a broad, diffuse absorption is observed known as *collision-induced absorption*.

2. Where *bound dimers* are formed and transitions occur between the discrete levels in the well. Here sharp absorption lines are observed, usually superimposed on the broad background from 1.

Because both effects are very small, large path lengths—up to 200 m—have been employed to observe such spectra. In the case of the dimers of diatomic molecules and atoms, more detailed spectra can usually be obtained.

3.2.2. Polar molecules

In the case of polar molecules other techniques are available for the study of dimers. One, known as molecular beam electric resonance, is based on the fact that each of the rotational energy levels, j, of a molecule with a dipole moment is split by an electric field into $j + 1$ components, characterized by a quantum number $|m_j|$ in the *Stark effect*. Each of these component states has a different energy in the field, characterized by the pair of quantum numbers $(j, |m_j|)$ and, in an inhomogeneous field will experience a force depending on $(j, |m_j|)$. Figure 3.2 contains a schematic diagram of a molecular beam electric resonance spectrometer of the type employed to study the absorption spectra of dimers. A beam of van der Waals dimers is produced in a supersonic nozzle beam (Chapter 2) by the expansion of the parent gas or gas mixture from a low-temperature, high-pressure zone in a very low-pressure region. The beam first enters a zone in which an electric field is applied perpendicular to the initial direction of the beam and the magnitude of the field varies in the z-direction. This field causes molecules in different $(j, |m_j|)$ states to be deflected by different amounts and is called the *defocusing field*. Subsequently the beam enters a region in which there is a homogeneous electric field, and then a region in which there is a further inhomogeneous electric field which deflects the

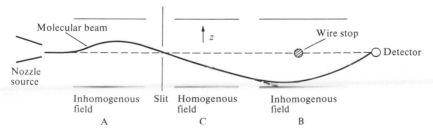

Fig. 3.2 Principle of operation of electric resonance spectrometer.

molecules back towards the axis of the spectrometer again, by an amount depending on their $(j, |m_j|)$ state. This is the *refocusing field*. By a suitable choice of the dimensions of the spectrometer and the electric field gradients it is possible to arrange that molecules in only one $(j, |m_j|)$ state are able to traverse the length of the spectrometer and impinge on the detector producing a measurable signal. Molecules in other states then strike the walls of the chamber, or a wire placed on the axis of the system, and do not reach the detector. If, between the two inhomogeneous fields, the beam is subjected to an oscillating electromagnetic field whose frequency corresponds to that necessary to induce an allowed transition in the dimer, then some of the molecules originally focused at the detector will transfer to a different $(j, |m_j|)$ state and will therefore not impinge on the detector, causing a reduction in the signal there. Consequently, by measuring the detector signal as a function of the frequency of the radiation (usually in the radio frequency or microwave region) the absorption spectrum between different $(j, |m_j|)$ states can be obtained.

Molecular beam spectrometers in which the beam is irradiated by laser light have also been employed. In such instruments, either the details of the induced fluorescence spectrum may be observed, or the total energy of the molecular beam at a detector may be determined. The latter effect reveals the increases or decreases in the internal energy of the beam caused by absorption of radiation.

Considerably higher resolution of the rotational spectrum of a van der Waals' complex in its vibrational ground state can be obtained by means of a technique known as pulsed-nozzle spectroscopy. In this technique a nozzle beam source is used to produce a very low-temperature, essentially collision-free pulse of dimers whose lifetime is sufficiently long for their rotational spectrum to be obtained by conventional spectroscopic methods. The technique is particularly suitable for the study of weakly bound complexes, and the information it yields is especially useful in defining the curvature of the potential surface in the region of the deepest minimum.

3.3. The interpretation of the spectra of van der Waals dimers

The most familiar analysis of the absorption spectra of chemically bound molecules begins from the assumption that the potential energy of the bond is a quadratic function of distance. That is, taking the zero of energy to be the bottom of the potential well,

$$U(r) = +\kappa(r - r_m)^2,$$

where r_m is the separation at the potential energy minimum. In this case the allowed vibrational energy levels of the molecules are those of the simple harmonic oscillator

$$G(v) = hv(v + \tfrac{1}{2}) \tag{3.2}$$

where v is the fundamental frequency, $v = \dfrac{1}{2\pi}(\kappa/\mu)^{1/2}$, and v the vibrational quantum number. In this simple case it is clear that the transitions between the various vibrational levels ($\Delta v = \pm 1$) correspond to the same frequency, v, and therefore yield a single absorption line, the measurement of the frequency of which determines κ in the potential energy function. Consequently, the spectroscopic measurements serve to determine the potential energy in the well region as a function of its width. Another potential energy function for which an exact solution of the Schrödinger equation is possible is the Morse potential:

$$U(r) = \varepsilon[\{1 - e^{-\beta(r-r_{\mathrm{m}})}\}^2 - 1], \qquad (3.3)$$

written with the same zero for energy. In this case, the energy levels are given by the equation

$$G(v) = hv_{\mathrm{m}}(v + \tfrac{1}{2}) - hv_{\mathrm{m}}x_{\mathrm{e}}(v + \tfrac{1}{2})^2 \qquad (3.4)$$

in which v_{m} is the fundamental frequency $(\beta/\pi)(\varepsilon/2\mu)^{1/2}$ and x_{e} is the 'anharmonicity' constant $hv_{\mathrm{m}}/4\varepsilon$. In this case, the energy levels are not evenly spaced but again, a determination of the absorption spectrum serves to determine them. The representation of these levels by means of eqn (3.4) then allows v_{m} and x_{e} to be determined and, again, the intermolecular pair potential as a function of the width of the well may be obtained.

Unfortunately, neither the quadratic potential nor the Morse potential are good representations of the intermolecular pair potential for any molecular interaction. Consequently, the procedures outlined above should be viewed as illustrations of the type of information contained in the spectroscopic data rather than definitive methods for its extraction. The most satisfactory procedure for deriving intermolecular pair potentials from spectroscopic absorption studies takes the form of a direct inversion of the experimental data, and is based on the so-called *Rydberg–Klein–Rees* (*RKR*) *analysis*. The first step in the analysis is the determination of the allowed vibration–rotation energy levels of the van der Waals dimer $G(v,j)$. This step evidently requires the assignment of vibrational and rotational quantum number changes to each absorption line in the observed spectrum. The process is relatively straightforward for the vibrational levels, because many of the lines corresponding to these transitions can be resolved. However, for the rotational lines a greater resolution is required of the spectrometer in order to observe the rotational fine structure, and this has not always proved possible. Nevertheless, even a knowledge of just the vibrational energies can be used to yield some information about the intermolecular pair potential, which is then enhanced if the rotational levels are also known.

Figure 3.3 shows a portion of the effective potential energy curve $V(L, r)$ for a pair of structureless particles

$$V(L, r) = U(r) + K/r^2 \qquad (3.5)$$

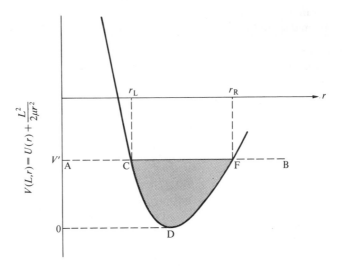

Fig. 3.3 Effective energy and parameters for RKR analysis. The zero of energy is taken to be the well minimum for this analysis.

where $K = L^2/2\mu$. Again, the zero of energy has been taken to be at the bottom of the potential well for convenience. The line AB corresponds to the energy of an oscillator with an energy V' so that r_L and r_R correspond classically to the extremes of the motion (the minimum and maximum separations of the two particles). The shaded area, S, contained between AB and the potential curve, CDF, may be obtained by the integration

$$S = \int_{r_L}^{r_R} (V' - V)\,dr. \tag{3.6}$$

Differentiation with respect to V' and with respect to K leads to the results

$$\left(\frac{\partial S}{\partial V'}\right)_K = \int_{r_L}^{r_R} dr = r_R - r_L \tag{3.7}$$

and

$$\left(\frac{\partial S}{\partial K}\right)_{V'} = -\int_{r_L}^{r_R} \frac{dr}{r^2} = \frac{1}{r_R} - \frac{1}{r_L}. \tag{3.8}$$

It is now convenient to introduce a quantity, x, which is related to the vibrational quantum number v by the equation

$$x = (v + \tfrac{1}{2}) \tag{3.9}$$

because it is then possible to express the integral of eqn (3.6) as an integral over x (or essentially the vibrational quantum number). In terms of this variable, when the differentiations of eqn (3.7) are carried out we find that for one particular vibrational level corresponding to, say $x = n$, where the potential energy is U_n, the width of the potential energy function is

$$r_R - r_L = (1/2\pi^2\mu)^{1/2} h \int_0^n \frac{h\,dx}{\{U_n - U_x\}^{1/2}} . \tag{3.10}$$

Thus the width of the potential function an energy U_n above the bottom of the well may be obtained by performing the integration on the right-hand side numerically. Repetition of this process for increasing values of n, (and hence U_n) builds up the width of the potential well as a function of energy, which, as anticipated by our earlier examples, is the information contained in the vibrational absorption spectrum. Indeed, in many cases this is the best analysis that can be carried out because the rotational fine structure associated with each vibrational line is usually unresolved. However, if the rotational fine structure can be resolved it is possible to perform an improved analysis. This arises because, in terms of the variable x, the differentiation in eqn (3.8) leads to the result that

$$r_L^{-1} - r_R^{-1} = \left(\frac{1}{2\pi^2\mu}\right)^{\frac{1}{2}} h \int_0^n \frac{dx}{\bar{r}_v^2 (U_n - U_x)^{1/2}} \tag{3.11}$$

where $\bar{r}_v$ is an effective mean separation of the pair of molecules for the vibrational energy level with quantum number v. The resolution of the rotational fine structure allows $\bar{r}_v$ to be determined for each vibrational level so that eqns (3.10) and (3.11) may be used together to determine r_L and r_R independently for each value of U_n. Thus, it is possible to establish the full curve of $r(U)$ or, equivalently, $U(r)$ measured from the bottom of the well.

By the preceding methods the inner and outer branches of the potential energy curve can, in principle, be determined from the bottom of the well up to the dissociation limit, $U_n = +\varepsilon$ using the present origin for energy. However, it is not generally possible to determine vibration–rotation levels very close to the top of the well, so there is usually an upper limit to the energy U_n for which eqn (3.10) is directly useful. It is therefore necessary to employ an extrapolation procedure to determine the well depth ε accurately. The most successful extrapolation procedure is based upon two approximations. First, near the top of the potential well the potential energy function for non-polar molecules is well represented by the function

$$U(r) - \varepsilon = -\frac{C_6}{r^6} \tag{3.12}$$

where the second term is the leading term of the London dispersion potential. Second, under the same conditions, only a small error is incurred by assuming that for levels high up in the well, the inner turning point $r_L = 0$. It may then be shown that the spacing between adjacent vibrational energy levels near the top of the well conforms to the equation

$$[G(v+1)-G(v)]^{1/2} = H(v_{max}-v-\tfrac{1}{2}) \tag{3.13}$$

in which H is a constant for a particular system, depending upon the dispersion coefficient C_6, and v_{max} is the maximum value of the vibrational quantum number corresponding to dissociation. This result means that if values of $G(v)$ are known for some states below dissociation a plot can be made of $(\Delta G_{v+1/2})^{1/2} = [G(v+1)-G(v)]^{1/2}$ against v. The plot may then be extrapolated to yield $G(v)$ for values of v up to v_{max}, which yields the dissociation energy or potential well depth, ε. Figure 3.4 contains a plot of this kind for Ar_2 in which $v_{max} \simeq 8$. Plots of this kind have been employed to determine the well depths for a number of different systems. The analysis may also be extended to include the rotational fine structure near the dissociation limit.

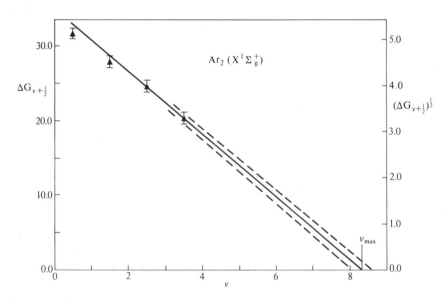

Fig. 3.4 Vibrational energy level extrapolation for Ar_2. (LeRoy, R. J. (1972). *J. chem. Phys.* **57,** 573.)

3.4. Experimental results for the inert gases

The absorption spectra of the homonuclear dimers of four of the inert gases have been observed in a series of studies. In the initial study of argon dimers, nine discrete band systems were observed by Tanaka and his co-workers, and six vibrational levels $v = 0$–5 assigned, but the rotational structure was so poorly resolved that the corresponding levels could not be assigned. In a later series of experiments Colbourn and Douglas resolved the rotational fine structure for one band system and so obtained the energies of the rotational levels associated with each of the six vibrational levels. By means of a full RKR analysis of both rotational and vibrational levels together with data on macroscopic properties and theoretical calculations of the dispersion energy coefficients, they obtained an intermolecular potential well for Ar with $\varepsilon/k = 143.3$ K and $r_m = 0.3759$ nm.

For helium the well depth is probably too low to allow the formation of bound dimers, but for neon, krypton, and xenon spectroscopic studies have been carried out leading to results at varying levels of detail. In each case an RKR analysis, supported by independent information on the bulk properties, has allowed the characterization of the potential well. The parameters of the well for each system determined in this way have been used to construct Fig. 3.5 which shows the reduced well-width function determined by RKR analysis, $(r_R - r_L)/r_m$, as a function of energy. The figure serves to illustrate the high degree of conformality between the potentials of the inert gases in the well region.

In the case of mixed dimers among the inert gases, the spectroscopic

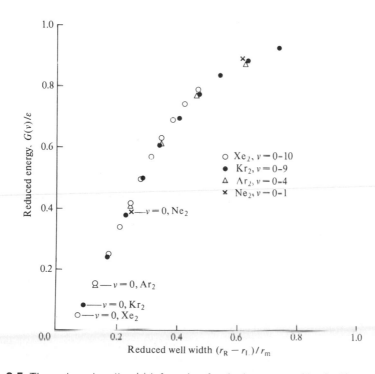

Fig. 3.5 The reduced well-width function for the inert gases Ne, Ar, Kr, and Xe, as determined by RKR analysis of spectroscopic data.

information is much less complete. These mixed dimers are formed in gas mixtures of the parent pure gases, but their concentrations are generally much lower than those of the homonuclear dimers. Consequently, increased sensitivity is required in the optical system used to observe their spectra and it has not yet been possible to carry out any systematic studies of such systems.

3.5. The interpretation of spectra for non-spherical systems

van der Waals dimers may also be formed from a pair of molecules in which one or both are polyatomic. However, in such cases, the absorption spectrum and its interpretation is much more complicated. First, a polyatomic molecule has internal degrees of freedom that may contribute to the observed absorption spectrum. Second, the intermolecular pair potential characterizing the interaction of the molecules is anisotropic, depending on their relative orientation as well as their separation. Finally, no formal inversion procedure exists whereby the potential may be determined directly from the spectroscopic data. These complications are reminiscent of those encountered in Chapter 2 in connection with the treatment of molecular collisions among polyatomic systems. Indeed, the full solution of the problem of determining the stable energy levels of such a dimer is essentially the same as that required in the treatment of molecular scattering and is beyond the limits of present-day computing facilities on a routine basis. Consequently, it has been necessary to develop a number of approximate methods of dealing with the problem. For the present purposes, it is sufficient to consider the case of dimers formed from a diatomic molecule and an atom which serves to illustrate the kinds of effect which can be observed and the information which may be derived from them.

For dimers of the type X_2–Y, rotation can occur internally in which X_2 rotates about its centre of mass characterized by a rotational quantum number j. Furthermore, rotation of the dimer of X_2 and Y can occur about their joint centre of mass which is characterized by the quantum number l. The total rotational motion is therefore characterized by a quantum number $J = j + l$, $j + l - 1 \ldots |j - l|$. Because the intermolecular potential for the interaction of X_2 and Y is not spherically symmetric, the rotation of X_2 about its centre of mass is hindered by a potential energy barrier as shown schematically in Fig. 3.6 for one particular case. This means that the liberty of X_2 to rotate freely depends upon the height of the barrier which itself depends upon the anisotropy of the potential. The effect of this is to couple j and l together in such a way that the energy levels corresponding to the total angular momentum quantum number J are shifted away from those corresponding to the case of free rotation.

To see this more clearly let us split the total intermolecular pair potential for X_2–Y into two parts so that

$$U(\mathbf{r}, \omega) = U_0(r) + U_{an}(\mathbf{r}, \omega) \tag{3.14}$$

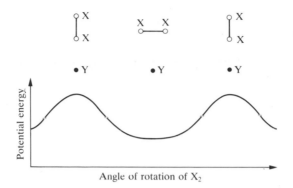

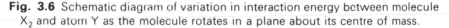

Fig. 3.6 Schematic diagram of variation in interaction energy between molecule
X_2 and atom Y as the molecule rotates in a plane about its centre of mass.

in which $U_0(r)$ is a spherically symmetrical part, $U_{an}(\mathbf{r}, \omega)$ the anisotropic part and ω describes the relative orientation of the atom and the molecule. Furthermore, we denote by $\Delta\varepsilon_{X_2}$ and $\Delta\varepsilon_{X_2-Y}$ the rotational energy spacings of the diatomic molecule and the X_2-Y dimer respectively. It is then possible to distinguish three classes of X_2-Y system.

(a) *Weak coupling system* $(\Delta\varepsilon_{X_2-Y} \lesssim U_{an} \ll \Delta\varepsilon_{X_2})$. In such systems, the anisotropy of the intermolecular potential is small, the barrier to rotation of X_2 is small, and the energy levels corresponding to the total quantum number J are only slightly perturbed from those corresponding to the case of a free rotor X_2. This is illustrated in Fig. 3.7, which contains a schematic representation of the energy levels of the system. Examples of van der Waals' molecules of this type are H_2–inert gas dimers.

(b) *Strong coupling system* $(\Delta\varepsilon_{X_2-Y} < \Delta\varepsilon_{X_2} \lesssim U_{an})$. Here, the barrier to rotation is larger than the spacing between the rotational energy levels of X_2 and the energy levels for the quantum number J are more seriously affected by the anisotropy. An example of such a system is Ar–HCl.

(c) *Semi-rigid system* $(\Delta\varepsilon_{X_2Y}, \Delta\varepsilon_{X_2} \ll U_{an})$. In this case the anisotropy of the potential is so large that the dimer adopts an equilibrium configuration in which X_2 executes only small-amplitude motions, similar to those that occur in covalently bonded molecules. A system that displays such behaviour is Kr–ClF. The equilibrium configuration may be 'T'-shaped, in which the atom lies on a line perpendicular to the X_2 bond, or colinear. In the former case, the energy level diagram appears as that on the extreme right of Fig. 3.7.

The changes in the energy level diagram indicate that significant differences are to be expected between the absorption spectra exhibited by the different classes of system. To illustrate this we consider the system H_2–Ar, which is an

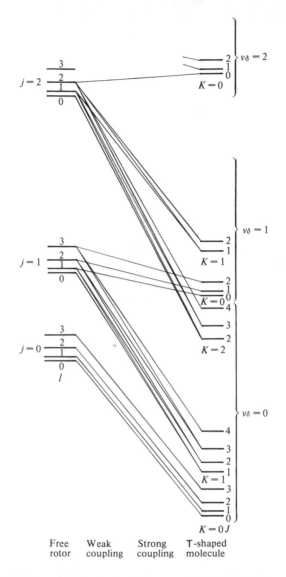

Fig. 3.7 Correlation diagram of rotatory motions of X_2–Y van der Waals molecules. (Notice that the spacing of the l levels is much finer than that of the j levels. This is because l indicates rotation about the long X_2–Y van der Waals' bond, while j denotes rotation about the short X_2 chemical bond.) v_δ is the vibrational quantum number of the dimer. (Henderson, G. and Ewing, G. E. (1974). *Mol. Phys.* **27,** 903).

example of a case of weak coupling, and the system N_2–Ar, which is a case of strong coupling. Figure 3.8 contains the absorption spectrum of the H_2–Ar dimer and Fig. 3.9 that of the N_2–Ar dimer. In the weak coupling case, the vibration–rotation frequencies for the dimer are very close to those of H_2 itself, which are indicated by the labels. Furthermore, because the moment of inertia of H_2 is small, the vibration–rotation features of the spectrum are well separated and relatively easily resolved. The detail contained in this spectrum has enabled quite precise information to be obtained about the intermolecular pair potential. On the other hand, for the strong coupling case of N_2–Ar the spectrum is much more diffuse and the rotation–vibration features are more closely spaced owing to the larger moment of inertia of N_2. Furthermore, the energy level splitting is now so large that many of the features of the spectrum are significantly shifted from those of freely rotating nitrogen. The lack of

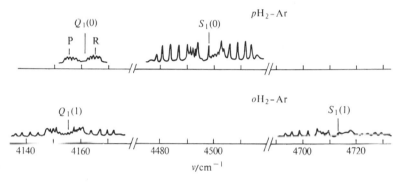

Fig. 3.8 Infra-red spectrum of *ortho* and *para* hydrogen–argon mixtures at 0.5 bar, 86 K, path length 165 m. Labels indicate free H_2 transitions. (McKellar, A. R. W. and Welsh, H. L. (1971). *J. chem. Phys.* **55**, 595.)

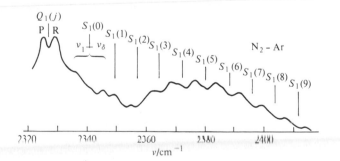

Fig. 3.9 Infra-red spectrum of N_2–Ar mixture at 1 bar, 87 K, path length 122 m. Labels indicate free N_2 transitions. (Henderson, G. and Ewing, G. E. (1974). *Mol. Phys.* **27**, 903.)

detail in this spectrum indicates that the extraction of the precise nature of the intermolecular pair potential from it is a difficult task. For the reasons indicated above, the greatest progress has been made for weakly anisotropic systems, which we consider briefly here. The resolution of the absorption spectra for more strongly anisotropic systems is steadily improving, particularly in molecular beam electric resonance studies. It is likely that in the near future, spectra for a system such as N_2–Ar of a quality comparable with that currently attainable for H_2–Ar will become available, allowing a detailed analysis to be carried out.

3.5.1. Weakly anisotropic systems

For simplicity, we consider just a small set of the energy levels of the X_2–Y in order to illustrate the manner in which particular aspects of the intermolecular pair potential reveal themselves in the absorption spectrum of the dimer. We consider the atom–diatom system in the coordinate system defined in Fig. 3.10, and define the following quantities:

(a) $\xi = (R - R_0)/R_0$ where R_0 is the average value of R in the ground rotation–vibration state of isolated X_2. Thus ξ pertains to the stretching of the X–X bond.

(b) j = internal rotational angular momentum quantum number for X_2.

(c) l = quantum number for angular momentum of the complex X_2–Y.

(d) J = total angular momentum quantum number.

(e) v = vibrational quantum number of X_2.

(f) n = vibrational quantum number of X_2–Y, that is, for stretching of r.

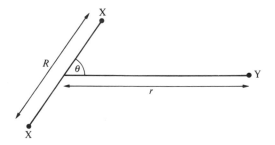

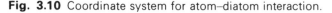

Fig. 3.10 Coordinate system for atom–diatom interaction.

The intermolecular pair potential is expressed as a function of r, ξ, and θ and may be expanded in terms of Legendre polynomials,

$$U(r, \xi, \theta) = U_0(r, \xi) + U_2(r, \xi) P_2(\cos \theta) + U_4(r, \xi) P_4(\cos \theta) + \dots$$

$$= \sum_{\substack{k=0 \\ k, \text{even}}}^{\infty} U_k(r, \xi) P_k(\cos \theta) \tag{3.15}$$

where the summation includes only the even values of k because of the symmetry of the system. We consider the potential energy surface to consist of a whole range of potential energy curves for the complex one for each pair of values of v and j. This is illustrated in Fig. 3.11 for the $v = 0, j = 0$, and $v = 1$, $j = 0$ states of H_2–Ar. The asymptotes of these two curves are then separated by the energy corresponding to the transition between the $v = 0$ and $v = 1$ vibrational states of hydrogen. Both curves are drawn for $n = 0$, that is, for no excitation of the H_2–Ar vibration.

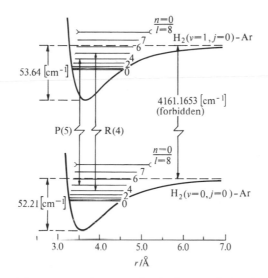

Fig. 3.11 Potential curves and energy levels for $v = 0, j = 0$, and $v = 1, j = 0$ states of H_2–Ar (schematic). (LeRoy, R. J. and Van Kranendonk, J. (1974). *J. chem. Phys.* **61**, 4750.)

Transitions such as those designated P(5) and R(4) in the diagram correspond to changes of the vibrational state of the H_2 from $v = 0$ to 1 accompanied by changes in the l state from 5 to 4 in the first case and from 4 to 5 in the second case. Thus if the two curves for $v = 0$ and $v = 1$ were identical, the average of the energy changes accompanying these transitions would be exactly equal to the difference in energies between the first two vibrational states of hydrogen. From the fine structure around the $v = 0$ to 1 transition in the hydrogen–argon dimer, which arises from changes in l, it is possible to determine the average energy of the two transitions indicated. It is found that their mean value differs from the $v = 0$ to $v = 1$ transition in hydrogen by a small amount (~ 1.5 K), which reflects differences in the two potential curves caused by the different value of ξ in the two cases. Hence studies of transitions of this type can be employed to elucidate the dependence of $U(r, \xi, \theta)$ on ξ.

The wave function of a diatomic molecule in its rotational ground state ($j = 0$) is spherically symmetric. Therefore the energy levels of the complex formed by such a molecule will be mainly determined by the isotropic part of U, $U_0 (r, \xi)$, so that studies of the absorption band associated with transitions between the two curves illustrated in Fig. 3.11 provide information on this part of the potential. In particular, the relative frequencies of the transitions between the l levels can be used to define the parameters of the potential well such as r_{m} and ε/k.

Following a similar argument a transition between the $v = 0$ state and $v = 1$ state, which involves a change in j, the angular momentum quantum number for the hydrogen, is related to terms in the expansion of the potential (eqn 3.15), only including those up to $k \leqslant 2j$. Thus, for example, the transition from $v = 0, j = 0$ to $v = 1, j = 2$ yields information about $U_0 (r, \xi)$ and $U_2 (r, \xi)$. Successively higher terms in the expansion of the potential can then be investigated by considering transitions involving progressively higher values of j.

Although the above arguments yield a qualitative picture of the information contained in the spectra of weakly anisotropic X_2–Y systems, the approach has not been taken to a stage where it is possible to develop formal inversion procedures. Instead, it has been necessary to adopt a relatively simple model for the intermolecular pair potential containing a number of adjustable parameters. The Schrödinger equation for the X_2–Y dimer is then solved for a particular set of these parameters and the energy levels of the dimer calculated to yield a predicted absorption spectrum. The process is then repeated for a series of values of the parameters until the best agreement between the predicted spectrum and that observed is obtained. The intermolecular pair potential determined in this way is then identified as the true intermolecular potential. This approach is not entirely satisfactory because it is difficult to be sure that the functional from assumed does not affect the final result. Nevertheless, considerable success has been achieved by the application of the method to H_2–inert gas systems. In particular, for H_2–Ar Le Roy and his collaborators have employed the representation

$$U (r, \xi, \theta) = \sum_{n=0}^{\infty} \sum_{k=0}^{\infty} \xi^k P_n (\cos \theta) U_{n, k} (r), \qquad (3.16)$$

where P_n are the Legendre polynomials.

Figure 3.12 contains plots of just three of the contributions to this function determined from an analysis of spectroscopic data.

3.5.2. Strongly anisotropic systems

As well as being more difficult to study experimentally, there are differences in principle between the spectra of strongly and weakly anisotropic systems. In strongly coupled systems the spectra are dominated by transitions involving

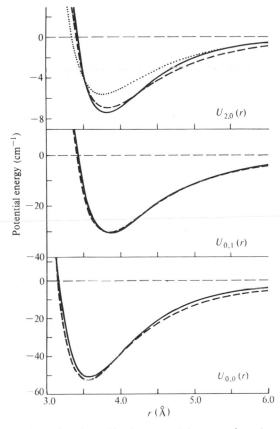

Fig. 3.12 Illustration of various H_2–Ar potential energy functions of the POTEX type (form of $U_{n,k}$ in parentheses). (———) HFD; (– – – –) LJ; (. . . .) LJ (beams). (Based on LeRoy, R. J., Carley, J. S., and Grabenstetter, J. E. (1977). *Faraday Dis. chem. Soc.* **62,** 169.)

changes in the total angular momentum quantum number J, rather than by contributions from transitions among the individual quantum numbers j and l. Consequently, the observed spectrum reflects more the motion of the dimer as a whole than motions within it. For this reason the information contained within the spectrum about the pair potential between the two components of the dimer is less easily extracted. In the extreme case of semi-rigid systems this fact becomes particularly apparent. If the two components of the dimer are more or less completely fixed in one orientation, for example the T configuration, by barriers in the intermolecular pair potential, then the spectrum can for the most part only tell us something about the valley between the barriers. Thus, although there have been some studies of the intermolecular pair potentials for such systems using absorption spectra, it seems unlikely that such information alone will be sufficient to define precisely the entire potential energy well.

Suggested further reading

Maitland, G. C., Rigby, M., Smith, E. B., and Wakeham, W. A. (1981). *Intermolecular forces: their origin and determination*. Chapter 4. Clarendon Press, Oxford. (Referred to in text as MRSW.)

Ewing, G. E. (1972). *Angew. Chem. Int. Edn. Eng.* **11**, 486.

—— (1975). *Acc. chem. Res.* **8**, 185.

LeRoy, R. J. (1980). *Semi-classical methods in molecular scattering and spectroscopy* (ed. M. S. Child) Chapter 3. Reidel, Dordrecht.

LeRoy, R. J. and Carley, J. S. (1980). *Adv. chem. Phys.* **42**, 353.

Exercises

E3.1. Plot the effective potential energy function for two identical atoms each of mass 1.4×10^{-25} kg, which approach each other with a relative speed of 280 m s^{-1}, and an impact parameter $b = 0.36$ nm. The two atoms interact through a Lennard-Jones 12–6 potential for which $\varepsilon/k = 200$ K and $\sigma = 0.36$ nm. Does the effective potential possess a positive outer maximum?

E3.2. A van der Waals dimer with zero angular momentum is made up of two identical atoms of mass 6×10^{-26} kg, which interact through a quadratic potential energy function. The single frequency characteristic of the absorption spectrum is 6×10^{11} Hz. Plot a graph illustrating all the features of the potential energy function that it is possible to deduce from this information.

E3.3. A van der Waals dimer with zero angular momentum is formed from two identical atoms of mass 3×10^{-26} kg, which interact through a Morse potential. The two highest frequencies in the absorption spectrum occur at $v = 4 \times 10^{11}$ Hz and $v = 3 \times 10^{11}$ Hz. Deduce as much as is possible about the Morse potential function from this information. (Planck's constant $= 6.63 \times 10^{-34}$ J s)

4
Gas imperfection

4.1. Introduction

For more than a century studies of the deviations of gases from the perfect gas law have been used as a valuable source of information about the interactions between molecules. If the molecules of a gas exert no forces on each other and behave as point masses, they may be shown to follow the perfect gas equation of state:

$$P\bar{V} = RT \qquad (4.1)$$

where $\bar{V}$ is the molar volume of the gas and R the gas constant ($8.31\,\mathrm{J\,K^{-1}\,mol^{-1}}$). The degree to which gases deviate from perfect behaviour provides a measure of the strength of molecular interactions. These deviations may be expressed by plotting the compression factor, $Z = \dfrac{P\bar{V}}{RT}$ (often called the compressibility factor) as a function of pressure at several temperatures, as illustrated in Fig. 4.1.

At high temperatures (e.g. T_5) Z increases steadily from the perfect gas value as the pressure is raised. As the temperature decreases, Z falls below unity and exhibits a characteristic minimum in its pressure dependence. At one particular temperature, called the Boyle temperature $T_B (= T_4)$, the limiting slope $(\partial Z/\partial P)_{T, P\to 0}$ is zero and the gas obeys the perfect gas equation up to moderate pressure. The shapes of these compression factor curves may be used to characterize the forces between molecules.

It is found that below a critical temperature characteristic of each substance, discontinuities occur in the curves, indicating that liquefaction is taking place. Andrews' classic measurements of the P–V isotherms of carbon dioxide established the nature of the gas–liquid critical point. He demonstrated clearly that the equilibrium of a pure liquid and its vapour, which is observed in a closed vessel, could occur only at temperatures below a value, characteristic of the substance, called the gas–liquid critical temperature T_c. At temperatures below T_c a gas may be compressed only until a certain pressure, the saturated vapour pressure, is reached. Further reduction in volume then leads to condensation of the gas, which continues until complete conversion to liquid has occurred. When this state is reached further reduction in volume leads to a

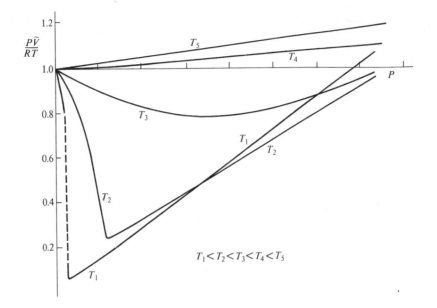

Fig. 4.1 The compression factor, $P\overline{V}/RT$, as a function of pressure at several temperatures. T_2 is the critical temperature, T_4 is the Boyle temperature.

large increase in the pressure as the liquid is not very compressible. The saturated vapour pressure depends on the temperature, and has a maximum value, called the critical pressure, P_c, at the critical temperature. The pattern of behaviour revealed by Andrews in his study of various isotherms for carbon dioxide is shown in Fig. 4.2. Studies on other gases reveal very similar behaviour. In general it is found that small, simple molecules such as N_2 or CH_4, where the attractive interactions are relatively weak, have low values of T_c, and these substances are gaseous under normal conditions. Those substances with stronger attractive forces, such as water or benzene, have larger values of T_c and are often liquids or solids at room temperature and pressure.

4.2. Joule–Thomson effect

Direct evidence for the existence of intermolecular forces is to be found in the Joule–Thomson effect. When a gas expands through a porous plug or nozzle the mean distance between the molecules increases. The resulting change in energy is reflected in a change in the temperature of the gas, usually a decrease (Fig. 4.3). The temperature change depends on the drop in pressure and the

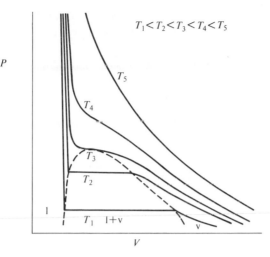

Fig. 4.2 Isotherms for an imperfect gas, near to the critical point. T_3 is the critical temperature. The coexistence curve for the liquid, l, and vapour, v, is indicated by the dotted line.

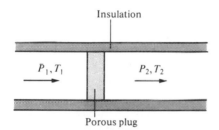

Fig. 4.3 A schematic representation of the adiabatic Joule–Thomson experiment.

Joule–Thompson coefficient, μ_{JT}, may be defined:

$$\mu_{JT} = \lim_{P_2 \to P_1} \left(\frac{T_2 - T_1}{P_2 - P_1}\right)_H = \left(\frac{\partial T}{\partial P}\right)_H. \tag{4.2}$$

The process takes place under conditions of constant enthalpy, H, and by the application of standard thermodynamic manipulations the Joule–Thomson coefficient may be expressed in terms of the molar heat capacity, C_P, and the equation of state of the gas:

$$\mu_{JT} = \frac{1}{C_P}\left\{T\left(\frac{\partial V}{\partial T}\right)_P - \bar{V}\right\}. \tag{4.3}$$

A related experiment may be performed in which heat is supplied to (or removed from) the low-pressure side to maintain the temperature constant.

The isothermal Joule–Thomson coefficient, ϕ_{JT}, studied in this way is directly related to the isenthalpic coefficient μ_{JT} by the equation

$$\phi_{JT} = \left(\frac{\partial H}{\partial P}\right)_T = -C_p \mu_{JT}. \tag{4.4}$$

For a perfect gas with no forces between the molecules, $T(\partial \overline{V}/\partial T)_P = \overline{V}$, and both coefficients are zero, so the occurrence of the effect is direct confirmation of the existence of molecular interactions. Although for most gases at low and moderate pressures μ_{JT} is positive, i.e. cooling occurs when the gas expands, there exists a temperature above which μ_{JT} is negative, and the gas warms up on expansion. The temperature at which $\mu_{JT} = 0$ is called the Joule–Thompson inversion temperature, and at low pressure is approximately twice the Boyle temperature for simple substances. The existence of both the inversion and Boyle temperatures reflects the changing balance between the importance of attractive and repulsive forces as the physical conditions of a fluid vary.

4.3. van der Waals equation of state

Many attempts have been made to represent the PVT behaviour of real substances over wide ranges of temperature and pressure by what are called equations of state. Indeed, for many substances very complicated equations have been devised which describe their compression factor from the low-pressure gas state through to the liquid region. However, the role of intermolecular forces in determining the gaseous state behaviour can be qualitatively understood in terms of a very simple model due to van der Waals, which led to the equation

$$\left(P + \frac{a}{\overline{V}^2}\right)(\overline{V} - b) = RT. \tag{4.5}$$

This attempts to modify the perfect gas equation in such a way as to allow for the effects of intermolecular interactions. The short-range intermolecular repulsions were dealt with by treating the molecules as small spheres which could not overlap. The volume unavailable to the centre of *both* molecules involved in a binary collision is $\frac{4}{3}\pi d^3$ where d is the diameter of the molecules, (see Fig. 4.4). Hence the excluded volume per molecule is $\frac{2}{3}\pi d^3$ and the effective reduction in the molar volume, the so-called covolume, is given by:

$$b = \frac{2}{3}\pi N_A d^3.$$

This quantity is four times the actual volume of the hard sphere molecules.

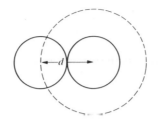

Fig. 4.4 Volume excluded in a binary collision of hard-sphere molecules.

Because the volume available to the molecules is reduced, the effect of molecular size (that is, of the repulsive forces) is to increase the pressure above the perfect gas value for a given molar volume, $\bar{V}$. A term was also introduced to account for the role of attractive forces. These were considered to reduce the pressure exerted on the walls of the vessel in a manner proportional to the number of binary interactions. This number increases as the square of the density $(1/\bar{V})$, so that the reduction in pressure may be written $(a/\bar{V}^2)$, where a is another constant.

The equation may be rewritten in the form

$$\frac{P\bar{V}}{RT} = \frac{\bar{V}}{\bar{V}-b} - \frac{a}{RT\bar{V}}. \tag{4.6}$$

This may be expanded in powers of the reciprocal volume to give

$$\frac{P\bar{V}}{RT} = 1 + \frac{b-a/RT}{\bar{V}} + \frac{b^2}{\bar{V}^2} + \frac{b^3}{\bar{V}^3} + \dots \tag{4.7}$$

This form clearly reveals that repulsive interactions raise the pressure above the value for a perfect gas at the same density, while attractive forces have the opposite effect. Temperature and density have important roles in determining the overall sign and size of the deviations from perfect gas behaviour, as seen in Fig. 4.1. At high pressures, where $(1/\bar{V})$ is large, or at high temperature for any pressure, the positive repulsive terms dominate. At low temperatures (where a/RT becomes significant) and at low pressures the deviation is negative. The initial slope of the compressibility plot is $b - a/RT$, again reflecting the balance between attractive and repulsive forces.

The constants a and b (which are given for a selection of molecules in Table 4.1) for real substances can be expressed in terms of the pressure P_c, and volume, V_c, at the gas–liquid critical temperature T_c. At this critical point, $(\partial P/\partial V)_T$ and $(\partial^2 P/\partial V^2)_T$ are both zero (see Fig. 4.2). Applying these

Table 4.1

van der Waals constants

Gas	$a \times 10^{-6}$ (cm^6 atm mol^{-1})	b (cm^3 mol^{-1})
He	0.034	23.7
Ne	0.211	17.1
Ar	1.35	32.2
Kr	2.32	39.8
Xe	4.19	51.1
H_2	2.44	26.6
N_2	1.39	39.1
O_2	1.36	31.8
Cl_2	6.49	56.2
CO_2	3.59	42.7
CH_4	2.25	42.8
C_2H_6	5.49	63.8

conditions to eqn (4.6) leads to

$$a = \frac{9}{8} RT_c V_c = 3 P_c V_c^2$$

$$b = \frac{1}{3} V_c.$$

However, although the van der Waals model has been a major influence in the study of molecular interactions, the correlation of physical properties, the development of more sophisticated equations of state, and the theories of liquids, it cannot represent accurately the detailed PVT behaviour of any substance. This is not surprising in view of its rather crude representation of intermolecular forces. For a more quantitative link with realistic interactions we must consider a more generalized equation of state.

4.4. The virial equation of state

Very many, often quite complex, equations of state have been proposed, and these have been successful to varying degrees in representing the behaviour of real fluids. However, when the relationship between intermolecular forces and the equation of state is of primary interest, one particular equation of state, the *virial equation*, is of central importance. This equation represents the compression factor of a gas or a gas mixture as an infinite series expansion in the density:

$$\frac{P\bar{V}}{RT} = 1 + \frac{B(T)}{\bar{V}} + \frac{C(T)}{\bar{V}^2} + \frac{D(T)}{\bar{V}^3} + \dots \quad (4.8)$$

The virial coefficients B, C, D etc. depend only on temperature and the interactions between the molecules of which the gas is composed. The most important coefficient, $B(T)$, is termed the *second virial coefficient* and is related to the interactions between isolated pairs of molecules. The higher coefficients are determined by molecules interacting three at a time (C), four at a time (D) and so on. Sometimes an alternative expansion in terms of the pressure is used:

$$\frac{P\bar{V}}{RT} = 1 + \hat{B}(T)P + \hat{C}(T)P^2 + \hat{D}(T)P^3 + \dots \qquad (4.9)$$

The coefficients of this series are closely related to those of the density expansion, for instance

$$\hat{B} = \frac{B}{RT} \text{ and } \hat{C} = \frac{C - B^2}{(RT)^2}.$$

The importance of the virial expansion lies in the fact that it arises naturally from the application of statistical mechanics to a real gas and its coefficients are explicitly related to the forces between molecules.

4.5. Intermolecular forces and virial coefficients

For systems with spherical symmetry and no internal degrees of freedom, i.e. atoms, the second virial coefficient is simply related to the intermolecular pair potential $U(r)$ by the equation

$$B(T) = -2\pi N_A \int_0^\infty f_{12} r^2 \, dr = -2\pi N_A \int_0^\infty [\exp(-U(r)/kT) - 1] r^2 \, dr$$

$$(4.10)$$

where f_{12}, the term in square brackets, is the *Mayer f-function*:

$$f_{12} = \exp(-U(r)/kT) - 1.$$

A derivation of this equation may be found in Appendix 4A.

For most values of r less than the collision diameter σ, $U(r) \gg kT$ and $f_{12}(r) \simeq -1$. The repulsive region of the potential therefore makes a *positive* contribution to $B(T)$, which changes relatively little with temperature. By contrast, for $r > \sigma$, where $U(r) < 0$, $f_{12}(r)$ is positive and increases markedly as the temperature is decreased (see Fig. 4.5), as does the corresponding *negative* contribution to $B(T)$ from this attractive region of the potential. The net result is that at low temperatures B is negative, increasing in value with increasing temperature until at $T = T_B$, the *Boyle temperature*, it becomes zero. On increasing T further, B becomes positive, rises to a maximum and then slowly falls. For most gases this maximum does not occur until inaccessibly high temperatures (greater than those illustrated in Fig. 4.5) and it has only been observed experimentally for the small, light molecule helium (Table 4.2).

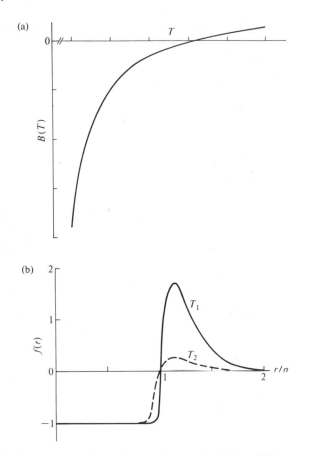

Fig. 4.5 (a) Temperature dependence of second virial coefficients.
(b) Temperature dependence of the Mayer function, $f(r)$. $T_2 > T_1$.

Equation (4.10) may be written in several alternative forms. Integration by parts gives

$$B(T) = \frac{2\pi N_A}{3kT} \int_0^\infty \exp\left(-U(r)/kT\right) \frac{dU(r)}{dr} r^3 dr \qquad (4.11)$$

If the potential well depth is ε and we define an energy ϕ measured from the potential minimum so that

$$\phi = U(r) + \varepsilon$$

then eqn (4.11) may be written

$$B(T) = \exp\left(\varepsilon/kT\right) \frac{2\pi N_A}{3kT} \int_0^\infty \Delta(\phi) \exp\left(-\phi/kT\right) d\phi \qquad (4.12)$$

Table 4.2
Second virial coefficients for some representative gases

Helium		Argon		Hydrogen		Nitrogen		Carbon tetrafluoride	
$T(K)$	$B(cm^3 mol^{-1})$	$T(K)$	$B(cm^3 mol^{-1})$	$T(K)$	$B(cm^3 mol^{-1})$	$T(K)$	$B(cm^3 mol^{-1})$	$T(K)$	$B(cm^3 mol^{-1})$
2.0	-174 ± 8	81	-276 ± 5	15	-230 ± 5	75	-275 ± 8	225	-172.5 ± 1
2.5	-134 ± 5	85	-251 ± 3	17	-191 ± 5	80	-243 ± 7	250	-137.5 ± 1
3.0	-109 ± 2	90	-225 ± 3	19	-162 ± 5	90	-197 ± 5	275	-109.0 ± 0.5
3.5	-92.6 ± 2	95	-202.5 ± 2	22	-132 ± 5	100	-160 ± 3	300	-87.0 ± 0.5
4.0	-80.2 ± 2	100	-183.5 ± 1	25	-110 ± 3	110	-132 ± 2	325	-69.0 ± 0.5
5.0	-62.7 ± 1	110	-154.5 ± 1	30	-82 ± 3	125	-104 ± 2	350	-55.0 ± 0.5
7.0	-40.9 ± 1	125	-123.0 ± 1	40	-52 ± 2	150	-71.5 ± 2	400	-32.0 ± 0.5
10.0	-23.1 ± 1	150	-86.2	50	-33 ± 2	200	-35.2 ± 1	450	-16.0 ± 0.5
15.0	-10.8 ± 1	200	-47.4	75	-12 ± 1	250	-16.2 ± 1	500	-4.0 ± 0.5
20.0	-3.4 ± 0.5	250	-27.9	100	-1.9 ± 1	300	-4.2 ± 0.5	600	14.0 ± 0.5
30.0	2.5 ± 0.5	300	-15.5 ± 0.5	150	7.1 ± 0.5	400	9.0 ± 0.5	700	25.0 ± 0.1
50.0	7.4 ± 0.5	400	-1.0 ± 0.5	200	11.3 ± 0.5	500	16.9 ± 0.5	800	33.0 ± 0.1
100.0	11.7 ± 0.5	500	7.0 ± 0.5	300	14.8 ± 0.5	600	21.3 ± 0.5		
200.0	12.1 ± 0.5	600	12.0 ± 0.5	400	15.2 ± 0.5	700	24.0 ± 0.5		
400.0	11.2 ± 0.5	700	15.0 ± 1						
700.0	10.1 ± 0.5	800	17.7 ± 1						
		900	20.0 ± 1						
		1000	22.0 ± 1						

Note: The low-temperature data for argon in MRSW (Table A4.2) are incorrectly tabulated.

where $\Delta(\phi)$ is the *well-width function*

$$\Delta(\phi) = r_{\mathrm{L}}^3 - r_{\mathrm{R}}^3 \qquad \phi \leqslant \varepsilon$$
$$= r_{\mathrm{L}}^3 \qquad \qquad \phi > \varepsilon$$

Here r_{L} and r_{R} are the value of the intermolecular separation for which the energy is ϕ. This form of $B(T)$ shows that the group $TB(T)$ is the Laplace transform of Δ. In principle, by fitting experimental values of $TB(T)$ to a function whose inverse Laplace transform is known, we could determine $\Delta(\phi)$ from $B(T)$. In practice, this has only proved possible for helium data at high temperatures, which have been used to determine the repulsive potential for this system. This is because at high temperatures $B(T)$ is determined mainly by $\Delta(\phi > \varepsilon)$, i.e. by $r_{\mathrm{L}}^3(\phi)$ or the part of $U(r)$ corresponding to the monotonic repulsive region. However, at lower temperatures $B(T)$ is determined by $\Delta(\phi < \varepsilon)$, i.e. by $r_{\mathrm{L}}^3 - r_{\mathrm{R}}^3$, or essentially by the size of the potential energy well. Hence the information about $U(r)$ contained in the second virial coefficient appears to be only the width of the well as a function of its depth. Nevertheless, as we shall see later, for the restricted class of functions of interest in the study of intermolecular forces for monatomic systems, the complete potential function can be extracted from second virial coefficient data.

Integration of eqn (4.10) for the simplest intermolecular potential, the hard sphere model for which

$$U = \infty, r \leqslant \sigma$$
$$U = 0, r > \sigma,$$

gives

$$B = \frac{2}{3}\pi N \sigma^3 = b_0 \qquad (4.13)$$

For the square-well model, where

$$U = \infty, r \leqslant \sigma$$
$$U = -\varepsilon, \sigma > r \geqslant R\sigma$$

and

$$U = 0, r > R\sigma$$

we obtain for B

$$B(T) = b_0 \{1 - (R^3 - 1)(\exp[\varepsilon/kT] - 1)\} \qquad (4.14)$$

Equation (4.10) can also be integrated for more realistic potentials; the results are most conveniently expressed in numerical form. These are usually tabulated in reduced form, $B^*(T) = B(T)/b_0$ as a function of $T^* = kT/\varepsilon$ (see, for example, Appendix 4).

For non-spherical molecules the relative orientation of the molecules must also be considered. The general expression for the second virial coefficient of a gas composed of molecules which interact through a non-central force field is

$$B(T) = -\frac{N_A}{2V\Omega^2} \iiiint [\exp(-U_{12}/kT) - 1]\, d\mathbf{r}_1\, d\omega_1\, d\mathbf{r}_2\, d\omega_2 \quad (4.15)$$

where ω_1 and ω_2 represent the coordinates necessary to specify the orientations of molecules 1 and 2, and $\mathbf{r}_1$ and $\mathbf{r}_2$ are the centre-of-mass positions of the molecules; U_{12} is the pair potential, which here depends on the relative orientation of the molecules as well as their separation; V is the volume of the system; and Ω is a normalization factor whose value depends on the number of angular variables needed to specify the relative orientation of the molecules. For linear molecules three angles are required and Ω is 4π.

The third virial coefficient arises from the interaction of three molecules. If the energies of interaction are pairwise additive (i.e. $U_{123} = U_{12} + U_{23} + U_{13}$) C for spherical systems may be written in terms of an integral of the corresponding Mayer f-functions over the pair separations r_{ij}:

$$C = -\frac{8\pi^2 N_A}{3} \iiint f_{12} f_{23} f_{13} r_{12} r_{23} r_{13}\, dr_{12}\, dr_{23}\, dr_{13}. \quad (4.16)$$

For most substances C is positive in the accessible temperature range and decreases with increasing temperature (Fig. 4.6). At low temperatures C should again decrease and become negative as the attractive forces begin to dominate, but this has been observed experimentally in only a few cases.

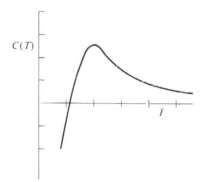

Fig. 4.6 Temperature dependence of third virial coefficients.

For real systems, eqn (4.16) is only an approximation, since there are further non-pairwise additive contributions to U_{123} and hence to C.

$$U_{123} = U_{12} + U_{13} + U_{23} + \Delta U_3. \quad (4.17)$$

Studies for those cases in which the pair interaction is well characterized suggest that the non-additive term, ΔU_3, is adequately represented by the three-body dispersion energy term as given by the Axilrod–Teller triple-dipole energy, U_{DDD} (see Section 1.9). This term stabilizes linear arrangements of three molecules and destabilises triangular arrangements relative to the pairwise additive energy. The effect of U_{DDD} is a large and positive additional contribution to C. For instance, for the rare gases near their critical temperature, the correction amounts to about 80 per cent of the pairwise contribution to C. Although this correction decreases with increasing temperature, it remains significant up to the highest temperatures that are experimentally accessible, falling to about 30 per cent by $2T_C$ and to about 15 per cent by $4T_C$.

Short-range repulsive non-additive contributions to C have been estimated using various theoretical models to be negative and approximately half the size of the triple-dipole contributions. The practical success of using the latter alone therefore implies a fortuitous cancellation of these negative repulsive non-additive contributions and other positive contributions that arise from higher-order multipole terms in the long-range non-additive energy. Experimental values of C for spherical molecules could, if the pair potential were known accurately, provide a probe of the non-additive three-body contributions to the intermolecular potential energy. In practice however, the accuracy of the measurements is usually not sufficiently high to distinguish between the Axilrod–Teller approximation and more extended representations. U_{DDD} in fact turns out to be an extremely good practical representation of the net non-additive multibody potential for spherical systems. We shall see in Chapters 6 and 7 that in addition to describing three-body contributions to the compressibility of a fairly dilute gas, it can also be used in conjunction with the pair potential to evaluate the properties of dense phases where many molecules are interacting simultaneously.

In the case of a gas composed of molecules interacting with an anisotropic potential, the expressions for C are modified in a similar fashion to those for the second virial coefficient to take account of the relative orientations of the molecules.

The expressions we have given relating virial coefficients to intermolecular potential functions are all obtained assuming classical mechanics to be appropriate. This is a good assumption for reasonably heavy molecules at all but the lowest temperatures (where such molecules are unlikely to exist in the gaseous state). For example, for neon at room temperature the correction is less than 1 per cent. These corrections depend on the value of the de Broglie wavelength, λ, associated with the translational motion of the molecules:

$$\lambda = h/p = \frac{h}{(3mkT)^{1/2}} \tag{4.18}$$

where p is the momentum, h is Planck's constant, and m is the mass of the molecule. Since the ratio of λ to the range of the interaction is largest for light molecules at low temperatures, the effects of quantum mechanical behaviour on virial coefficients become most significant for these situations. Indeed, for He at 30 K the quantum corrections are estimated to be greater in magnitude than the classical value of B itself.

4.6. The determination of intermolecular forces from second virial coefficients

The traditional way of using bulk properties to determine potentials is to assume a particular functional form for $U(r)$ that contains a number of disposable parameters. Values of $B(T)$ for this potential may then be calculated using the equations of section 4.5; the disposable parameters can be determined by optimizing the fit of calculated to experimental values of $B(T)$. Such a procedure is fraught with many difficulties. The initial assumptions made about the functional form of $U(r)$ impose unwanted constraints on the potential that is determined. In addition it turns out that many differently shaped potentials are able to represent the same virial coefficient data equally well, especially over a narrow temperature range. Attempts to overcome these problems have included the use of very flexible functions containing many disposable parameters, and virial coefficient data over a wide range of temperature, usually in conjunction with other properties. In some cases this approach has proved fruitful.

Recently, alternative procedures have been devised to enable the potential to be determined from a particular property without making any prior assumptions about its form. These are called *inversion methods*. In the particular case of the second virial coefficient, a pair of values (B, T) can be used to give a corresponding pair of points (r, U) on the associated potential curve. This transformation can be understood by analogy with the exact results for soft spheres which interact with an inverse power repulsion:

$$U(r) = C_n r^{-n} = \varepsilon(\sigma/r)^n$$

for which we have

$$B(T) = (C_n kT)^{3/n} \Gamma[1 - 3/n] b_0$$

where Γ is the gamma function and $b_0 = \frac{2}{3}\pi N\sigma^3$. In other words, the gas behaves as a collection of spheres whose effective diameter $\sigma(T)$ decreases with increasing temperature:

$$B(T) = \frac{2}{3}\pi N\sigma^3(T)$$

where

$$\sigma(T) = (C_n/kT)^{1/n}\{\Gamma[1 - 3/n]\}^{1/3}.$$

We can extend this result to real molecules and write

$$B(T) = \frac{2}{3}\pi N\bar{r}^3(T) \tag{4.19}$$

where $\tilde{r}(T)$ is a temperature-dependent characteristic length (or effective diameter). We can now investigate how the intermolecular potential energy $U(\tilde{r})$ is related to the temperature T.

The simplest situation is to assume that two molecules approach one another until their potential energy is equal to their initial kinetic energy, which is of order kT. We can then postulate that

$$U(\tilde{r}) = kT, \tag{4.20}$$

so through eqns (4.19) and (4.20) we have an immediate parametric relation between each value of the second virial coefficient and a point on the potential energy function ($U = kT, \tilde{r}$). This simple hypothesis has been tested using simulated results, where the experimental values of $B(T)$ have been calculated from known realistic potentials. We find that it can be used to define $U(r)$ to within ± 5 per cent using virial coefficients at high temperatures ($kT/\varepsilon > 30$), but fails badly at lower temperatures. Since it is only for helium that such high temperature data exist, and these probe only the high repulsive wall of the potential, such a method is of little practical value. However, it can be dramatically improved by modifying these simple postulates in two ways:

1. For real molecules the definition of $\tilde{r}$ through eqn (4.19) is unsuitable, since $B(T)$ is negative over most of the experimental range. However the quantity $B + T\mathrm{d}B/\mathrm{d}T$ is positve at all temperatures, decreasing as temperature increases. This functional of B is, in fact, the Laplace Transform of $U(r)\Delta(\phi)$ and it may be shown that the definition of $\tilde{r}$ can be improved by writing

$$\tilde{r}(T) = \left[\frac{B + T\,\mathrm{d}B/\mathrm{d}T}{\frac{2}{3}\pi N} \right]^{1/3} \tag{4.21}$$

where the term $T\mathrm{d}B/\mathrm{d}T$ can be thought of as allowing for the presence of attractive forces between the molecules.

2. The energy $U(\tilde{r})$ is not now equated to kT but instead is related to it by an *inversion function* $G(T)$:

$$U(\tilde{r}) = G(T)kT. \tag{4.22}$$

The function $G(T)$ is not known exactly but can be estimated using an initial approximation to the potential $U_0(r)$ e.g. a 12-6 Lennard–Jones function. Values of $G_0(T)$ can then be used in eqns (4.21) and (4.22) to generate a series of points ($\tilde{r}, U(\tilde{r})$) from the data (B, T) which define a new function $U_1(r)$. Tests using simulated data show that this function is a closer approximation to the true potential than $U_0(r)$. $U_1(r)$ is used to calculate a new function $G_1(T)$, which can in turn be used to invert $B(T)$ to give a new potential $U_2(r)$. The iterative application of this procedure quickly converges on the true potential. Three iterations are usually sufficient to define the potential with as high precision as the range and accuracy of the experimental data allow—typically ± 1 per cent in U (Fig. 4.7).

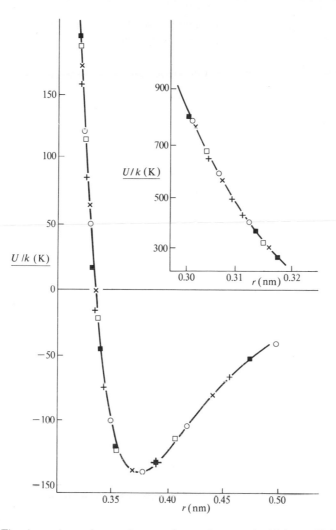

Fig. 4.7 The inversion of pseudo-experimental second virial coefficient data calculated from the BBMS potential energy function (solid line). Results after the third iteration. Initial approximate potential: (□) 9–6; (×) 11–6–8; (+) 12–6; (○) 20–6; (■) 18–6.

The remarkable success of such methods in practice appears at first sight to contradict the assertions quantified in Section 4.5, that $B(T)$ contains information only on the repulsive energies and the width of the potential well as a function of its depth. However, the potential and derivative are continuous at $r = 0$, the point at which the well-width function $\Delta(\phi)$ possesses a discontinuity. It is these continuity and similarity characteristics, built into the method through $G(T)$, that presumably enable the full potential to be determined. Further details of the inversion procedure are given in Appendix 5.

4.7. Principle of corresponding states

We saw in Section 4.3 that the parameters a and b of the van der Waals' equation of state can be related to the critical temperature, pressure, and volume of a gas which conforms to this equation. Making use of these relations enables the van der Waals' equation to be written in the form

$$\left[\frac{P}{P_c} + \frac{3}{(\overline{V}/V_c)}\right]\left[3\frac{\overline{V}}{V_c} - 1\right] = 8\frac{T}{T_c}$$

The ratios P/P_c, V/V_c, T/T_c are a dimensionless (or *reduced*) pressure, volume, and temperature respectively. All substances that obey the van der Waals equation therefore have identical values of reduced pressure if they have the same reduced temperature and volume. This statement is just one example of the *principle of corresponding states*. In a more general form the principle of corresponding states can be derived from a consideration of the intermolecular potential. Substances with spherical molecules, where the interaction energy is pairwise additive, and whose pair potential is of the form

$$U(r) = \varepsilon F(r/\sigma)$$

where F is a universal function, may be shown to possess identical thermodynamic properties when these are expressed in suitable dimensionless form. In this more general case, the reduction parameters are appropriate combinations of the length and energy scale parameters, ε and σ, which are characteristic of each particular substance.

An example of this more general statement of the principle of corresponding states can be clearly seen for the case of second virial coefficients. For a potential of the general form above, the classical expression for $B(T)$, eqn (4.10), becomes

$$B(T) = -2\pi N_A \sigma^3 \int_0^\infty [\exp(-F(r/\sigma)/T^*) - 1](r/\sigma)^2 \, d(r/\sigma).$$

The value of the integral depends only on the reduced temperature $T^* (= kT/\varepsilon)$ and on the form of the function F, i.e.

$$B(T) = \frac{2\pi N_A}{3} \sigma^3 B^*(kT/\varepsilon) = b_0 B^*(T^*).$$

Hence the reduced second virial coefficient $B^*(T^*)$ can be evaluated from the potential expressed in reduced units $U^*(r^*)$ i.e.

$$U^*(r^*) = \frac{U(r/\sigma)}{\varepsilon} = F(r/\sigma)$$

$$B^*(T^*) = 3 \int_0^\infty [1 - U^*/T^*] r^{*2} \, dr^* = B(T)/b$$

All the substances with the same *reduced potential function*, F, will therefore have the same *reduced* second virial coefficient B^* at the same reduced temperature T^*.

Because for many substances ε and σ are still unknown, it has become common practice to reduce data by experimental quantities that are in some way related to ε and σ. Traditionally the critical parameters T_c and V_c have been employed in this reduction in an analogous way to that illustrated earlier for the van der Waals equation. However, the critical properties are characteristic of many-body (high density) interactions and hence are not entirely appropriate replacements for the two-body scale parameters ε and σ. For this reason length and energy parameters based on second virial coefficients, which reflect two-body interactions, are now preferred. Particularly appropriate choices are the Boyle temperature T_B, (the temperature at which $B(T) = 0$) and the Boyle volume, $V_B = T_B(dB/dT)_{T=T_B}$, though the latter is sometimes replaced by a quantity $B_0 = -B(T = 0.7 \, T_B)$ which is more easily determined experimentally. Figure 4.8 shows the second virial coefficients in reduced form calculated from a number of different potential energy functions. Only at low temperatures $(T < 0.4T_B)$ do significant differences occur, which illustrates the importance of having data at the extremes of the temperature range in order to be able to discriminate between potential functions of different shape using second virial coefficients. Should experimental data of sufficient quality and range be available, then the parameters of the potential can be obtained from the Boyle parameters T_B and B_0 by

$$\varepsilon/k = T_B/T_B^*, \quad \sigma = \left(\frac{B_0}{\frac{2}{3}\pi N B_0^*}\right)^{1/3}$$

where T_B^* and B_0^* are the values of the reduced Boyle parameters for the potential function that is found to be consistent with the data. However, where good data exist the inversion methods described earlier are the preferred way of obtaining potential functions from second virial coefficient data.

The corresponding states behaviour of molecules of increasing complexity is compared in Fig. 4.9; here T_c and V_c have been used as reducing parameters since experimental Boyle parameters are not available for all of the substances. It is seen that the effects of moderate deviations from spherical symmetry are small (e.g. compare N_2 with Ar) but as the molecular anisotropy increases e.g. (Ar $\rightarrow C_3H_8 \rightarrow n-C_5H_{12}$), the reduced second virial coefficients become

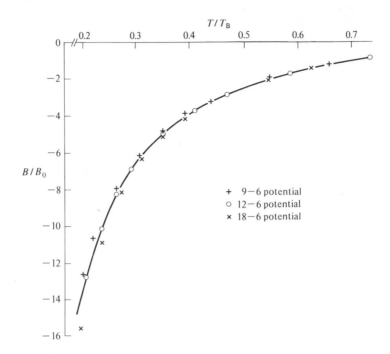

Fig. 4.8 Reduced second virial coefficients for some n–6 potential energy functions. The line represents the 12–6 results. The reductions are performed using the Boyle temperature, T_B, and the characteristic volume, B_0, defined as $B_0 = -B(T = 0.7T_B)$.

increasingly negative, especially at low temperatures. Even pseudo-spherical molecules, like the 'globular' $C(CH_3)_4$, CF_4 or SF_6, lie significantly below the inert gas line. The effects of increasing polarity (e.g. CH_3Cl) are qualitatively similar to those of shape.

These observations suggest that many types of change in the intermolecular potential can lead to broadly similar effects on the second virial coefficient. In a powerful analysis of deviations from simple corresponding states behaviour, Pitzer has shown that almost any increase in molecular complexity has a similar effect on the angle-averaged intermolecular potential, which dominates the behaviour of the second virial coefficient. These angle-averaged interactions are characterized by steeper repulsive walls and narrower potential wells than those found for simple spherical molecules. Pitzer showed that a single additional parameter, which he called the *acentric factor* (ω) was sufficient to characterize the extent of most types of deviation from simple (spherical molecule) corresponding states behaviour. It is defined by

$$\omega = -\log_{10}(P_s/P_c) - 1.000$$

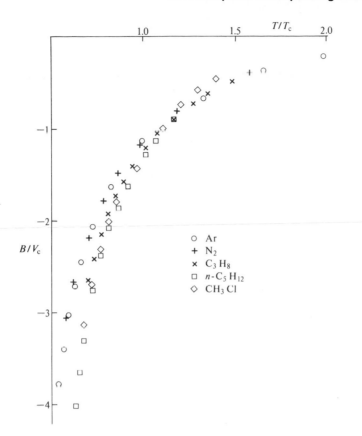

Fig. 4.9 Reduced second virial coefficients for several gases.

where P_s is the saturated vapour pressure of the substance at $T = 0.7\,T_c$ and P_c is the critical pressure. Values for several substances are given in Appendix 1. Pitzer was able to give analytical expressions for $B(T)$ and many other properties of both simple and complex molecules in terms of just reduced temperature and the acentric factor. Although such correlations are extremely useful from the point of view of property prediction, their very existence suggests that second virial coefficients are unlikely to be a very sensitive probe of the precise form of the intermolecular potential for non-spherical molecules. Nevertheless the theoretical relationships between potentials and the virial coefficients are well established and, at the risk of labouring an apparently obvious point, it must be emphasized that a proposed pair potential function that cannot reproduce measured second virial coefficients to within their experimental error cannot be correct.

4.8. Mixtures

The virial coefficients of gas mixtures are related to the gas composition and to the intermolecular potential energy functions that characterize the different types of possible interactions. For an n-component mixture, the second and third virial coefficients may be written:

$$B_m = \sum_{i=1}^{n} \sum_{j=1}^{n} x_i x_j B_{ij}$$

$$C_m = \sum_{i=1}^{n} \sum_{j=1}^{n} \sum_{k=1}^{n} x_i x_j x_k C_{ijk}$$

Hence B_m and C_m are the virial coefficients of a mixture containing mole fractions x_i of component i. For binary mixtures these equations may be written explicitly

$$B_m = x_1^2 B_{11} + 2x_1 x_2 B_{12} + x_2^2 B_{22}$$
$$C_m = x_1^3 C_{111} + 3x_1^2 x_2 C_{112} + 3x_1 x_2^2 C_{122} + x_2^2 C_{222}$$

In these equations B_{11} and B_{22} are the second virial coefficients of the pure components, and B_{12}, the second cross-virial coefficient or *interaction second virial coefficient*, is related to the pair potential U_{12} characterizing the 1–2 interaction in just the same way that B_{11} and B_{22} depend on the potentials for 1–1 and 2–2 interactions:

$$B_{12} = -2\pi N_A \int_0^\infty (e^{-U_{12}(r_{12})/kT} - 1) r_{12}^2 \, dr_{12}.$$

The third cross-coefficients C_{112} and C_{122} are also related to the different potential energy functions via equations analogous to eqn (4.16).

Measurements on gas mixtures may thus be used as a source of information about the interactions between unlike molecules. In practice, applications have been confined almost entirely to the second virial coefficient, B_{12}. B_{12} may be measured by using the procedures described below both on gas mixtures and, separately, on the pure components. The resultant errors in derived values of B_{12} tend to be large, owing to the cumulative effects of the errors in B_{11} and B_{22}. Alternative methods of measuring B_{12} which can give greater accuracy, have also been used. For example, the change in pressure that occurs when two gases, initially at the same pressure, are mixed at constant temperature and volume may be measured, and is largely determined by the excess second virial coefficient, $B_{12} - \frac{1}{2}(B_{11} + B_{22})$. This method has been used successfully to study B_{12} for simple gas mixtures at low temperatures. The related experiment, in which the volume change needed to achieve mixing at constant pressure, (again this is simply related to the excess second virial coefficient) has also been used.

When values of B_{12} have been established, they may be used to study the appropriate potential energy function for the unlike interaction, U_{12}. In the past, much work on unlike molecule interactions has been based on the assumption that the pair potential energy function for both pure components, and for the unlike pairs, were of the same shape, i.e. that they were conformal. Such conformality was considered in Section 4.7 in connection with the principle of corresponding states. Attention is most commonly focused on the relationships between the parameters ε and σ characterizing the three types of interaction. Various combining rules relating the like and unlike parameters have been proposed, notably the Lorentz–Berthelot rules:

$$\sigma_{12} = (\sigma_{11} + \sigma_{22})/2$$

$$\varepsilon_{12} = (\varepsilon_{11}\varepsilon_{22})^{1/2}$$

The first rule is exact for mixtures of hard spheres, and the second owes its origins to mixing rules for the dispersion energy, $(C_6(12) = [C_6(11)C_6(22)]^{1/2})$. With the development of more direct routes to the pair potential from the measured properties it has become apparent that in many cases the assumptions of potential conformality, and of simple combining rules for the parameters are incorrect. In particular ε_{12} is generally found to be less than the value given by the geometric mean rule. Although the harmonic-mean rule (see Section 1.8.3) was in some cases found to be a better empirical approximation, no single set of combining rules has met with universal success.

4.9. Experimental methods

Gases under normal conditions are often very nearly perfect and the second virial coefficient makes only a small correction to the equation of state. Thus for a gas at 1 atm and room temperature with the fairly sizeable second virial coefficient of $250 \text{ cm}^3 \text{ mol}^{-1}$, the compression factor is given by

$$Z = \frac{P\bar{V}}{RT} = 1 - \frac{B}{\bar{V}} = 1 - \frac{250}{25\,000} = 0.99.$$

The deviation from perfect gas behaviour is only 1 per cent. If B is to be measured with a precision of $\pm 1 \text{ cm}^3 \text{ mol}^{-1}$ then Z must under these conditions be determined to one part in 25 000 (0.004 per cent)—a formidable requirement. The most difficult measurement is that of pressure, which is not easy to determine to the required accuracy even with the best mercury manometers, and modern technology offers little help. To circumvent this difficulty, at least partially, comparative methods must be used in which absolute errors in pressure measurement are not directly reflected in the values of B. Thus the accuracy of an apparatus in which the gas can be compressed into a series of globes of known volume (Fig. 4.10) can be much improved if used as a comparative method. In this case two series of identical bulbs are

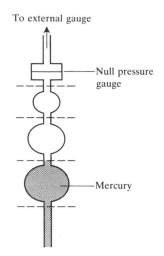

To external gauge

Null pressure gauge

Mercury

Fig. 4.10 Low-pressure virial coefficient apparatus.

linked and the pressure difference between the two sets determined with a reference gas in one series and the gas under investigation in the other. This pressure difference can be directly related to the difference in the second virial coefficients of the two gases.

Alternatively, the determinations can be made at high pressure, where the deviation from perfection will be greater. This introduces a further difficulty. Because the virial equation is an infinite series, approximating it by a truncated polynomial can give rise to errors in the coefficients unless care is taken to ensure that the omitted higher order terms are negligible. At low to moderate pressures, where the deviations from ideality are usually small, only a few terms need be retained, but at high pressures the deviations are more marked and considerably more terms must be included.

At high pressures expansion procedures are often employed (Fig. 4.11). The gas is allowed to expand from the original container, V_1, into an evacuated vessel, V_2, and the new pressure determined. The original volume is then isolated, the expansion vessel evacuated and the procedure is repeated. B is given by the limiting slope of $P_n/(P_{n+1})$ (as $P \rightarrow 0$) as a function of P_n, where n is the number of expansions carried out. Polynomial fits to high pressure data can be used to estimate third virial coefficients, C, but it is even more difficult to determine than B. The values quoted in the literature are often subject to considerable uncertainty.

The Joule–Thomson effect may be used to obtain information about second virial coefficients, as the low pressure limit of the isothermal Joule–Thomson coefficient is given by

$$\phi_{JT}(P \rightarrow 0) = B - T\left(\frac{dB}{dT}\right).$$

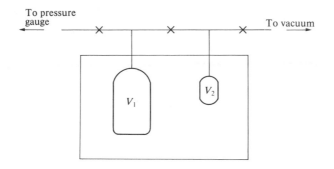

Fig. 4.11 High-pressure virial coefficient apparatus.

In practice, however, the Joule–Thomson coefficient has proved extremely difficult to measure accurately.

4.10. Conclusions

Gas imperfection data, in particular second virial coefficient measurements, have proved a valuable source of information about intermolecular forces. Though corresponding-states analysis suggests that data over a wide range of temperatures is necessary if the shape of the pair potential function is to be determined, second virial coefficient data over a modest range readily permit the elimination of inadequate potentials. Even with data over the widest possible temperature range, theoretical analysis shows that *in general* the data cannot be inverted to give a unique potential function. However, for the limited classes of function that arise in intermolecular forces, direct inversion procedures have been devised that are applicable to data of high quality.

Third virial coefficients, though hard to determine to high accuracy, can provide valuable information about non-additive contributions to inter-molecular energy.

Appendix 4A. Intermolecular forces and virial coefficients

Virial coefficients may be directly related to the interactions between the molecules of a gas. The compression factor of a system of N molecules may be related to its partition function Z_N:

$$\frac{PV}{kT} = \left(\frac{\partial \ln Z_N}{\partial \ln V}\right)_T \tag{4A.1}$$

Z_N is related to the total energy of the system by

$$Z_N = \frac{1}{N!h^{3N}} \int \cdot \cdot \int \exp[-E/kT] \, d\mathbf{p}^N \, d\mathbf{r}^N.$$

where $\mathbf{p}_i$ and $\mathbf{r}_i$ are the momenta and coordinates of the molecules. For molecules without internal energy modes such as vibration and rotation, E may be written as the sum of the kinetic energy and the intermolecular configurational energy U_N.

$$E = \sum_i^N p_i^2/2m + U_N(r^N).$$

For systems with no intermolecular interactions, $U_N = 0$, and the integration over $\mathbf{r}^N$ gives V^N. Subsequent integration over the momenta gives the perfect gas partition function

$$Z_N = V^N/\lambda^{3N} N!$$

where $\lambda = h/(2\pi mkT)^{1/2}$. Substitution of this expression for Z_N into eqn (4A.1) yields $PV/NkT = 1$, the perfect gas equation of state.

If U_N is not zero we may write for Z_N:

$$Z_N = Q_N/\lambda^{3N} \qquad (4A.2)$$

where Q_N is the configurational integral, defined

$$Q_N = \frac{1}{N!} \int .. \int \exp[-U_N/kT] \, d\mathbf{r}^N.$$

This integration extends over the positions of all N molecules in the volume V. It may be expressed in the equivalent form

$$Q_N = \frac{V^N}{N!} \langle \exp[-U_N/kT] \rangle$$

where $\langle \rangle$ represents the average value of the Boltzmann factor, $\exp[-U_N/kT]$, over all possible configurations. If the configurational energy U_N is written as a sum of pair energies

$$U_N = \sum_{j>i} U_{ij}$$

we may write

$$\langle \exp[-U_N/kT] \rangle$$
$$= \langle \exp(-U_{12}/kT)\exp(-U_{13}/kT) \ldots \exp(-U_{N-1,N}/kT \rangle.$$

Employing the definitions

$$\varphi_N = e^{-U_N/kT} \quad \text{and} \quad \varphi_{ij} = e^{-U_{ij}/kT}$$

this equation can be expressed

$$\langle \varphi_N \rangle = \langle \varphi_{12}\varphi_{13} \ldots \varphi_{N,N-1} \rangle.$$

Many of these pair interactions are quite independent. Thus

$$\langle \varphi_{12}\varphi_{34} \rangle = \langle \varphi_{12} \rangle \langle \varphi_{34} \rangle = \langle \varphi_{12} \rangle^2.$$

This last form reflects the fact that all U_{ij} are equivalent. However some contributions are not independent. We cannot in general write

$$\langle \varphi_{12}\varphi_{13}\varphi_{23} \rangle = \langle \varphi_{12} \rangle \langle \varphi_{13} \rangle \langle \varphi_{23} \rangle.$$

This simple product form may nevertheless be used as a first-order approximation to the exact result, and will be valid at low densities. If any contributing pair of molecules is widely separated, $U_{ij} = 0$, $\varphi_{ij} = 1$, and the above form is correct. At low densities, configurations in which groups of three molecules are simultaneously close together are rare, and so this expression may be used.

Thus, for low densities we may write

$$Q_N = \frac{V^N}{N!} \langle \varphi_{ij} \rangle^{N(N-1)/2}$$

where

$$\langle \varphi_{ij} \rangle = \int \exp\left(-U_{ij}/kT\right) \frac{dr_i \, dr_j}{V \; V}$$

$$= \frac{1}{V} \int \exp\left(-U_{ij}/kT\right) dr_{ij}$$

since $\int \int dr_i \, dr_j = \int dr_i \int dr_{ij} = V \int dr_{ij}$. It proves convenient to write

$$\langle \varphi_{ij} \rangle = 1 + \frac{1}{V} \int \left[\exp\left(-U_{ij}/kT\right) - 1\right] dr_{ij}$$

For large N, $N(N-1) \simeq N^2$. If we allow $N \to \infty$, and $V \to \infty$, while maintaining the density $\rho = N/V$ constant

$$Q_N = \frac{V^N}{N!} \left[1 + \rho/N \int \left[\exp\left(-U_{ij}/kT\right) - 1\right] dr_{ij}\right]^{N^2/2}.$$

Using the relation

$$\exp\left(x\right) = \lim_{N \to \infty} \left(1 + \frac{x}{N}\right)^N$$

we may rewrite this equation and obtain

$$Q_N = \frac{V^N}{N!} \left\{ \exp\left[\frac{N^2}{2V} \int \left[\exp\left(-U_{ij}/kT\right) - 1\right] dr_{ij}\right] \right\}.$$

From eqns (4A.1) and (4A.2) we have

$$\left(\frac{PV}{NkT} - 1\right) = \frac{1}{N} \left(\frac{\partial \ln Q_N}{\partial \ln V}\right)_T = \frac{N}{2V} \int \left[\exp\left(-U_{ij}/kT\right) - 1\right] dr_{ij}.$$

As

$$\left(\frac{PV}{NkT}\right) = 1 + \frac{B(T)}{V} + \ldots \ldots$$

we have obtained an expression for the second virial coefficient. As $dr = 4\pi r^2 \, dr$ this may be written, for one mole of gas for which $N = N_A$, as

$$B(T) = -2\pi N_A \int f(r) r^2 \, dr$$

where $f(r)$ is the Mayer f-function

$$f(r) = \exp\left(-U(r)/kT\right) - 1.$$

This gives the correct result for B but does not provide an estimate of the third virial coefficient C. This can be shown to arise from the difference between the average over the triplet and the cube of the pair term.

$$\langle e^{-U_{12}/kT} e^{-U_{13}/kT} e^{-U_{23}/kT} \rangle / \langle e^{-U_{12}/kT} \rangle^3.$$

Introduction of this ratio as a correction term leads to the expressions for C:

$$C = -\frac{8\pi^2 N_A}{3} \int\int\int f_{12} f_{23} f_{13} r_{12} r_{23} r_{13} \, dr_{12} \, dr_{23} \, dr_{13}.$$

Similar but more complicated expressions for the higher virial coefficients can be obtained in terms of the Mayer functions.

The approach followed in this Appendix is based on that given by N. G. Van Kampen, (1961). *Physica*, **27**, 783, which should be consulted for a more detailed treatment.

Suggested further reading

Maitland, G. C., Rigby, M., Smith, E. B. and Wakeham, W. A. (1981). *Intermolecular forces: their origin and determination.* Chapter 3. Clarendon Press, Oxford. (Referred to in text as MRSW.)

Mason, E. A. and Spurling, T. H. (1969). *The virial equation of state.* Pergamon Press, Oxford.

Hirschfelder, J. O., Curtiss, C. F. and Bird, R. B. (1954). *The molecular theory of gases and liquids*, Chapter 3. Wiley, New York.

Exercises

E4.1. The constant b in the van der Waals equation is found to be 39.1 cm³ mol⁻¹ for nitrogen. Estimate the collision diameter of the molecules. Why is the value you obtain not the same as that given in Appendix 2?

E4.2. Calculate $(\partial T/\partial P)_H$ for CO_2 at 294 K using the parameters of Appendix 2 in conjunction with the reduced properties given in Appendix 4. The heat capacity of CO_2 at constant pressure at this temperature is $37.5 \text{ J K}^{-1} \text{mol}^{-1}$.

E4.3. Using the table in Appendix 4 and the parameters given in Appendix 2, calculate the second virial coefficient, B, for argon at 142 K.

5
The transport properties
of gases

5.1. Introduction

It is a commonplace observation that whenever a sample of material is subject to a gradient of temperature there is a flux (or transport) of energy in the form of heat from the hotter to the colder region down the temperature gradient. This process of heat conduction is just one example of a group of phenomena known as transport processes, which occur whenever the parameters that characterize the thermodynamic state of the system are non-uniform over the material. The remaining, primary transport processes are associated with gradients of macroscopic velocity (the phenomenon of viscosity) and with gradients of composition (the phenomenon of diffusion). Associated with each transport process there is a flux of some dynamic variable of the system: energy for heat conduction, momentum for viscosity, and mass for diffusion. In each case it turns out that the flux of the dynamic variable, J, is related in a linear fashion to the gradient of the corresponding macroscopic quantity, X, so that

$$J = - K \frac{dX}{dx}$$

The proportionality constant K is known as the *transport coefficient* and represents the thermal conductivity for energy transport, the viscosity for momentum transport, and the diffusion coefficient for mass transport.

In the particular case of dilute gases the only mechanism available for the transport of any of these quantities is through the motion of the molecules themselves. Thus, in a gas subject to a temperature gradient, the molecules in the neighbourhood of the higher temperature have a higher energy and, during the course of their motion, they tend to move towards the colder regions of the gas carrying their energy with them and leading to a net flux of energy. Of course on their way to this colder region of the gas the molecules inevitably collide with other molecules of the gas. Consequently the rate of transport of energy, and therefore the value of the transport coefficient (thermal conductivity) is determined by both the number and nature of these molecular collisions. As we have seen in Chapter 2, the outcome of a molecular collision is determined by the intermolecular pair potential according to which two molecules interact. It follows that the value of the transport coefficients depends in some way upon the forces between molecules. In order to establish this connection exactly it is necessary to formulate a complete kinetic theory of the gas, but considerable insight can be gained from the simpler treatment that we provide here. It begins with a consideration of the motion of molecules in a gas composed of spherically symmetrical, structureless molecules.

The distribution of molecular speeds in gases is given by the Maxwell–Boltzmann distribution:

$$dn\,(C) = 4N \left(\frac{m}{2\pi\,kT} \right)^{3/2} C^2\,e^{-mC^2/2kT}\,dC$$

where $dn\,(C)$ is the number of molecules whose speeds lie in the interval C to $C + dC$ and N is the total number of molecules. m is the molecular mass and T the temperature. The mean molecular speed corresponding to this distribution is given by

$$\bar{C} = \frac{1}{N} \int_0^\infty C\,dn\,(C)$$

$$= 4\pi \left(\frac{m}{2\pi\,kT} \right)^{3/2} \int_0^\infty C^3\,e^{-mC^2/2kT}\,dC$$

i.e.

$$\bar{C} = \left(\frac{8kT}{\pi m} \right)^{1/2}. \tag{5.1}$$

In order to evaluate the transport properties we require an expression for the mean value of the component of molecular velocities in a specified direction, for example along the z axis (in Cartesian coordinates), which we write $\bar{C}_z$. We write

$$\bar{C}_z = \overline{C \cos \theta} = \bar{C}\,\overline{\cos \theta} = \bar{C}/2$$

$$\overline{\cos \theta} = \frac{1}{2\pi} \int_0^{2\pi} \int_0^{\pi/2} \cos \theta \sin \theta\,d\theta\,d\phi$$

$$= [\tfrac{1}{2} \sin^2 \theta]_0^{\pi/2} = \tfrac{1}{2}.$$

We can use this result to obtain the rate with which molecules cross (in one direction) a unit area in the xy plane (Fig. 5.1). The number crossing the plane will be those contained in a column of height $\bar{C}_z$ whose velocities are in a downward direction (that is half the total). Therefore

$$\text{Collision rate/unit area} = \tfrac{1}{2}\,n\bar{C}_z$$

$$= \tfrac{1}{4}\,n\bar{C}$$

where n is the number of molecules per unit volume.

Another quantity we need to evaluate is the mean distance a molecule travels

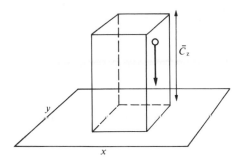

Fig. 5.1 The flux of molecules in the z-direction.

between collisions—the *mean free path*, l. As the mean speed of the molecules is $\overline{C}$, they sweep out, in unit time, a cylinder of length $\overline{C}$ and radius d, where d is the diameter of the molecule. If the centre of another molecule falls within this cylinder a collision will occur (Fig. 5.2). Thus the number of collisions in unit time will be $\pi d^2 \, \overline{C} n$. The mean distance a molecule travels between such collisions, l, is therefore given by

$$l = \frac{\text{distance travelled in unit time}}{\text{number of collisions in unit time}} = \frac{\overline{C}}{\pi d^2 \, n\overline{C}}$$

$$= \frac{1}{\pi d^2 \, n}. \tag{5.2}$$

If we make allowance for the fact that all the molecules are moving simultaneously and that we are concerned with their *relative* velocities we obtain a more accurate expression

$$l = \frac{1}{\sqrt{2\pi d^2 n}}.$$

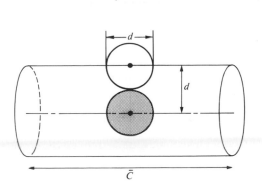

Fig. 5.2 A hard-sphere collision.

5.2. Viscosity

In order to understand first how the viscosity of a gas arises, we consider the gas contained between two plates (Fig. 5.3(a)), the upper one of which is moving with a velocity **u** in the positive x-direction. The gas in contact with the lower, stationary plate has no flow velocity in the positive x-direction and thus a velocity gradient exists in the gas, which causes the gas to exert a drag on the upper plate. In order to maintain the velocity of the upper plate a force must be applied to overcome the viscous drag. Newton's law of viscosity defines the coefficient of shear viscosity, η, in terms of the viscous force, F, on a plate of area A, and the velocity gradient (d**u**/dz) by the equation

$$F = -\eta A \frac{d\mathbf{u}}{dz}. \tag{5.3}$$

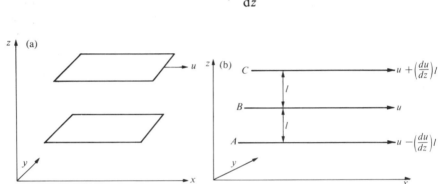

Fig. 5.3 (a) Shear in a fluid, (b) momentum transport between planes.

The origin of viscous forces can be illuminated by a pleasing analogy. We imagine two trains moving on parallel tracks passing each other with different speeds and that parcels of mail are exchanged between the trains. The result of this exchange is that the parcels arriving on the slower train from the faster one have a higher velocity than the slow train and thus tend to speed it up. Conversely, the parcels landing on the faster train tend to slow it down. The net effect will be to reduce the difference in speed of the two trains, and a distant observer would conclude that they exerted a frictional force on one another. In the case of the frictional force in a gas it is the layers in the gas that correspond to the trains and the molecules moving from one layer to another that correspond to the parcels.

We consider a reference plane in the gas lying in the xy-plane, in which the gas moves with a flow velocity **u** in the positive x-direction only (Fig. 5.3(b)). The velocity gradient (d**u**/dz) is assumed to be uniform. The viscous forces can be deduced by considering the molecules that reach the reference plane B.

These molecules will, on average, have travelled since their last collision a distance l, the mean free path. Those which arrive in plane B from above (Fig. 5.3(b)) will have originated in plane C and will have a flow velocity in the positive direction of

$$\mathbf{u} + \left(\frac{d\mathbf{u}}{dz}\right)l$$

and a positive x-direction flow momentum of

$$m\left\{\mathbf{u} + \left(\frac{d\mathbf{u}}{dz}\right)l\right\}$$

where m is the mass of a molecule. As discussed earlier, we assume that in the downward direction the number of molecules that will cross a unit area in the xy-plane in unit time will be all those contained within a column of height $\bar{C}_z$ and unit cross-sectional area and moving in the correct direction (Fig. 5.1), that is $n\bar{C}/4$.

The molecules reaching the reference plane, B, from above will therefore transport downwards an amount of positive x-direction momentum

$$\tfrac{1}{4}n\bar{C}m\left\{\mathbf{u} + \left(\frac{d\mathbf{u}}{dz}\right)l\right\}$$

across unit area in unit time. The molecules that reach plane B from below (plane A of Fig. 5.3(b)) will transport upwards an amount of positive x-direction momentum

$$\tfrac{1}{4}n\bar{C}m\left\{\mathbf{u} - \left(\frac{d\mathbf{u}}{dz}\right)l\right\}$$

across unit area in unit time. The next transport of momentum across unit area of the reference plane B in unit time is the frictional force, F, on this plane in the positive x-direction:

$$F = -\tfrac{1}{4}nm\bar{C}\left\{\mathbf{u} + \left(\frac{d\mathbf{u}}{dz}\right)l\right\} + \tfrac{1}{4}nm\bar{C}\left\{\mathbf{u} - \left(\frac{d\mathbf{u}}{dz}\right)l\right\} = -\tfrac{1}{2}nm\bar{C}\left(\frac{d\mathbf{u}}{dz}\right)l \ (5.4)$$

The frictional force per unit area for a unit velocity gradient is, according to (5.3), the coefficient of viscosity, η, so that we may identify η as

$$\eta = \tfrac{1}{2}nm\bar{C}l = \tfrac{1}{2}\rho\,\bar{C}l \tag{5.5}$$

where ρ is the mass density of the gas. Substituting for the mean free path of the gas, l, from (5.2) and the mean molecular speed from eqn (5.1) we obtain the alternative expressions:

$$\eta = \frac{1}{2}\frac{m\bar{C}}{\pi d^2} = \frac{1}{2}\frac{m}{\pi d^2}\left(\frac{8kT}{\pi m}\right)^{1/2}. \tag{5.6}$$

This equation predicts that the viscosity of a dilute gas of hard spheres is independent of density. This surprising result was first obtained theoretically by Maxwell, who subsequently tested it for real gases by measuring their viscosity as a function of pressure. He found that this prediction of the simple hard-sphere model was in keeping with the behaviour of *real* gases. This was a triumph for the newly emergent kinetic theory and did much to convince the sceptics of its validity. The physical reason for this independence is that in denser gases, though more molecules pass from one layer to another, the mean free path is correspondingly shorter and the excess momentum carried by each molecule is therefore less. More careful measurements on real gases show that the result is not in fact exact, but it is a very reasonable approximation at moderate densities. Equation (5.6) also predicts that the viscosity of a rigid sphere gas should be proportional to $T^{1/2}$. This is a less satisfactory approximation for real gases, whose viscosity varies more rapidly with temperature.

5.3. Thermal conductivity

The viscosity of a gas arises from the transport of momentum along a velocity gradient, whereas for a rigid sphere gas thermal conduction is due to the transport of kinetic energy along a temperature gradient. The phenomenological law of heat conduction was given by Fourier as

$$Q = -\lambda A \left(\frac{\mathrm{d}T}{\mathrm{d}z} \right) \tag{5.7}$$

where Q is the energy (heat) flow across an area A and λ is the coefficient of thermal conductivity. In order to obtain an expression for this transport coefficient we consider a reference plane in a gas in which there is a uniform temperature (and energy) gradient in the z-direction alone. If we denote the mean energy of a molecule by E, then a molecule reaching the reference plane from above (the higher temperature region) will have an energy

$$E + \frac{\mathrm{d}E}{\mathrm{d}z} l.$$

Those reaching the reference plane from below will have an energy

$$E - \frac{\mathrm{d}E}{\mathrm{d}z} l.$$

By similar arguments to those used in the case of viscosity, the net transport of energy across unit area of the reference plane in unit time in the direction of the energy gradient is

$$\tfrac{1}{2} n \overline{C} \left(\frac{\partial E}{\partial z} \right) l.$$

However

$$\frac{dE}{dz} = \left(\frac{dE}{dT}\right)\left(\frac{dT}{dz}\right) = c_v\left(\frac{dT}{dz}\right)$$

where c_v is the heat capacity of the gas per molecule. Thus, for a unit temperature gradient the transport of kinetic energy across unit area in unit time, which is the thermal conductivity coefficient, λ, is

$$\lambda = \tfrac{1}{2} nc_v l\bar{C}$$

or, using eqn (5.2)

$$\lambda = \frac{c_v}{2\pi d^2} \bar{C} = \frac{c_v}{2\pi d^2}\left(\frac{8kT}{\pi m}\right)^{1/2}. \tag{5.8}$$

The thermal conductivity of a hard-sphere gas is therefore predicted to be independent of density and proportional to $T^{1/2}$ as was the viscosity. In fact, our simple model leads to the conclusion that there is a proportionality between the viscosity and thermal conductivity coefficients of a rigid sphere gas, namely

$$\lambda = \eta c_v/m.$$

This proportionality turns out to be an extremely good approximation for a real monatomic gas, albeit with a different proportionality constant.

5.4. Diffusion

Diffusion is the transport of mass along a concentration gradient. Since the argument for two gases diffusing into each other is complicated, let us imagine a gas composed of two isotopes, whose properties, including their molecular mass, are sufficiently similar so that we can treat the values of $\bar{C}$ and l as identical. We select one of the isotopes as a reference and suppose that n is its number density in a reference plane that is situated in the gas normal to a concentration gradient of the isotope [d $(nm)/dz$]. Then, following our earlier arguments, the mass of the reference isotope reaching the reference plane, per unit area in unit time, from a plane of higher concentration a distance l above, is

$$\tfrac{1}{4}\bar{C}\left[nm + \frac{d\,(nm)}{dz}\,l\right].$$

This represents a downward flux of mass. The mass of molecules of the reference isotope reaching the plane from below is

$$\tfrac{1}{4}\bar{C}\left[nm - \frac{d\,(nm)}{dz}\,l\right].$$

The net mass flow across unit area of the reference plane in the direction of the concentration gradient is therefore

$$-\tfrac{1}{2}\overline{C}l\frac{d\,(nm)}{dz}\,.$$

The transport coefficient for this process, known as the self-diffusion coefficient, D, is defined by the equation of Fick's Law

$$J = -AD\frac{d\,(nm)}{dz}$$

where J is the mass flow of molecules of the reference isotope. We can isolate an expression for D by considering transport of mass across unit area in Fick's Law and we find

$$D = \tfrac{1}{2}\overline{C}l$$

$$= \tfrac{1}{2}\overline{C}\frac{1}{\pi n d^2} = \frac{1}{2\pi d^2 n}\left(\frac{8kT}{\pi m}\right)^{1/2}.$$

Thus, the diffusion coefficient is inversely proportional to the number of molecules per unit volume. Furthermore, for a perfect gas

$$n = P/kT$$

so that we can write

$$D = \frac{1}{2\pi d^2}\left(\frac{8kT}{\pi m}\right)^{1/2}\frac{kT}{P} \qquad (5.9)$$

The self-diffusion coefficient of a hard-sphere gas is therefore predicted to be inversely proportional to pressure and directly proportional to $T^{1/2}$.

The exact kinetic theory for hard-sphere molecules gives the same general form of the equation for the transport properties as derived above for our simple model. That is the dependences on temperature, density, molecular mass, and diameter predicted by our simple argument, are all identical with those of the rigorous kinetic theory. However, the numerical coefficients in the expressions are quite different in the two treatments (see Table 5.1). The correct functional dependences are a result of our use of an essentially correct physical mechanism for the transport processes. The discrepancies in the numerical coefficients arise, not surprisingly, from false assumptions made in the evaluation of some of the quantities involved, e.g. $\overline{C}$.

5.5. Application to real gases

Even the results of the rigorous theory given in Table 5.1 relate only to gases composed of hard-sphere molecules, and each expression contains (through the mean free path, l) a cross-section πd^2 that is independent of temperature. However, for real substances, with intermolecular forces that can be both

Table 5.1

Transport properties of hard-sphere gases

	Transport of	*Simple theory coefficient* ξ†	*Rigorous theory coefficient* ξ†	*SI units of transport coefficient*
Viscosity	Momentum	$\dfrac{\sqrt{2}}{\pi} = 0.450$	$\tfrac{5}{16} = 0.313$	$\mathrm{N\,s\,m^{-2}(Pa\,s)}$
Thermal conductivity	Kinetic energy	$\dfrac{\sqrt{2}}{\pi} = 0.450$	$\tfrac{25}{32} = 0.781$	$\mathrm{W\,m^{-1}\,K^{-1}}$
Diffusion	Mass	$\dfrac{\sqrt{2}}{\pi} = 0.450$	$\tfrac{3}{8} = 0.375$	$\mathrm{m^2\,s^{-1}}$

†These are the coefficients in the equations: $\eta = \xi\{\pi m k T)^{1/2}/\pi d^2\}$: $\lambda = \xi\{(\pi k T/m)^{1/2}/\pi d^2\}c_v$: $D = \xi\{(\pi k T/m)^{1/2}/n\pi d^2\} = \xi\{(\pi k^3 T^3/m)^{1/2}/\pi d^2 P\}$.

attractive and repulsive according to separation, the situation is more complicated, and the cross-sections that influence the transport properties depend on temperature. The rigorous kinetic theory for real gases therefore introduces into the expressions for the transport coefficients temperature-dependent factors, which may be thought of as corrections to the hard-sphere cross-section to allow for the effects of intermolecular forces.

Some insight into the nature of these corrections can be obtained by considering a very simple molecular model: one in which the molecules interact according to the inverse power repulsive potential

$$U = C/r^n.$$

The discussion can be further simplified by considering only head-on collisions. If the relative kinetic energy of the two molecules before the collision is E then at the distance of closest approach r_0 (where the relative kinetic energy will be reduced to zero) we obtain

$$E = C/r_0^n \text{ so that } r_0 = \left(\frac{C}{E}\right)^{1/n}.$$

The average relative kinetic energy of two molecules will be proportional to kT. So that

$$E = \alpha k T$$

where α is a constant.

Thus the average distance of closest approach r_0 at temperature T is given by

$$r_0 = \left(\frac{C}{\alpha k T}\right)^{1/n}.$$

The expression for the viscosity coefficient of a hard-sphere gas is given by

$$\eta = \frac{5}{16} (\pi m k T)^{1/2} \frac{1}{\pi d^2}.$$

If we assume that, for molecules interacting with an inverse power inter-molecular potential, the hard-sphere diameter d can be replaced by the average distance of closest approach r_0 in this expression, we obtain

$$\eta = \frac{5}{16} (\pi m k)^{1/2} \frac{1}{\pi} \left(\frac{\alpha k}{C}\right)^{2/n} T^{(1/2 + 2/n)}$$

In this case the coefficient of viscosity increases as $T^{(1/2 + 2/n)}$, a result which, despite the many approximations we have made, is the exact result for this model. This can be compared with the $T^{1/2}$ dependence given by the hard-sphere theory. The result shows us that the temperature dependence of the viscosity of a gas composed of molecules interacting with a repulsive inverse-power function reflects the steepness of the potential. As the temperature is increased the higher kinetic energy allows molecules to approach each other more closely, leading to a smaller 'effective' collision diameter.

This simple argument is far from exact, even though it leads to the correct temperature dependence. It does, however, reveal the essential physics of the problem and suggests we write

$$\eta = \frac{5}{16} (\pi m k T)^{1/2} \frac{1}{\bar{\Omega}(T)}$$

where $\bar{\Omega}(T)$ is the thermally averaged cross-section. $\bar{\Omega}(T)$ is called a *collision integral*. It is often more convenient to replace $\bar{\Omega}(T)$ by

$$\pi d^2 \, \Omega^* \, (T)$$

where Ω^* is called the *reduced collision integral* and reflects how a temperature independent cross-section πd^2 must be modified to take account of inter-molecular forces. In practice the various transport properties involve different collision integrals. Thus

$$\left.\begin{array}{l} \eta = \dfrac{5 \, (m \pi \, k T)^{1/2}}{16 \pi d^2 \, \Omega^{(2,2)*}} \\[3mm] \lambda = \dfrac{25 \, (\pi k T/m)^{1/2} \, c_v}{32 \pi d^2 \Omega^{(2,2)*}} \end{array}\right\} \tag{5.10}$$

and

$$D = \frac{3 \, (\pi k^3 T^3/m)^{1/2}}{8 P \, \pi d^2 \, \Omega^{(1,1)*}}$$

where the reduced collision integrals $\Omega^{(l,s)*}$ are defined by

$$\Omega^{(l,s)*} = \frac{1}{\pi d^2} [(s+1)! \, (kT)^{s+2}]^{-1} \int_0^\infty Q^{(l)} \, (E) e^{-E/kT} E^{s+1} \, dE \tag{5.11}$$

where E is the relative kinetic energy of collisions and the transport cross section $Q^{(l)}(E)$ is defined as:

$$Q^{(l)}(E) = \frac{2\pi}{\left[1 - \frac{1}{2}\left(\frac{1 + (-1)^l}{1 + l}\right)\right]} \int_0^\infty (1 - \cos^l \chi)\, b\, db. \qquad (5.12)$$

The classical deflection angle, χ, has been defined in Chapter 2. As χ is determined by the intermolecular forces, a knowledge of $U(r)$ enables the collision integrals and hence the transport properties to be computed. We note that different collision integrals are involved for diffusion compared with viscosity and thermal conductivity. Diffusion is the transport of mass and is favoured by collisions involving only small deflections, after which the molecule is able to continue on virtually the same path. Viscosity and thermal conductivity, on the other hand, arise from the transport of momentum and energy. For these properties collisions that involve a significant angle of deflection are necessary in order for significant momentum and energy to be transferred. The definitions of the appropriate collision integrals reflect these factors.

The expressions for the transport properties given above are only first approximations, and they must be multiplied by correction factors close to unity (which themselves depend on further collision integrals) if the properties are required to high accuracy. The higher order equations together with expressions for the transport properties of mixtures are given in Appendixes A5.2 and A5.3 of MRSW.

There is a further transport process, thermal diffusion, which is of more subtle origin and cannot be described by the simple kinetic theory. When a gas mixture is subjected to a temperature gradient a partial separation of the components of the mixture occurs, so that in general the lighter component becomes more concentrated in the region of the higher temperature. The corresponding transport coefficient, the thermal diffusion factor α_T, determines the extent of the separation of the gas mixture which occurs in the presence of a temperature gradient. It is defined by

$$\frac{\partial x_1}{\partial z} = -\alpha_T x_1 x_2 \left(\frac{\partial \ln T}{\partial z}\right)$$

where x_i are the mole fractions of the component gases and $(\partial T / \partial z)$ the temperature gradient. If the experiment is performed with two isotopes with very similar masses m_1 and m_2

$$\alpha_T = \frac{15}{16}\left(\frac{m_2 - m_1}{m_1 + m_2}\right)\frac{6C_{12}^* - 5}{A_{12}^*}$$

where

$$C_{12}^* = \frac{\Omega_{12}^{(1,2)*}}{\Omega_{12}^{(1,1)*}} \qquad \text{and} \qquad A_{12}^* = \frac{\Omega_{12}^{(2,2)*}}{\Omega_{12}^{(1,1)*}}$$

Thus thermal diffusion depends on the magnitude of ratios of collision integrals. It turns out that the thermal diffusion factor is, at the same time, the transport coefficient most sensitive to the steepness of the repulsive branch of the intermolecular pair potential and the property which it is most difficult to measure accurately.

5.6. Polyatomic gases

In the preceding sections we have been concerned with the transport properties of gases composed of spherically symmetrical, structureless molecules, that is atomic gases. For gases composed of polyatomic molecules this simple description is inadequate because the molecules are generally not spherically symmetrical, inevitably possess energy in rotational and vibrational modes of motion, and can convert this energy to translational energy as a result of collisions. The kinetic theory of the transport properties of such gases has been fully developed, and for viscosity and diffusion at least its formal results are identical with those of the kinetic theory of monatomic species. The collision integrals that enter the expressions for the transport coefficients are, however, different from those of the atomic case. They reflect the new collision processes that can occur in polyatomic systems. The evaluation of these collision integrals is correspondingly more time-consuming than for the atomic case, so much so that only a few exact calculations for realistic intermolecular pair potentials have yet been performed. Thus, while it is still possible to assert that the intermolecular forces between polyatomic molecules influence the values of the viscosity and diffusion coefficient of the gas, the study of the form of the influence is still in its early stages. The most that can be said with certainty at present is that these two transport coefficients are not merely sensitive to the spherical average of the intermolecular pair potential but also reflect some features of its anisotropy.

   In the case of the thermal conductivity of polyatomic gases the situation is radically different because, in addition to the translational energy of the molecules, the internal energy can be transported down the temperature gradient. Thus the thermal conductivity consists of two contributions,

$$\lambda = \lambda_{\text{trans}} + \lambda_{\text{int}},$$

in place of the single translational term characteristic of atomic gases. The kinetic theory of atomic gases predicts a proportionality between the viscosity and thermal conductivity:

$$\lambda = \lambda_{\text{trans}} = \eta \frac{C_{\text{v}}}{M}$$

in our simple theory, or

$$\lambda = \lambda_{\text{trans}} = \frac{5}{2} \eta \frac{C_{\text{v}}}{M} \tag{5.13}$$

for the more rigorous treatment (Table 5.1). However, this proportionality is not maintained for polyatomic gases. If we neglect any processes whereby internal energy and translational energy may be interconverted (inelastic collisions), it is possible to make an estimate of the thermal conductivity of a polyatomic gas by assuming that the internal energy of the molecules is transported by a diffusion mechanism. This leads to a result, first derived by Eucken,

$$\lambda = \frac{5}{2}\eta\frac{C_{v\,trans}}{M} + \frac{\rho D}{M}(C_v - C_{v\,trans})$$

in which C_v is the total molar heat capacity of the gas and $C_{v\,trans} = 3R/2$, its translational part. It is found that this result is only accurate for those molecules that interact through very weakly anisotropic pair potentials, such as hydrogen. For other systems significant deviations occur. These must be ascribed to the neglect of inelastic collisions, which are more frequent for strongly anisotropic potentials. The implication of these findings is that the thermal conductivity is more sensitive to the anisotropy of the pair potential than viscosity or diffusion, but again owing to the difficulties of calculation the nature of this sensitivity has not yet been explored.

In addition to all of the normal transport properties of the gas that we have already considered, a new set of transport coefficients arise for polyatomic gases that simply do not occur for atomic species. These transport coefficients have their origin in the anisotropic pair potentials for polyatomic species and hence are uniquely sensitive to that part of the potential. Whenever a polyatomic gas is subject to a macroscopic gradient, there is a tendency for the molecules to adopt a preferential alignment with respect to the gradient. If an electric or magnetic field is applied to the gas so as to make the molecules precess, this alignment can be partially destroyed. Thus, for example, it is found that the thermal conductivity of a gas in the direction of an applied temperature gradient depends on the magnitude of a magnetic field applied perpendicular to the temperature gradient. It is even possible to observe in such circumstances a heat flow perpendicular to both the applied field and the temperature gradient. Phenomena of this type, which may be observed for all of the transport processes, are known collectively as the *Senftleben–Beenakker effects*. The magnitude of the effects is very small and specially designed equipment is necessary for measurements. However, the transport coefficients that characterize the magnitude of the effects depend mainly upon the anisotropic part of the pair potential and, in principle, provide a method of investigating it. Again, owing to the difficulties of calculation a systematic study of these coefficients is only just beginning.

5.7. Transport properties and intermolecular forces

The outcome of a collision between structureless molecules with spherically symmetrical potentials may be characterized simply by the deflection angle χ

(Chapter 2). This depends on the relative kinetic energy, E, of the colliding molecules, the impact parameter, b, and on the potential function $U(r)$ (eqn. 2.4). Thus, given a knowledge of the latter, it is possible to calculate the deflection angle at various values of E and b and, by integration over these variables according to eqns (5.11) and (5.12), to evaluate the collision integrals, $\Omega^{(l,s)*}$. These are usually tabulated in a form where they are reduced by the parameters σ and ε that characterize the potential function:

$$\Omega^{(l,s)*}(T^*) = \frac{\Omega^{(l,s)}(T^*)}{\pi\sigma^2}$$

where $T^* = kT/\varepsilon$ is the reduced temperature, i.e. for real molecules, d in eqns (5.10)–(5.12) is replaced by σ, where $U(\sigma) = 0$. Such tabulations are available for many of the functional forms that have been employed to represent the forces between spherical molecules.

The traditional method of obtaining information about intermolecular forces from transport properties involved first selecting a functional form for $U(r)$ that might be expected to adequately represent the forces. Then, comparison of the collision integrals obtained from experimental data with the reduced values tabulated enabled σ and ε/k to be estimated. This procedure, though widely used, was subject to the obvious limitation that it relied on a knowledge of an appropriate functional form for $U(r)$. In fact those most commonly employed, such as the Lennard-Jones (12–6) function are now known to have the wrong shape.

A more desirable method of tackling the problem would be to obtain $U(r)$ directly from the experimental measurements by a *data inversion* procedure. Inspection of eqns (2.4), (5.11) and (5.12) suggests that it will not be easy to devise a formal inversion procedure that would be of practical value. However, an effective method is available based on the behaviour of the transport properties of molecules which interact with an inverse power potential,

$$U(r) = \frac{C_m}{r^m}.$$

For such molecules it can be shown that

$$\overline{\Omega}^{(2,2)} = F(m, \text{ sign of } C_m) \left(\frac{C_m}{kT}\right)^{2/m}$$

where F is a constant.
We define characteristic values of separation $\tilde{r}$, such that

$$\tilde{r}(T) = [\overline{\Omega}^{(2,2)}(T)]^{\frac{1}{2}} \tag{5.14}$$

and noting that $U(\tilde{r}) = C_m/\tilde{r}^m$, we obtain

$$[\tilde{r}(T)]^2 = F(m, \text{sign of } C_m)\left(\frac{C_m}{kT}\right)^{2/m} = \left(\frac{U(\tilde{r})}{C_m}\right)^{-2/m}.$$

Thus
$$U(\tilde{r}) = [F(m, \text{sign of } C_m)]^{-m/2} kT$$
and writing $F^{-m/2}$ as G we obtain
$$U(\tilde{r}) = G(m, \text{sign of } C_m) kT.$$

For inverse power potential functions G is a numerical constant, which ranges from -0.58 for $m = 6$ and C_m negative to $\simeq 0.85$ for C_m positive and $m = 10\text{--}15$. For real potentials we find that G varies with temperature, since the collisions have different energies and probe different parts of the potential function (which, in the terms of this model, have different effective values of m). We find that the variation of G with temperature is very similar for all realistic potential functions and that we may write $U(\tilde{r}) = G_0(T)kT$, where $G_0(T)$ is that calculated using an approximate potential function $U_0(r)$ such as a 12–6 potential. Then a knowledge of a series of values of $\tilde{r}(T)$ obtained via eqns (5.10) and (5.14) from experimentally measured transport properties and $G_0(T)$ obtained from an approximate potential, enables pairs of values $(\tilde{r}, U(\tilde{r}))$, i.e. $U(r)$, to be determined. In more sophisticated applications the potential obtained can then be used to obtain a better $G(T)$ function and hence an improved estimate of $U(r)$.

5.8. Experimental measurements

The experimental methods for carrying out measurements of gas transport properties have, in most cases, been known for at least 50 years. However, only in the last 10–15 years have reliable measurements been made of the transport coefficients over a wide range of temperatures. The reasons for this were principally poor design of apparatus and an inadequate knowledge of the theory underlying the experimental methods in the early work. Since the accuracy of the information that can be obtained about intermolecular forces from transport coefficient measurements is limited by the accuracy of the measurements themselves, we discuss here only the more recent experimental work of proven reliability.

5.8.1. Viscosity

Reliable measurements of the viscosity of pure, dilute gases and binary gas mixtures have been carried out by two different techniques in different laboratories over a wide temperature range. Smith and his collaborators have employed the familiar capillary flow method of viscometry, in which the measured efflux time, τ, of a known volume of gas from a closed vessel through a small diameter circular section tube, may be related to the viscosity of the gas at the temperature of the tube by the Hagen–Poiseuille equation for laminar flow.

Figure 5.4 shows a schematic diagram of the apparatus. In an experiment,

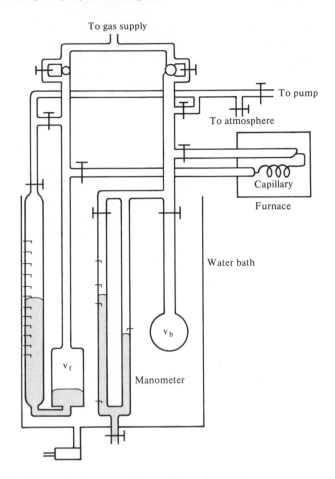

Fig. 5.4 A schematic diagram of a capillary viscometer.

gas initially contained in the front vessel, v_f, is allowed to pass through the capillary to the back vessel v_b. The pressure in the front vessel is monitored by means of the mercury level in the side arm connected to it. The time taken for the mercury level to fall from one pointer to another in this side arm is accurately determined during the course of the flow. By using the entire series of pointers it is possible to measure the efflux time for the gas at a series of pressures upstream of the capillary during a single experimental run.

Careful design of a capillary viscometer is essential in order to obtain accurate measurements. Under appropriate conditions the efflux times for two different gases at the same temperature are related by the equation

$$\frac{\tau_1}{\tau_2} = \eta_1 \frac{(1+\delta)}{\eta_2}$$

where δ is a small (~ 1 per cent) correction term, which can be estimated. This technique has enabled the viscosities of several gases and gas mixtures, both monatomic and polyatomic, to be measured over the temperature range 77–1600 K, with an estimated accuracy of ± 1.0 per cent.

Kestin and his research group have employed an oscillating disc viscometer for measurement of the viscosity of nineteen pure gases and most of their binary mixtures within the temperature range 298–973 K. Figure 5.5 contains a schematic diagram of their apparatus. In this, a horizontal circular quartz disc (1) is suspended by a thin quartz strand (4) between two horizontal fixed plates (2 and 3). This disc is free to undergo damped, simple harmonic oscillations in a horizontal plane, which are observed by means of a mirror attached to the disc (5). The viscosity of the gas surrounding the disc can be related to the period of the oscillations and the damping coefficient.

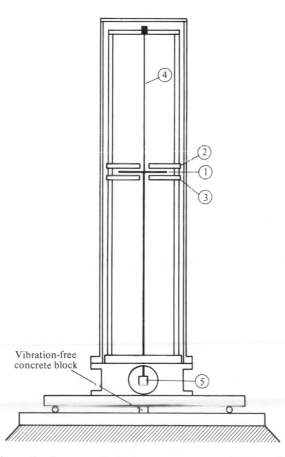

Fig. 5.5 A schematic diagram of a high-temperature oscillating-disc viscometer.

A judicious choice of the characteristics of the suspension system permits absolute viscosity measurement to be made by this method. The results have an estimated accuracy of ± 0.1 per cent near room tempeature, falling to ± 0.3 per cent at 973 K. The two sets of viscosity data obtained by these different methods are in agreement within their mutual uncertainty bounds.

5.8.2. Thermal conductivity

The thermal conductivity of dilute gases has been measured by a variety of techniques. The majority have been of the steady-state type, wherein the temperature gradient across the gas contained in a cell of accurately known geometry is measured when a heat flux passes through it. Both parallel plate and concentric cylinder instruments have been used. It has been demonstrated conclusively that the accuracy of such measurements is usually considerably inferior to that of viscosity by application of the exact form of eqn (5.13) to experimental data for both properties.

The most likely cause of the uncertainties in thermal conductivity is natural convective heat transfer. Recently, a technique operating in a transient mode has been refined and applied over a limited temperature range to a few gases. The method consists of observing the transient temperature rise of a thin wire immersed in the gas following the essentially instantaneous initiation of a heat flux within it. The temperature rise of the wire is monitored over a period of only 1 s, so that convective heat transfer is eliminated. The accuracy of the experimental results is estimated to be ± 0.2 per cent, and the technique offers the opportunity for measurements of the thermal conductivity of monatomic and polyatomic gases over a wide range of conditions.

5.8.3. Binary diffusion coefficient

The binary diffusion coefficient of gas mixtures has also proved an extremely difficult property to measure accurately despite the apparent simplicity of the apparatus required and the varied experimental methods employed. The most common measurement technique has been the two-bulb method, in which two samples of a gas mixture of unequal compositions, each contained initially in a separate bulb, are allowed to mix through a connecting tube. The entire assembly is immersed in a thermostatted enclosure.

The approach of the system to a uniform composition following the opening of the connecting tube is monitored by measuring the composition in one bulb as a function of time. The time constant of this relaxation process is related to the geometry of the apparatus and the diffusion coefficient for the gases. For mixtures of the monatomic gases a series of measurements with an accuracy comparable with that of the viscosity results has been carried out over the temperature range 60–400 K.

5.8.4. Thermal diffusion factor

The thermal diffusion factor has proved the most difficult transport coefficient to measure accurately. This is because the separation of the gas mixture in a temperature gradient, by thermal diffusion, is very small.

The original type of apparatus consists of two bulbs joined by a connecting tube, each maintained at a different temperature. The different mole fractions of one of the species in the two bulbs at the steady state is measured. The separation typically amounts to 0.05 in mole fraction for a temperature difference of 100 K. This small value implies that the measurement of α_T with an accuracy of a few per cent requires analyses of gas mixtures far more accurate than are normally attainable. In the case of isotopic mixtures this problem is even more severe, since the separation is usually much smaller. Two methods have been employed in order to amplify the thermal separation. In the first, the Trennschaukel, many two-bulb systems are effectively coupled in series between the same temperatures, whereas in the second, the thermal diffusion column, natural convective currents are used to increase the separation arising from a given temperature gradient. Although the methods increase the separation, their theory is more complicated and somewhat less certain. Consequently, the overall accuracy of the thermal diffusion factor is not greatly improved. Nevertheless, the column method has been employed with some success by Saviron and his collaborators in recent years for studies on monatomic gas mixtures. However, in general, despite the special sensitivity of the thermal diffusion factor to the steepness of the intermolecular pair potential noted earlier, its use as a probe of the potential has been hampered by the difficulty of accurate measurement.

Suggested further reading

Maitland, G. C., Rigby, M., Smith, E. B., and Wakeham, W. A. (1981). *Intermolecular forces: their origin and determination.* Chapters 5 and 6. Clarendon Press, Oxford. (Referred to in text as MRSW.)

Ferziger, J. H. and Kaper, H. G. (1972) *The mathematical theory of transport processes in gases.* North Holland, Amsterdam.

Chapman, S. and Cowling, T. G. (1970). *The mathematical theory of non-uniform gases* (3rd edn) Cambridge University Press, London.

Beenakker, J. J. M. and McCourt, F. R. (1970). *Ann. Rev. phys. Chem.,* **21**, 47.

Exercises

E5.1. Using the data in Appendixes 2 and 3, estimate the viscosity of CO_2 at 245.3 K.
E5.2. Calculate the ratio of the self-diffusion coefficients of N_2 and SF_6 at 332.3 K from the data given in Appendixes 2 and 4.

E5.3. Using the expression for the isotopic diffusion factor

$$\alpha_0 = 15\,(6C^* - 5)/16A^*$$

where $C^* = \dfrac{\Omega^{(1,2)*}}{\Omega^{(1,1)*}}$ and $A^* = \dfrac{\Omega^{(2,2)*}}{\Omega^{(1,1)*}}$, calculate its value for O_2 at 316 K using the data in Appendixes 2 and 4.

6
The solid state

6.1. Introduction

It is known from the behaviour of systems of hard-sphere molecules that at high density the most stable phase is the solid state. For real substances with attractive intermolecular forces, additional factors contribute to the relative stability of the solid and liquid phases. Thermodynamic analysis indicates that the stable phase at a given temperature T and pressure P is the one that minimizes the total Gibbs free energy G of the system. G is defined by the equation

$$G = U + PV - TS$$

where U is the internal energy, V is the volume and S is the entropy. At low temperatures the solid state is found to become the stable high density phase for all substances other than helium, whose behaviour is modified by quantum mechanical factors. Under these conditions the free energy is dominated by the internal energy, and at the absolute zero the structure adopted by the solid will be one that minimizes U by maximizing the attractive intermolecular energy. This maximum attractive energy is generally achieved by placing the molecules in a regular pattern, which may be conveniently represented using the sites of an appropriate unit cell. The whole crystal structure then consists of repetitions of this unit cell and the solid state is thus characterized by the presence of both long- and short-range order.

At 0 K in a classical model the molecules would be found stationary on these lattice sites. However we know from quantum mechanics that even at absolute zero the molecules undergo zero-point vibrations about these sites. The occurrence of these vibrations will slightly modify the maximum interaction energy and the lattice spacing. As the temperature is raised, the amplitude of these vibrations will increase as the molecules acquire thermal energy. In quantum-mechanical terms, some higher vibrational states become excited. Under these circumstances the entropy of the solid increases as the system acquires increased disorder, and the entropic contribution to the free energy, TS, will become significant. A temperature is eventually reached at which the solid melts. The greater entropy of the liquid then compensates for its energetically less favourable structure. The temperature at which melting occurs is related to the strength of the attractive intermolecular forces between

Table 6.1

Melting points, T_m, at 1 atmosphere

Substance	$T_m(K)$
Ar	84
Xe	161
HCl	159
C_2H_6	90
C_2H_4	104
C_6H_6	279
$C_{10}H_8$	354
NaCl	1074
CuO	1508

the molecules (or ions). This is demonstrated by the data in Table 6.1. Here we observe that ionic solids, with strong attractive Coulombic forces, melt at very high temperatures, while molecular solids have generally much lower melting points, which may be approximately correlated with the strength of the attractive forces. A large, polarizable molecule such as naphthalene gives a relatively high-melting solid, but small molecules normally form solids only at very low temperatures at ordinary pressure, and are generally gaseous at room temperature. It is clear then that the properties of solids must be intimately related to the intermolecular interactions and should be a valuable source of information about them.

In addition, many molecular solids are found to adopt different crystal structures in various regions of temperature and density. The occurrence and location of such transitions is clearly sensitively dependent on the inter-molecular energy, and in particular on its orientational dependence. Studies of these effects must provide useful information on the relations between interactions and crystal structure.

It is evident from the above discussion that an analysis of the structures of solids and their variation with temperature can provide valuable information about the interactions between molecules. Furthermore the vibrations of molecules within the solid, which determine many of the thermal properties such as heat capacity, are also governed by the intermolecular forces and may provide additional information about these interactions.

One general point concerning the solid state should be noted. As was mentioned in Chapter 1 the intermolecular energy of clusters of three or more molecules is only approximately equal to the sum of the constituent two-body pair energies. In the solid state many molecules are inevitably close together at all times, and the properties of solids must therefore be expected to reflect to

some extent the non-additive contributions to the total energy. These
contributions should be included in an accurate treatment of the solid state.

6.2. Experimental measurements

There are many classes of measurement that can provide useful information
about intermolecular interactions in the solid state. These include *structural*,
thermodynamic, and *spectroscopic* measurements, and give results that relate
both to static and dynamic aspects of the solid. In the case of simple substances,
for which the solid state is only observed at low temperatures, the measurements may be rather difficult—in particular problems may arise in the
preparation of suitable samples. For some purposes large, well-formed single
crystals are needed, and these may be very difficult to produce. For other
classes of investigation polycrystalline samples may be acceptable; these are
more easily prepared.

The primary experimental measurement for solids is the determination of
the underlying crystal structure. The interference patterns that result when
monochromatic beams of X-rays or neutrons are diffracted by crystalline
solids may be analysed to yield the shape and dimensions of the unit cell. If the
structural parameters are measured over a range of temperature it is then
possible to estimate the characteristic value at 0 K, and the results may also
give information about the thermal expansivity of the solid. For simple solids,
the nearest-neighbour separation, a, is very close to the separation at the
minimum of the pair potential, r_m, and may be used to establish the value of
this parameter.

The lattice energy of a solid is a very important experimental quantity and is
directly related to the well depth of the potential, ε. The lattice energy may be
inferred from studies of the enthalpy of sublimation of the solid. The
sublimation enthalpy at 0 K may be derived from heat capacity data, measured
from the lowest accessible temperature up to the triple point, together with
values of the enthalpies of fusion and the enthalpy of vaporization of the liquid
at the triple point. Provided that the deviations of the vapour from ideality are
known, these results may be combined to give the enthalpy of sublimation over
the whole solid-state temperature range, and hence the value at 0 K may be
deduced. Alternatively, measurements of the vapour pressure of the solid as a
function of temperature may be used to obtain the enthalpy of sublimation
directly, using the Clapeyron equation:

$$\frac{dP}{dT} = \frac{\Delta H_{sub}}{T \Delta V_{sub}}$$

where P is the saturated vapour pressure at temperature T, ΔH_{sub} is the
enthalpy of sublimation and ΔV_{sub} is the change in molar volume on
sublimation.

The vibrational properties of the molecules in the solid (usually called lattice vibrations, because they involve all the molecules in the solid) are most commonly approached through the heat capacity of the solid at constant volume, C_v, which depends largely on the curvature of the pair potential function, d^2U/dR^2, in the well region. C_v may be related to the more easily measured heat capacity at constant pressure, C_p, by use of the thermodynamic identity

$$C_p - C_v = \beta^2 T/\rho\chi_T$$

provided that the density, ρ, compressibility, χ_T, and the thermal expansivity, β, are known. Heat capacity data provide a major body of experimental results against which theoretical predictions may be tested. For molecular solids they also provide a means of identifying the occurrence of solid-state phase transitions, which are often characterized by anomalous 'lambda point' behaviour of the heat capacity in the vicinity of such transitions. Other thermodynamic data relating to such transitions, such as changes in the molar volume may also be useful, and for example dilatometric measurements of such volume changes have provided valuable additional data.

More direct probes of lattice vibrations have become available in recent years using coherent inelastic scattering of thermal neutrons. The lattice vibrations may be characterized in terms of their wavelength, λ, (or more commonly the wave vector, $k(= 2\pi/\lambda)$) and frequency, ν. The dependence of the frequency on the wave vector is known as the dispersion relation and may be deduced from neutron scattering studies. In addition, infra-red and Raman spectroscopy can also give valuable information about the vibrational modes of the solid.

In spite of the experimental difficulties associated with the low-temperature measurements required for simple solids, a substantial body of accurate information exists for most simple substances, for structural, thermodynamic, and vibrational properties. This information makes possible the use of solid-state properties in the development and refinement of intermolecular potential energy functions.

6.3. Theory: static lattice properties

The solid state is characterized by a very high degree of structural regularity, and for a given lattice type the numbers, relative separations, and (where appropriate) the orientations of molecules in the first, second, and subsequent neighbour shells are readily calculated. For the simple close-packed cubic and hexagonal lattices, such values are summarized in Table 6.2. If an inter-molecular potential $U(R)$ is assumed, and the approximation of pairwise additivity is made, the static lattice energy, ϕ, may be obtained by summing the intermolecular energy between all pairs of molecules in the solid. This is

Table 6.2

Neighbours shells for cubic and hexagonal close-packed lattices

Shell number	fcc (ccp)		hcp	
	r_i/a	n_i	r_i/a	n_i
1	1	12	1	12
2	$\sqrt{2}$	6	$\sqrt{2}$	6
3	$\sqrt{3}$	24	$\sqrt{(8/3)}$	2
4	2	12	$\sqrt{3}$	18
5	$\sqrt{5}$	24	$\sqrt{(11/3)}$	12

r_i/a is distance of shell i from the central molecule in units of the nearest neighbour distance, *a*. n_i is the number of molecules in shell *i*.

conveniently accomplished by considering one central molecule, and its surrounding neighbour shells. Thus, for a cubic close-packed (f.c.c.) lattice we may write

$$\phi(a) = \frac{N}{2}[12U(a) + 6U(\sqrt{2}a) + 24U(\sqrt{3}a) + \ldots]$$

and for a hexagonal close packed lattice we have

$$\phi(a) = \frac{N}{2}[12U(a) + 6U(\sqrt{2}a) + 2U(\sqrt{8/3}a) + 18U(\sqrt{3}a) + \ldots]$$

In these equations a is the nearest-neighbour distance. The total energy is obtained by multiplying the interaction energy involving the central molecule by $N/2$, where the factor $1/2$ prevents double counting of each pair interaction. (For some classes of potential, consisting of sums of terms in inverse powers of R, these calculations may be simplified.) The calculated static lattice energy is seen to be a function of the assumed nearest neighbour distance, a, and has the general appearance shown in Fig. 6.1. As discussed earlier, the low-temperature lattice energy and spacing will correspond classically to the minimum of the function $\phi(a)$, and these quantities may be readily deduced for a given structure, when a particular form of intermolecular potential has been proposed. The value of ϕ is found to be dominated by the contribution from the nearest-neighbour shell, which may contribute over 90 per cent of the total lattice energy.

Using a model potential, such calculations may be performed for various plausible types of lattice, and the structure giving rise to the largest lattice energy can be identified. A prediction can thus be made of the preferred crystal

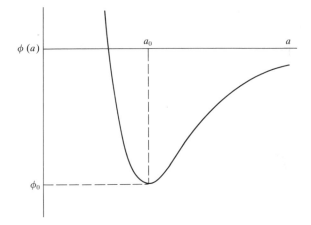

Fig. 6.1 The lattice energy, ϕ, as a function of nearest-neighbour distance, a. The classical minimum, ϕ_0, for nearest-neighbour separation, a_0, is shown.

structure at low temperatures. In the case of molecular solids the crystal structure may involve more parameters, including the orientations of the molecules. Once more, the structure predicted for a given intermolecular potential may be established by optimizing the lattice energy with respect both to separations and orientations.

In more precise calculations, allowance must also be made for the non-additivity of the intermolecular energy. It is believed that the major correction to pairwise additivity is that due to non-additive three-body effects, and the appropriate contribution to the total energy may be calculated by means of modified lattice sums, in which all triplets of molecules involving the central molecule are considered. This is a rather larger calculation than that of the two body lattice sums, but may be simplified if a non-additive energy term such as the Axilrod–Teller triple dipole correction is used. A single summation then permits calculation of the energy correction for all values of the nearest neighbour distance. (This correction is positive and typically 5–10 per cent of the pairwise lattice energy for simple molecules.) A further factor that must be included in precise calculations is the effect of the zero-point vibrations of the molecules. These contributions will usually differ for different crystal structures. For a light molecule such as methane the zero-point energy may be as much as 20 per cent of the static lattice energy, though it is usually less than this for heavier molecules.

6.4. Lattice vibrations

Each of the N atoms in a crystal lattice undergoes a complex three-dimensional vibration about its lattice site. Since each atom interacts with many neighbours, the motions are strongly coupled, and it is not generally possible to resolve the motions of separate atoms. However the problem may be overcome by performing a normal mode analysis, in which the vibrations of the entire lattice are decomposed into $3N$ independent normal modes of vibration. Each normal mode represents an independent vibration of the set of N molecules in which all N atoms move in phase; the frequency and amplitude of motion is characteristic of the normal mode. With this point of view the vibrational motion of the lattice is seen as a superposition of the $3N$ independent normal modes. (Such a normal mode analysis is similar to that widely used in spectroscopic studies of the vibrations of polyatomic molecules.) The normal mode approach relies on the assumption that the vibration of each molecule is simple harmonic in character. In turn, this implies that the potential energy field in which the atoms move is quadratic in the separation of the atom from its rest position. Provided that the amplitude of the molecular vibrations is small, this assumption makes a reliable starting point for a description of the lattice vibrations. However, the true intermolecular potential field is never exactly quadratic, as the existence of thermal expansion reveals. It is therefore often necessary to include corrections for the anharmonic nature of the oscillations as perturbations in a more exact treatment.

In the case of molecular solids, two classes of vibration may be distinguished. These are described as *optical* and *acoustic* modes of vibration, respectively. The first class may be identified with the vibrations within the isolated molecules, and are usually found at frequencies characteristic of the vibrations of isolated molecules. On the other hand, the acoustic modes are associated with movements of an entire molecule about its lattice position, and are generally found at considerably lower frequencies than the optical modes.

We now consider in more detail the relatively simple case of a monatomic solid. If the vibrational frequencies are known, the solid may be regarded as an assembly of $3N$ independent quantum mechanical harmonic oscillators, of frequencies v_1 to v_{3N}. The thermodynamic properties of the solid may then be calculated using the well-known statistical mechanical result for harmonic oscillators. The partition function for a simple harmonic oscillator of frequency v may be written

$$q_{\text{vib}} = \frac{1}{(1 - \exp(-x))}$$

where $x = hv/kT$. The heat capacity, C_v, is then given by the equation

$$C_v = \frac{kx^2 \exp(x)}{(\exp(x) - 1)^2}$$

The heat capacity of the solid may then be written as the sum over $3N$ such terms, one for each of the normal modes:

$$C_v = k \sum_{i=1}^{3N} \frac{x_i^2 \exp{(x_i)}}{(\exp{(x_i)} - 1)^2}$$

where $x_i = h\nu_i/kT$.

In order to calculate properties in this way a knowledge of the normal mode frequencies is required. A very simplified model may be used to demonstrate the relation between the vibration frequency and the intermolecular potential. This is illustrated in Fig. 6.2, and shows part of a one-dimensional crystal. The interaction energy of the central molecule with its neighbours is shown, assuming that the neighbours are stationary on their lattice sites. The vibration frequency of this molecule is given by the simple harmonic oscillator formula

$$\nu = \frac{1}{2\pi} \sqrt{\frac{\kappa}{m}}$$

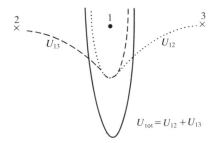

Fig. 6.2 The potential field in which a central molecule, 1, vibrates in a linear solid. The energies U_{12} and U_{13} due to interactions with neighbours 2 and 3 are shown, together with their sum.

where $\kappa = \mathrm{d}^2U/\mathrm{d}r^2$ and U is the sum of the intermolecular pair energies. The vibration frequency thus depends on the curvature of the pair potential in the well region. In this model, the neighbours are assumed fixed, whereas in practice, as we have discussed, their movements are strongly coupled together. However this assumption of independent vibrations of the atoms played an important part in the development of the theory of the solid state, and is central to the Einstein model for monatomic solids. In this model all $3N$ vibrations are assumed to have the same frequency, ν_E, and the vibrational properties of the N-atomic solid are then identical to those of $3N$ quantum mechanical harmonic oscillators all of frequency ν_E.

Further progress towards a complete description of the properties of an atomic solid requires the relaxation of one or both of the assumptions of the Einstein model. In the Debye model the assumption that all of the normal mode vibrations have the same frequency is replaced by the assignment of a distribution of frequencies, $f(v)$, defined so that there are $f(v)\,dv$ normal modes with a frequency between v and $v + dv$. However, the assumption that the vibrations are simple harmonic is retained, together with its implication that the potential energy field is quadratic in separation. By adopting a frequency distribution for the normal modes characteristic of an isotropic, continuous solid, Debye was able to evaluate the thermodynamic properties of the solid. In particular, he found that at low temperatures the constant volume heat capacity of the solid is proportional to T^3, which is in agreement with experimental results for monatomic solids. However, the Debye model fails to reproduce the experimental behaviour at higher temperatures, partly because of the use of an approximate frequency distribution and partly because the true intermolecular potential cannot be represented by a quadratic function except very near its minimum, which is the most important range only at low temperatures.

These limitations of the Debye model mean that although it provides physical insight into the behaviour of the thermodynamic properties of the solid it cannot be used to investigate intermolecular forces in the solid in any detail. For this purpose it is necessary to adopt the technique of lattice dynamics developed originally by Born and von Karman. In this method, for a given crystal structure and an *assumed* intermolecular potential, the complete frequency distribution of the normal modes, $f(v)$, is evaluated numerically. Just as for the simple Einstein model, in the case of harmonic oscillations the frequency distribution is determined by the second derivatives of the pair potential at the relevant separations, but the form of the distribution is quite different from either the single value of the Einstein model or the assumed distribution of the Debye model. Figure 6.3 shows a typical frequency distribution obtained by the lattice dynamics method for a face-centred cubic lattice together with the corresponding Debye distribution. It can be seen that

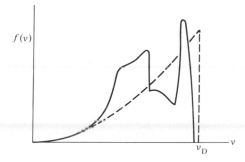

Fig. 6.3 Frequency distributions for normal modes of an fcc lattice. Solid curve from lattice dynamics; dashed curve from Debye theory.

the true distribution of frequencies has a much more complex appearance than the Debye function, but that the latter is accurate at low frequencies (long wavelengths) when the atomic structure of the real solid is unimportant and it behaves as the continuum for which the Debye model is appropriate.

So far our discussion of the thermodynamic properties of a solid has concentrated upon the analysis of the frequency distribution of the lattice vibrations, in which the motion has been assumed to be simple harmonic. There is considerable evidence that this assumption is not valid. Simple harmonic motion follows from the assumption that the restoring forces between atoms are proportional to their displacement from the equilibrium separation, and hence that the potential energy curve for a pair of atoms is quadratic, with the symmetrical appearance shown in Fig. 6.4(a). For such a curve the mean separation, $\bar{r}$, is independent of the energy. In the anharmonic (or non-quadratic) case the potential curve is unsymmetrical (Fig. 6.4(b)) and the value of $\bar{r}$ increases as the energy is raised. Since the mean energy of a system of oscillators rises as the temperature is increased, the experimental observation that crystals expand on heating indicates that anharmonic effects are not negligible. Provided that the amplitude of the oscillations is fairly small, perhaps less than 5–6 per cent of the nearest neighbour separation, the effects of anharmonicity may be treated as a small perturbation to the harmonic results. The anharmonic corrections may then be calculated as lattice sums for an assumed potential, and depend on its higher derivatives at the neighbour separations. This approach is not applicable to light molecules such as neon, for which the amplitude of the lattice vibrations is too large, but is suitable for the heavier inert gases at temperatures up to about one third of the melting point. At higher temperatures and for light atoms other theoretical approaches have been devised.

For simple molecular solids, lattice dynamics calculations may also be

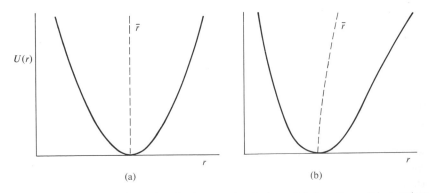

Fig. 6.4 (a) Potential function for harmonic motion; (b) function giving anharmonic behaviour. $\bar{r}$ is the mean separation.

carried out, and group theoretical classification of the vibrations can indicate which symmetry classes of vibration are active in Raman and in infra-red spectroscopy. Most calculations of this type have used rather simple models for the intermolecular potential functions.

In any event, the preceding discussion indicates that, for an assumed intermolecular potential, it is possible to evaluate both the lattice dynamics of a solid and its thermodynamic properties which may then be compared with experimental results.

6.5. Molecular interactions from solid state data

The procedures described in the preceding sections have been most thoroughly applied to the inert gases. Argon was the first substance whose intermolecular potential was determined with precision, and in the early development of this potential, solid-state data played an important part. Results for the lattice energy and nearest-neighbour distance provided a means of distinguishing between potentials that appeared to be compatible with other classes of experimental and theoretical data. Calculations of low-temperature heat capacities, which, as we have seen, depend strongly on the second derivative of the pair potential in the well region, provided another important source of information about the form of the potential. In these calculations the importance of including non-additivity corrections, particularly the triple-dipole term, was established. The total non-additive contribution to the low-temperature lattice energy was found to be around 7–8 per cent, whereas the zero-point energy contributed about 11 per cent in this case. Compressibility data covering pressures up to about 20 kbar were also reproduced with high accuracy using the best Ar pair potential, and in general solid-state data of many types can be reproduced within the experimental error.

Results for the other inert gases were later obtained and illustrated the changing importance of the minor contributions as the mass and polarizability of the molecules alter. Thus for Xe the total non-additive energy amounts to about 9 per cent of the lattice energy, but the zero-point energy makes a much smaller contribution than for Ar, about 3 per cent of the total. The accurate intermolecular potentials now available for all the heavier inert gases have been developed using solid-state properties as one important class of input data, and these potentials are capable of reproducing the experimental properties of such solids to a high degree of accuracy.

One anomalous result for the inert gases that had long puzzled investigators was the preference of the heavier gases, from Ne to Xe, for the fcc structure rather than the hcp form. Many varied pair potentials were found to predict that the hcp lattice should be preferred, although the energy difference between the two structures was very small. Early studies of the triple-dipole energy were applied to this problem, but the inclusion of this term was not found to be sufficient to account for this experimental result. It has been recently suggested that the origin of this phenomenon is a many-body perturbation of the leading term in the dispersion energy, caused by the first shell of neighbours. The sensitivity of even such a basic property as the crystal structure to the fine detail of the intermolecular interactions is a clear indication of the value of solid-state studies.

For molecular solids, where the development of accurate intermolecular potentials is far from complete, quantitative results of the type found for the inert gases are not yet generally available. There has been, however, considerable activity in studies of the properties of simple molecular solids such as nitrogen. Much of this work has been carried out using relatively simple model intermolecular potentials, such as the site–site Lennard-Jones model. Despite the obvious inadequacies of these potentials, some useful general conclusions have been reached concerning the relationships between the anisotropy of the molecular interactions and the crystal structures adopted at low temperatures.

At low temperatures, several diatomic and linear polyatomic molecules of small or moderate anisotropy such as hydrogen and nitrogen adopt a cubic crystalline form, which is shown in Fig. 6.5(a). This structure does not permit a very high packing density for elongated molecules, but does allow nearest neighbours to adopt an orientation with a favourable quadrupole–quadrupole energy. For molecules of moderate anisotropy and fairly large quadrupole moments, such as CO_2, it is found that this structure persists up to the triple point. For molecules with smaller quadrupole moments, such as N_2 or CO, a transition to an orientationally disordered form (Fig. 6.5(b)) is observed as the temperature is raised. The important role of the quadrupole–quadrupole interactions may be seen in a comparison of N_2 with CO. These molecules are

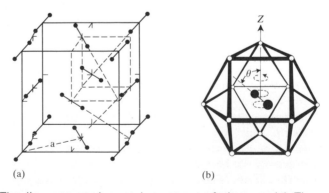

(a)   (b)

Fig. 6.5 The (low pressure) crystal structures of nitrogen. (a) The cubic α-N_2 structure. (b) The hexagonal β-N_2 form. The molecules are orientationally disordered in the x–y plane.

structurally very similar, and have similar triple point and critical temperatures (see Table 6.3), suggesting close similarity in their intermolecular interactions. However, the quadrupole moment of CO is considerably greater than that of N_2, and it is found that whereas N_2 undergoes a phase transition to the disordered structure at around 36 K, in the case of CO the analogous transition occurs only at 61 K, very close to the triple point. The extra stability conferred on the low-temperature structure of CO by the stronger quadrupolar interactions is thus evident.

Table 6.3
Characteristic properties of N_2 and CO

	$T_m(K)$	$T_c(K)$	$T_{tr}(K)$	$10^{40}\Theta\ (Cm^2)$
N_2	63	126	36	-4.9
CO	68	133	62	-8.2

T_m is the normal melting point.
T_c is the gas–liquid critical point.
T_{tr} is the solid transition temperature.
Θ is the quadrupole moment, defined with respect to the centre of mass.

When the low-temperature structures of more elongated molecules are studied, it appears that the unfavourable packing of the cubic structure becomes important, and alternative crystal forms, with layered monoclinic or orthorhombic structures, are preferred. These are observed for example in the halogens. Such changes with molecular shape and with variations in the strength of the quadrupolar interactions have been successfully accounted for in terms of a simple diatomic Lennard-Jones model, together with quadrupole–quadrupole terms.

There have also been many calculations of the vibrational properties of simple molecular solids, initially in order to compare with spectroscopic data, and more recently making comparison with phonon dispersion curves from inelastic neutron scattering. In most cases these calculations have been carried out using model potentials, such as the site–site Lennard–Jones, though in recent years there have been serious attempts to develop more precise representations of the molecular interactions, which have been used in such calculations. Virtually all of these studies have made the assumption of pairwise additivity and it is not at present clear to what extent non-additive effects will modify their conclusions. It again seems likely that the dominant non-additive term will be the triple-dipole energy, which now, however, becomes a function of the relative orientations of the molecules as well as of their positions. The effects of anharmonicity on the lattice vibrations again appear to be significant in molecular solids, and this is particularly the case in respect of low-frequency librational (rocking) motions, whose amplitudes are quite large, since the rotational energy barriers are relatively low.

It is clear from the wealth of information that exists for molecular solids, and the richness of their behaviour, that future investigation of the relationships between molecular interactions and the properties of such systems will be fascinating and rewarding. In particular, the importance of the orientational dependence of the intermolecular energy in determining solid-state characteristics suggests that such studies will be of particular value in establishing this aspect of the molecular interactions.

Suggested further reading

Maitland, G. C., Rigby, M., Smith, E. B., and Wakeham, W. A. (1981). *Intermolecular forces: their origin and determination.* Chapter 8. Clarendon Press, Oxford. (Referred to in text as MRSW.)

Kittel, C. (1971). *Introduction to solid-state physics.* Wiley, New York.

Klein, M. L. and Venables, J. A., ed. (1976/77) Rare gas solids, Vols 1 and 2. Academic Press, London.

Parsonage, N. G. and Staveley, L. A. K. (1976). *Disorder in crystals.* Clarendon Press, Oxford.

English, C. A. and Venables, J. A. (1974). *Proc. R. Soc* **A349**, 57.

Exercises

E6.1. The enthalpy of sublimation of solid Xe at 0 K is 15.8 kJ mol^{-1}, and the molar volume is 34.7 cm^3. Assuming that the contributions to the lattice energy from second and higher neighbours may be neglected, use these results to calculate the nearest neighbour distance, a, and the intermolecular energy at this separation, $U(a)$. The crystal structure is body-centered cubic, for which $V = Na^3/\sqrt{2}$, and there are 12 atoms in the first-neighbour shell.

E6.2. The above calculation neglects the effects of zero-point energy and of non-additive contributions to the intermolecular energy. These have been estimated to be 0.6 kJ mol^{-1} and 1.4 kJ mol^{-1}, respectively. What is the effect of including these terms on the calculated value of $U(a)$?

7
The liquid state

7.1. Introduction

Computer studies on systems of hard sphere molecules have shown that for such systems only two phases can exist, a fluid and a solid. There are no separate gaseous and liquid phases and the solid–fluid transition is determined simply by the packing of the spheres. These results show directly the important role of repulsive intermolecular forces in dense fluids, a theme that will recur throughout this chapter. We know also from the study of imperfect gases that the presence of both attractive and repulsive intermolecular forces leads, at appropriate temperatures and pressures, to the formation of two fluid states, the liquid and its vapour. The liquid is generally characterized by a rather greater density than its vapour, and thermodynamic measurements show that the transformation from liquid to vapour requires the input of energy, the 'latent heat of vaporization'. These observations suggest that in the liquid, each molecule is surrounded by a substantial number of relatively near neighbours, and feels their attractive intermolecular interactions. In the low-density vapour phase, molecules are generally isolated, and the intermolecular energy is very small in comparison with the kinetic energy of the molecules. The success of the van der Waals equation of state, which introduces (in an approximate way) the effects of molecular size and of relatively short-ranged attractive forces, adds further support to this picture.

Since the existence of liquids depends on intermolecular forces, we might expect that studies of the liquid state would provide much information about molecular interactions. This was not generally true in the past, as a consequence of the complex connection between the properties of liquids and the forces between molecules. This connection is provided by statistical mechanics and it is only quite recently that adequate theories of the liquid state have been developed. However, the deficiencies in statistical mechanics may be substantially by-passed by the use of a technique that has become increasingly important in recent years, the direct simulation of systems containing many molecules using computers.

These *computer simulation* procedures make it possible to determine the structural and thermodynamic properties of assemblies of molecules that interact with a known form of intermolecular potential, without introducing statistical mechanical approximations. They have produced essentially exact results for model systems with well-defined intermolecular forces, which are valuable in testing other approaches to the liquid state. Unfortunately, computer simulations are relatively costly, and they have not been widely used in the characterization of accurate intermolecular potentials from studies of liquid state properties. Indeed, almost all studies of liquids have adopted simplified representations of the intermolecular pair potential, and have generally made the further assumption that the intermolecular energy is pairwise additive.

Despite these limitations, computer simulations have provided invaluable evidence to support the belief that it is the repulsive intermolecular forces that determine the way in which the molecules pack together in the liquid, in the absence of strongly directional attractive forces such as hydrogen bonds. This simple picture of liquid structure provides the basis for the very successful *perturbation theories* of liquids, which probably provide the most reliable economical route to liquid-state properties at the present time.

In the brief account of theories of liquids that follows, we adopt the conventional assumption that the form of the intermolecular potential is known. It is only for the very simplest substances, the inert gases, that liquid-state studies have so far been used as a source of information about accurate pair potentials and the role of non-additive interactions in dense fluids.

7.2. Liquid structure

In spite of the high densities which characterize the liquid state, liquids do not show the regular periodic structure that is characteristic of solids, whose density is similar. The structure of liquids is characterized by a certain degree of molecular ordering at short separations, but no long-range order. The description of the structure may conveniently be carried out for spherical molecules using the radial distribution function, $g(r)$, which measures the probability of finding another molecule at a distance r from a central reference molecule. For a system of N molecules in a total volume, V, the number of molecules, $n(r)$, in the volume element, $4\pi r^2\, dr$, at a distance r from a central molecule is given by

$$n(r) = \frac{N}{V} g(r) 4\pi r^2\, dr. \tag{7.1}$$

The total number of pairs of molecules whose separations lie in the range r to $r + dr$, is then related to $g(r)$ by the expression

$$n'(r) = \frac{N^2}{2V} g(r) 4\pi r^2\, dr. \tag{7.2}$$

For a system in which the molecules interact only through a pairwise additive intermolecular potential, $U(r)$, the total intermolecular energy may be readily calculated.

$$U_N = \frac{2\pi N^2}{V} \int_0^\infty U(r)g(r)r^2\,dr \tag{7.3}$$

and the pressure may then be obtained in terms of the forces between the molecules using the virial theorem of Clausius (see Appendix 8A.1 of MRSW):

$$PV = NkT - \tfrac{1}{3}\overline{\sum_{i<j} r_{ij}F(r_{ij})}$$

or, in this case,

$$\frac{PV}{NkT} = 1 - \frac{2\pi N}{3kTV}\int_0^\infty g(r)\frac{dU(r)}{dr}r^3\,dr \tag{7.4}$$

Other properties may be obtained from these by standard thermodynamic manipulations.

The above expressions are valid only if the total intermolecular potential energy can be written as a sum of pair interactions. If non-additive many-body interactions are present, then higher order distribution functions must also be considered. The most important of these is the triplet distribution function, $g_3(\mathbf{r}_1, \mathbf{r}_2, \mathbf{r}_3)$, which measures the probability that a molecule will be found at a position $\mathbf{r}_3$, when two other molecules are at $\mathbf{r}_1$ and $\mathbf{r}_2$. If the only important non-additive interactions are the three-body terms (as seems usually to be the case), then a knowledge of the triplet function, together with the radial distribution function, is sufficient to determine the equilibrium properties of the system.

However, the principal structural information is contained in the radial distribution function, and the typical appearance of $g(r)$ for a simple liquid is shown in Fig. 7.1. It is seen that for a liquid, $g(r)$ is zero for small values of r, where owing to the large positive values of the intermolecular energy the molecules do not overlap. At a value of r near to the molecular collision diameter, σ, $g(r)$ increases rapidly, and reaches a maximum value of 2–3 near to $r = r_m$. Hence the probability of finding a molecule at such a distance from a central molecule is several times larger than for a random distribution. At larger separations, $g(r)$ then falls away to a minimum, followed by a smaller maximum, and then oscillates about the limiting long-range value of unity, showing that at long distances the influence of the central molecule has died away and that there is no long-range order. Also shown in Fig. 7.1 are the corresponding results for a simple solid, and for a gas at a moderate density. The regular long-range order of the solid is clearly shown, in contrast to the short-range order characteristic of the liquid. For the gas, $g(r)$ has a value of unity at almost all separations, with deviations at small r determined chiefly by the Boltzmann factor, $\exp(-U(r)/kT)$, based on the energy of a pair of molecules.

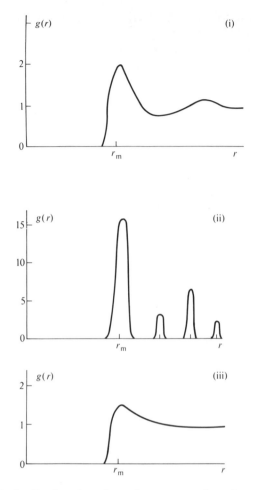

Fig. 7.1 Radial distribution functions for monatomic substances. (i) Liquid; (ii) solid; (iii) dilute gas.

For diatomic and polyatomic molecules, some structural information may again be conveyed by the radial distribution function for the centres of mass of the molecules. However, it is clear that such information is incomplete, and a fuller description of the structure requires a radial distribution function, $g(r, \omega)$ which is also a function of the relative orientation of the molecules, ω, as well as their separation. Even for a pair of diatomic molecules, the specification of the orientation requires three angular variables, and it is clear that the representation of such an orientation-dependent function presents difficulties. An alternative representation of the structure of molecular liquids uses sets of distribution functions based on the positions of the atoms, rather than of the centres of mass of the molecules. Atom–atom distribution functions, $g_{AB}(r_{AB})$ may be defined in a manner analogous to that used for $g(r)$, and describe the probability of finding an atom of type B at a distance r_{AB} from an atom of type A. Such a distribution function may have contributions from atoms that are in the same or different molecules. In order to describe the structure as completely as possible it is necessary to specify as many atom–atom distribution functions as there are different types of atom pairs. For example, in liquid H_2O (Fig. 7.2), we would need to know $g_{HH}(r_{HH})$, $g_{OO}(r_{OO})$, and $g_{OH}(r_{OH})$. However, in spite of the increased number of functions we observe that each separate function depends only on a single distance variable, and this representation of the structure is probably simpler than that using orientation-dependent functions. Nevertheless, both types of function are valuable.

Experimental values of $g(r)$ for liquids may be obtained from studies of X-ray or neutron diffraction. When monochromatic incident radiation is used, interference patterns arise in the diffracted radiation owing to correlations

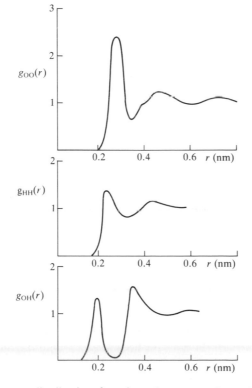

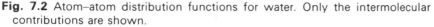

Fig. 7.2 Atom–atom distribution functions for water. Only the intermolecular contributions are shown.

between the positions of the atoms. This effect is similar to, though less sharply defined than, the diffraction effects produced by solids, where the atoms on their lattice sites behave in a manner resembling a three-dimensional diffraction grating. Interference occurs between components of the diffracted beam that have been scattered by different atoms, and this results in the almost total cancellation of intensity, except at a very few scattering angles, which are related to the wavelength of the radiation and the dimensions of the lattice. In practice, the perfect regularity of the solid crystal is modified by the vibrations of the atoms about their sites, and the diffraction pattern is less sharp than would be expected from the simple picture given above. In the liquid, this blurring of the pattern is carried further, since long-range structural correlations are absent, but the intensity variations nevertheless allow the recovery of the distribution function.

The analysis of diffraction data is carried out in terms of a reciprocal length, s, defined in terms of the wavelength, λ, and the scattering angle, α.

$$s = \frac{4\pi}{\lambda} \sin (\alpha/2). \tag{7.5}$$

Experimental measurements provide information about the scattered intensity as a function of s. After the scattering intensity due to the single atoms has been subtracted, the intensity is proportional to a function, $H(s)$, that is itself related to the radial distribution function, $g(r)$, by the equation

$$r[g(r) - 1] = \frac{2V}{N\sqrt{2\pi}} \int_0^\infty sH(s)\sin (rs)\,\mathrm{d}s. \tag{7.6}$$

Thus, experimental values of $H(s)$ may be transformed to give $g(r)$. It is seen that values of $H(s)$ for all values of s are needed. In practice the experiments give $H(s)$ for a limited range of s, and this truncation leads to uncertainties in the derived values of $g(r)$. Furthermore, there are numerous corrections that must be made to the raw experimental data, and the determination of accurate values of $g(r)$ requires extremely accurate measurements coupled with very careful treatment of the results.

For molecular liquids containing more than one type of atom, the recovery of all the different site–site distribution functions is particularly difficult. It requires the combination of results from scattering experiments using both X-rays and neutrons, in the latter case carried out using isotopically substituted molecules.

In spite of these very considerable problems, there is now a substantial body of experimental structural data on liquids of varying degrees of molecular complexity. These results may be compared with the predictions of statistical mechanical theories, and in recent years comparison has often been made with the distribution functions obtained in the course of computer simulations of liquids. Either route forms the basis for interpreting liquid properties in terms of the molecular interactions involved.

7.3. Computer simulation

Two rather different types of computer simulation procedure have been widely used in the study of liquids. These are known as the (Metropolis) *Monte Carlo* procedure and the method of *molecular dynamics*. In both types of calculation a cell is considered, which contains a specified number of molecules, usually between 100 and 1000, whose interactions are specified by the investigator. The coordinates of the molecules are stored within the computer, and enable the total energy of any configuration, U_N, to be calculated. When calculating the energy of a given configuration, the minimum image convention is generally adopted. The cell is considered to be surrounded by identical replicas of itself on each side (26 replicas in a three-dimensional case). The two-dimensional case is illustrated in Fig 7.3. The distance between any pair of molecules i and j in the cell is compared with those between i and all the images of j in the surrounding cells, and the interaction energy is based on the shortest distance so found. (With long-range potentials problems may arise, which we shall not consider here).

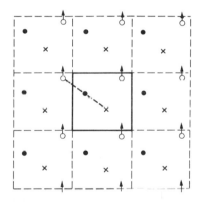

Fig. 7.3 Periodic boundary conditions and the minimum image convention. The central cell, bounded by solid lines, is surrounded by images of itself. Three molecules are indicated, ◯, ● and ×. In calculating the interaction energy of any molecule, e.g. ●, the nearest images of the other molecules are used, as shown by the dashed lines. If a molecule leaves the central cell, e.g. ◯, its image enters through the opposite face.

In the *Monte Carlo method* the coordinates of the N molecules within the cell are changed in such a way that the probability of occurrence of a given configuration is proportional to the Boltzmann factor, $\exp(-U_N/kT)$ associated with it. This is generally done by changing the coordinates of the molecules one at a time, by adding a small randomly chosen amount to the coordinate of a given molecule. If such a shift were to take the molecule through an edge of the central cell, its image in one of the neighbouring cells would have entered at the opposite face, and this molecule would then take the place of the molecule which left. The total number of molecules in the cell is thus constant, through the application of these 'periodic boundary conditions', and density fluctuations are suppressed.

The energy change produced by this tentative shift, ΔU, is then calculated. If the move has left the energy unchanged, or has lowered it, the new configuration is accepted. If the energy has been increased by the move, the new configuration is accepted in a proportion of cases which is given by the factor $\exp(-\Delta U/kT)$. Very many moves, sometimes millions, are made in this way, producing a series of configurations whose probability of occurrence is proportional to the Boltzmann factor, $\exp(-U_N/kT)$, and these can be analysed to give the properties of the system. For example, the intermolecular energy is known at each stage, and its unweighted average over a large number of configurations may be calculated, giving directly the configurational internal energy. Similarly, the virial function, $\Sigma_{i<j} r_{ij} dU(r_{ij})/dr_{ij}$, may be averaged and the pressure calculated using the virial theorem. An analysis of the distance between molecules and the numbers of pairs in various ranges can give values for the radial distribution function. In addition, it is possible also to investigate quantities that are not directly measurable in real experiments.

It is important to note that the movement of the molecules in a Monte Carlo simulation has no physical significance, and is not related to the true molecular movement. It only provides a way of sampling the configuration space over which the properties of the system must be averaged. This situation may be contrasted with that in the molecular dynamics simulation method.

In molecular dynamics simulations, a basic cell and its images are again established, but now, starting from an initial configuration in which the total (potential and kinetic) energy is defined, the motions of the molecules are followed. This is achieved by numerical integration of the equations of motion of all the molecules. For each molecule the forces resulting from all the other molecules are summed, again using the minimum image convention, and the new positions and velocities after a small time interval τ are calculated. The time step, τ, is chosen to be small compared with the time between collisions, and is typically of the order 10^{-14} s for simple systems. The procedure is repeated for many time steps, typically 10^3 to 10^4, during which period the motions of the molecules and their collisions may be observed. At each step in the time chain, contributions to averages similar to those studied in the Monte Carlo procedure may be evaluated. The partition of the total energy between kinetic and potential energy can also be noted, and the distribution of molecular velocities can be studied. The temperature is inferred from the mean kinetic energy, in contrast to the Monte Carlo simulations, where temperature is a variable selected by the investigator. Another difference from Monte Carlo calculations is that the molecular dynamics method permits the study of the transport properties of fluids. These may be obtained by the evaluation of suitable time-correlation functions.

These *correlation functions* measure the extent to which the value of a given dynamic variable, such as velocity, is related to the value of that variable at an earlier time. They thus indicate the extent to which a molecule remembers its earlier dynamic history. (At large time intervals, when the correlation has disappeared, the correlation functions approach a value of zero). The different transport properties may be related to appropriate correlation functions. For example, the diffusion coefficient D is related to the velocity auto-correlation function, $z(t)$, defined as:

$$z(t) = \frac{1}{N} \left\langle \sum_{i=1}^{N} \mathbf{V}_i(0) \cdot \mathbf{V}_i(t) \right\rangle, \tag{7.7}$$

by the equation

$$D = \frac{1}{3} \int_0^\infty z(t)\, dt.$$

The typical behaviour of $z(t)$ in a simple liquid is shown in Fig 7.4, where it is seen that $z(t)$ falls quickly from its initial value of unity, and becomes negative after a short time, indicating that on average the velocity of a molecule is reversed, presumably as a result of collisions with a surrounding 'cage' of neighbours. The calculation of such functions thus gives insight into the local behaviour of the molecules, as well as permitting the transport properties to be calculated.

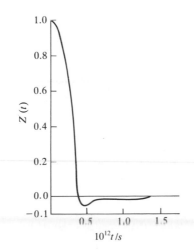

Fig. 7.4 A typical velocity autocorrelation function for a monatomic liquid. Note that on average the velocity is reversed in direction after about 4×10^{-13} s.

Early computer simulations were largely restricted to studies of molecules with very simple intermolecular potentials. The hard-sphere fluid was very extensively studied, and this work laid the foundations for many subsequent developments. The radial distribution functions of hard-sphere fluids were found to resemble in many ways the experimental results for real systems, and this observation provides the foundation for the perturbation theories of liquids, which are described in the following section. The detailed results obtained from simulations were also valuable in permitting the testing of various approximate statistical mechanical theories that had been used to calculate radial distribution functions. In addition, the important discovery was made that hard spheres could exist in only two dense phases, with the characteristics of a solid and a fluid. The existence of a liquid–gas equilibrium appears to require the presence of attractive as well as repulsive intermolecular forces. The melting of hard spheres has been extensively studied and gives insight into the melting of real substances.

More recently, very many simulations have been carried out, both for monatomic systems with a variety of potentials, and for diatomic and small polyatomic molecules. There have also been many studies of models for water using several intermolecular potentials, and aqueous solutions have also been investigated. There have even been studies of the solvation that occurs around biological molecules such as DNA, though this probably represents the limit of complexity that is presently feasible. Although for these large systems the detailed features of the molecular interactions are far from being defined quantitatively, the use of model potentials (see Chapters 1 and 8) in molecular dynamics simulations is increasing our understanding of how intermolecular forces influence the behaviour of molecularly complex systems, such as membranes and polymeric materials. At the opposite extreme, the simulation of very light molecules, such as helium, for which quantum effects are important, presents some difficulties, although methods of overcoming these are now being developed.

In summary, computer simulations are now able to give insights and detailed information about molecular arrangements and dynamics that was previously unobtainable. Their continued use seems certain, and the only serious limitations from which they presently suffer seem to lie in the deficiencies in intermolecular potentials, which are available for most molecules, and the considerable cost of the computer time needed to carry out the calculations.

7.4. Perturbation theories

One of the most successful approaches to the study of liquids in recent years has been through the development of perturbation theories. These may be thought of as modern versions of van der Waals theory, and their essential physical basis is the separation of the roles of attractive and repulsive intermolecular forces. It is proposed that the structure of simple liquids, as revealed by their radial distribution functions, is chiefly determined by the packing requirements of the molecules, which in turn reflect the repulsive intermolecular forces. The attractive forces are thought to serve essentially as the 'glue' that holds the molecules together, maintaining the high density, but otherwise playing no major structural role.

When the structures of hard-sphere liquids are compared with those of real monatomic liquids, close similarities are seen. This suggests that the effects of the soft repulsive forces of real molecules may be modelled with reasonable accuracy using a hard-sphere system. The properties of hard-sphere systems are well known from computer simulations and from statistical mechanical theories.

In the formal development of perturbation theories, the effects of changes in the form of the intermolecular potential on the properties of a system of molecules are studied. For pairwise-additive systems the pair potential energy function is written as a sum of terms, a reference potential, $U_0(r)$, plus a perturbation, $U_1(r)$:

$$U(r) = U_0(r) + U_1(r). \tag{7.8}$$

The properties of the system of molecules interacting through $U_0(r)$ are assumed to be known, and those of the perturbed system are expressed in terms of $U_1(r)$ and the properties of the reference system. For example, the configurational energy, U_N, for a system of N molecules interacting through $U(r)$ may be written, to first order in the perturbation theory

$$U_N = U_N^0 + \frac{N^2}{2V} \int_0^\infty 4\pi r^2 g^0(r) U_1(r)\,dr, \tag{7.9}$$

where U_N^0 is the configurational energy of the reference system, whose radial distribution function is $g^0(r)$. (This equation should be compared with eqn (7.3). Similar expressions for other properties may also be written, and these are also quite easily calculated if $g^0(r)$ is known. Higher-order perturbation terms may also be added, but their calculation is much more demanding, and the successful application of this theory depends on the rapid convergence of the expansion. This in turn will depend on the choice of a reference system whose structure faithfully mimics that of the system under study. The success of this approach has thus rested on the correct choice of the division of $U(r)$ into reference and perturbation potentials. By a suitable division of $U(r)$, the magnitude of the higher-order terms can be made very small, and rapid convergence achieved even at low temperatures.

Most perturbation theories have attempted to calculate the properties of a liquid whose molecules interacted through a model pair potential, usually the Lennard-Jones function. In the earliest studies, $U_0(r)$ was taken to be hard-sphere potential, with the hard-sphere diameter, d, slightly less than the Lennard-Jones collision diameter, σ, but with its value chosen in a slightly arbitrary manner. For all values of r greater than σ, $U_1(r)$ was taken to be the Lennard-Jones potential. This division of the potential is illustrated in Fig 7.5(a) and may be written

$$
\begin{aligned}
U_0(r) &= \infty, && r \leqslant d \\
&= 0, && r > d \\
U_1(r) &= 0, && r \leqslant \sigma \\
&= 4\varepsilon[(\sigma/r)^{12} - (\sigma/r)^6] && r > \sigma.
\end{aligned}
$$

The results of the first-order perturbation theory are found to be quite sensitive to the choice of the hard-sphere diameter, d. Significant progress in the application of perturbation theory to liquids was only made after reliable and well-founded methods for choosing d were established. In the first successful theory, due to Barker and Henderson, the effective hard-sphere diameter was defined by the equation

$$
d = -\int_0^\sigma [\exp(-U(r)/kT - 1]dr \tag{7.10}
$$

which gives a hard sphere diameter that is a function of temperature but not of density, and that decreases as the temperature is raised. Barker and Henderson were able to calculate the first- and second-order perturbation terms, using computer simulation results for the distribution functions of the reference system. Calculations of the properties of Lennard-Jones liquids were found to be in very good agreement with those obtained from direct computer simulation. The second-order term, though small, was found to be necessary to achieve the excellent level of agreement.

An alternative, very successful, perturbation theory was proposed by Weeks, Chandler, and Andersen, and is based on a novel choice of reference and perturbation potentials. This is illustrated in Fig 7.5(b), and may be written

$$
\begin{aligned}
U_0(r) &= U(r) + \varepsilon && r \leqslant r_m \\
U_0(r) &= 0, && r > r_m \\
U_1(r) &= -\varepsilon, && r \leqslant r_m \\
U_1(r) &= U(r), && r > r_m.
\end{aligned}
$$

This division of potentials assigns the whole of the *repulsive* region of $U(r)$ to the role of reference potential and determinant of structure, rather than just the *positive* portion of $U(r)$, as in the Barker–Henderson theory. A consequence of this division is that the perturbation energy, $U_1(r)$, is now a very smoothly varying function of r, and this seems to have the useful effect of reducing the higher-order fluctuation terms, giving a very accurate equation of

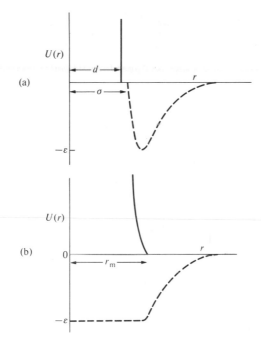

Fig. 7.5 Division of the total intermolecular potential into reference and perturbation components.
———— , $U_0(r)$, the reference potential
———— , $U_1(r)$, the perturbation.
(a) Barker–Henderson; (b) Weeks–Chandler–Andersen.

state even when restricted to a first-order treatment. However, a penalty is incurred also, in that the properties of the reference fluid are not now so simple as those of the hard-sphere fluid nor as well established. Weeks and co-workers were able to propose a relation between their reference fluid and a hard-sphere fluid, and used this to make calculations for the Lennard-Jones fluid that proved to be approximately as accurate in first order as those based on the second-order Barker–Henderson perturbation treatment.

Both of these perturbation theories provide remarkably accurate and reasonably simple procedures by which the properties of fluids of spherical molecules may be calculated. They have been extended in recent years to the study of more complex systems with non-spherical molecules, and some of these applications are considered in the next section. The wide range of successful applications of perturbation theories in the study of the liquid state has displayed with remarkable force the primary role of repulsive intermolecular interactions in determining the structural properties of liquids.

7.5. Molecular liquids

Following the development of generally satisfactory theories for liquids of monatomic substances, there has been much subsequent interest in molecular liquids, and considerable progress has been made. It is convenient for our purpose to distinguish two major groups of molecular liquids, which we may describe as 'simple' and 'hydrogen-bonded'. The former group includes such molecules as N_2, O_2, CS_2, HCl, small hydrocarbons, and many other substances. Hydrogen-bonded liquids that have been extensively investigated include H_2O, HCN, CH_3OH, HF, and others.

In all molecular liquids the intermolecular forces are functions both of separation and orientation, and the long-range interactions will include the electric multipole interactions considered in Chapter 1, which are absent in monatomic systems. For the substances we have designated as simple the orientation-dependent electrostatic terms will generally contribute significantly to the attractive energy, but will be of comparable magnitude to, or smaller than, the dispersion energy. In the hydrogen-bonded systems, the hydrogen-bond energies are generally much the largest contributors to the attractive energy.

The effects of relatively small orientation-dependent energies may be conveniently approached by means of perturbation theory, and there have been many studies in which the electrostatic terms have been treated in this way. Generally speaking, this approach is found to be satisfactory for molecules in which the repulsive interactions are reasonably spherical. Attempts to include substantial deviations from spherical shape in perturbation calculations based on spherical reference systems have not generally been successful. This observation is of course not unexpected, in view of the important structural role of repulsive forces. For molecules such as CO_2 or CS_2, whose shapes are markedly non-spherical, an alternative approach is needed, in which the non-spherical repulsion and its structural implications are incorporated into the reference system. Perturbation theories using this approach, and in which the molecules are treated as a number of suitably placed interaction sites, have been successfully applied in such cases. The effectiveness of these various theoretical approaches to molecular liquids may now be determined through comparisons with the results of several computer simulations, in which the effects of electrostatic interactions and of non-spherical repulsive interactions have been investigated. A comparison of the results of perturbation calculations and computer simulation for a model of liquid fluorine is shown in Fig 7.6.

Hydrogen-bonded liquids differ from simple molecular liquids in that the interaction energies associated with the hydrogen bonding, and the fairly stringent geometrical requirements of hydrogen bonds, lead to substantial structural effects. In these cases it is no longer sufficient to regard the structure as largely determined by the repulsive intermolecular forces and the packing of

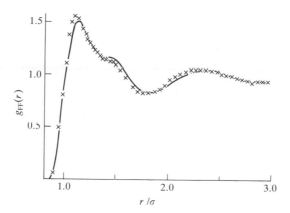

Fig. 7.6 Site–site distribution function, $g_{FF}(r)$, for a model of liquid fluorine, based on the site-site Lennard–Jones potential.
——————— results of computer simulation studies.
× × × × × × obtained from perturbation theory, using a non-spherical reference system.

the molecules. Water gives possibly the most obvious and striking example of this.

Ice at low pressures and at temperatures just below the melting point shows a characteristic open structure, in which each oxygen atom is surrounded by four hydrogen atoms, tetrahedrally disposed. Two of these are covalently bonded and two are hydrogen bonded to the oxygen. On melting, this extended network structure breaks down, and the liquid may be thought of as segments of ice-like material, of varying sizes. These are able to pack more efficiently than in ice, and the well-known contraction on melting is thus accounted for. It results from the low density and open structure of ice as well as from the unusual structure of the liquid. However, there remains a significant degree of hydrogen bonding in the liquid, and the structural properties, as revealed by the radial distribution functions, demonstrate this. X-ray diffraction results can yield the distribution function for the oxygen atoms, which is shown in Fig 7.2. The presence of the well defined secondary peak at about 0.45–0.5 nm is believed to support an extensively hydrogen-bonded structure. The extent to which tetrahedral arrangements persist in the liquid remains a subject of debate, but it is clear that a structural model based simply on the repulsive envelope of the molecule would yield qualitatively incorrect results.

Other hydrogen-bonded liquids display different, but related structural features, some of which were described in Chapter 1. In the cases of HF and HCN, chains of molecules are thought to occur, while in the lower alcohols, such as CH_3OH, small clusters, possibly cyclic, are found.

The structural characteristics of such molecules may be investigated using the conventional X-ray and neutron diffraction techniques, but the complete analysis of the diffraction results, involving atoms of several types, can be difficult. Some progress has been made by the use of neutron scattering with isotopically substituted molecules, but it is also often necessary to make some simplifying assumptions before a complete structure determination can be completed. Much recent work has been carried out using computer simulation, particularly for water and aqueous solutions, and considerable progress has been made in obtaining qualitative and in some cases semi-quantitative agreement with experimental results. In view of the continuing uncertainty in the intermolecular potentials for water and other hydrogen-bonding molecules, and the problems of non-additive cooperative effects that occur in clusters of three or more molecules, this represents a substantial achievement.

7.6. Liquid crystals

It seems appropriate at this point to mention briefly a group of molecules that show unusual properties resulting directly from extremely anisotropic intermolecular interactions. Such molecules, which are usually characterized by a fairly rigid structure, and have either long 'cigar-shaped' or flat 'plate-like' shapes, can exist in an unusual state of matter, intermediate between the crystalline solid and the normal liquid, known as 'liquid crystals'. For example, *p*-azoxyanisole (Fig. 7.7) exists as a crystalline solid below 118°C, at which temperature it undergoes a phase transition. The resulting cloudy fluid undergoes a further change at 136°C, above which it becomes a normal clear liquid. In the intermediate liquid crystalline region, the material combines some properties of a liquid, such as fluidity, with other characteristics of solids, such as marked anisotropy in optical properties.

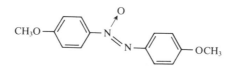

Fig. 7.7 *p*-azoxyanisole.

Structural studies are able to give considerable insight into this behaviour, and reveal that the liquid crystalline state retains much of the high level of orientational order which is found in the solid, although the long-range spatial ordering of the molecular centres has been lost. Various degrees of spatial and orientational order are found in several different types of liquid crystal, some of which are illustrated in Fig 7.8. In the normal liquid region both the orientational and spatial order are lost.

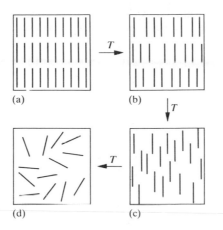

Fig. 7.8 Schematic representation of the ordering in (a) crystalline solid, (b) smectic liquid crystal, (c) nematic liquid crystal, and (d) isotropic liquid. (The orientational ordering in the liquid crystalline phases may not be complete.)

This behaviour is evidently a very dramatic example of the influence molecular shape has on the nature of liquids, and may be seen as a striking demonstration of the importance of repulsive intermolecular forces in determining the structures of the dense phases of matter. It may be contrasted with the considerable degree of orientational disorder, combined with the retention of spatial order, that is often observed in disordered molecular solids (plastic crystals) whose molecules are only slightly non-spherical.

7.7. Mixtures and solutions

Our considerations have so far been restricted to pure liquids. When liquid mixtures containing two or more components are studied we encounter an astonishing range of behaviour and properties, which reflect the diversity of interactions between the atoms, molecules, or ions involved. A unifying theme can however be detected, since many of the characteristics of mixtures can be explained, at least qualitatively, in terms of the relative strength of the intermolecular forces between unlike pairs of molecules and those acting between the pure components. Thus the limited miscibility of water and a liquid hydrocarbon such as cyclohexane is not an indication that molecules of water and cyclohexane repel each other, but rather that they attract each other less strongly than water attracts another water molecule, and cyclohexane attracts another cyclohexane. The old adage of solubility, 'like dissolves like', may then be seen as a reflection of the similarity of the intermolecular forces between molecules of similar chemical types.

The extent to which this general principle relating molecular interactions and properties can be carried through to give quantitative predictions, or precise information about molecular interactions, reflects the complexity of the species and interactions involved. We shall consider a number of classes in turn, in roughly increasing order of complexity.

7.7.1. Liquid mixtures of non-electrolytes

For the simplest liquid mixtures, consisting of two different monatomic species such as Ar + Kr, the perturbation theories described in Section 7.4 may be used, taking mixtures of hard spheres of different diameters as the reference state. Information about the interactions between unlike molecules may thus be derived from thermodynamic data. The intermolecular potentials for Ar–Kr and Kr–Xe have been studied in this way, using an extension of the Barker–Henderson theory, and including corrections for non-additive three-body forces.

In the case of slightly more complex molecules, such detailed theories are not yet available. Nevertheless, useful results can be obtained, since the emphasis in such work is on the changes that occur when the mixture is formed, rather than the prediction of the absolute values of the total thermodynamic properties. The results are generally presented in terms of the excess thermodynamic functions, usually for mixing under conditions of constant temperature and pressure. When n moles of a mixture are formed from its pure components, the associated change in an extensive thermodynamic property, X, may be represented $\Delta_{mix} X$. In an ideal mixture, these changes may be simply related to the composition of the mixture expressed in terms of the mole fractions, x_i, of the components. Specifically

$$\Delta_{mix}^{id} V = \Delta_{mix}^{id} H = 0$$

$$\Delta_{mix}^{id} G = -T \Delta_{mix}^{id} S = nRT \left[\sum_i x_i \ln (x_i) \right]. \tag{7.13}$$

Such an ideal mixture obeys Raoult's law (assuming that the vapour behaves as a perfect gas mixture) but, in practice, this ideal behaviour is rarely, if ever, observed. More commonly the mixing process is accompanied by a volume change, and the evolution or absorption of heat, and the mixture shows deviations from Raoult's law. The excess functions describing such changes are defined in terms of the observed mixing functions for one mole and those for an ideal mixture of the same composition. Thus

$$X^E = \Delta_{mix} X - \Delta_{mix}^{id} X, \tag{7.14}$$

and the excess functions differ from the mixing functions only in the cases of the free energy and entropy. If a mixture is formed with a positive excess free energy it is said to show positive deviations from ideality, and is thermodynamically less stable than the corresponding ideal mixture. These mixtures show positive deviations from Raoult's law and, in extreme cases, show character-istic behaviour, such as limited miscibility of the components, or the formation of azeotropes boiling at a minimum temperature. Mixtures that have negative excess free energies show negative deviations from ideality, and, when the deviations are large, may form azeotropes boiling at a maximum temperature.

It is clear that the excess thermodynamic functions reflect the differences between the intermolecular interactions in the pure components and in the mixture, and also the structural changes which accompany mixing. In the simplest theoretical model, the intermolecular potentials in a binary mixture may be characterized in terms of the associated well depths, ε_{11}, ε_{22} and ε_{12}. The difference, w,

$$w = \varepsilon_{12} - \tfrac{1}{2}(\varepsilon_{11} + \varepsilon_{22}) \tag{7.15}$$

then gives a measure of the relative strength of the like and unlike interactions. Positive values of w indicate relatively strong unlike interactions, associated with negative deviations from ideality, and vice versa. Using this analysis, major deviations from ideality, for example those associated with 'chemical' changes such as hydrogen bonding, may be qualitatively related to the intermolecular interactions. In the absence of such specific interactions and for systems in which the molecules are substantially different in size, this simple view is inadequate, and useful results can only be obtained using a more sophisticated approach.

In a widely studied approach, the one-fluid model, the properties of a binary mixture are taken to be those of a hypothetical pure liquid. It is usual to assume that this hypothetical fluid and the two pure components have conformal intermolecular potentials, and so satisfy the principle of corresponding states. The intermolecular potential for the hypothetical fluid is calculated as some composition-dependent average of the potentials for the pure components and for the unlike interactions. One of the simplest of such theories, the 'van der Waals' one-fluid' model, closely resembles the original extension to mixtures by van der Waals of his equation of state. In its modern form the one-fluid approach is followed, and the mixture parameters σ_m and ε_m are derived from the relations

$$\sigma_m^3 = x_1^2 \sigma_{11}^3 + 2 x_1 x_2 \sigma_{12}^3 + x_2^2 \sigma_{22}^3 \tag{7.16}$$
$$\varepsilon_m \sigma_m^3 = x_1^2 \varepsilon_{11} \sigma_{11}^3 + 2x_1 x_2 \varepsilon_{12} \sigma_{12}^3 + x_2^2 \varepsilon_{22} \sigma_{22}^3.$$

Using these prescriptions, the one-fluid model is now able to cope quite well with mixtures of simple liquids, even in cases where the molecules differ significantly in size. This theory has been extensively tested using results for mixtures of Lennard-Jones molecules obtained from computer simulations, and now provides a generally reliable framework for calculating the mixing properties of fairly simple liquids. When applied to real mixtures of simple liquids this approach has yielded useful information about the interactions between unlike molecules, and on the adequacy of the Lorentz–Berthelot combining rules. In particular, it has been demonstrated that the geometric mean rule

$$\varepsilon_{12} = \sqrt{(\varepsilon_{11}\,\varepsilon_{22})} \tag{7.17}$$

generally overestimates ε_{12}. The extent of the discrepancy can be expressed in terms of a parameter k_{12} defined by

$$\varepsilon_{12} = (1 - k_{12})\,(\varepsilon_{11}\,\varepsilon_{22})^{1/2}. \tag{7.18}$$

For similar molecules the deviation from the geometric mean is very small, but in some cases it may be as much as 10 per cent. Some typical values of $(1 - k_{12})$ estimated from the study of liquid mixtures are given in Table 7.1. These figures are subject to a moderate uncertainty, since the theory used to obtain them is not exact, but the general trends are found to be consistent with results obtained from the study of other properties, such as interaction second virial coefficients, B_{12} (see Chapter 4).

Table 7.1

Deviations from geometric mean rule

	$(1 - k_{12})$
$C_2H_6 + C_3H_8$	1.00
$Ar + O_2$	0.99
$N_2 + O_2$	0.99
$CO + CH_4$	0.99
$CH_4 + C_2H_6$	0.99
$C_6H_6 + c\text{-}C_6H_{12}$	0.97
$N_2 + CH_4$	0.97
$CH_4 + C_3H_8$	0.97
$CH_4 + CF_4$	0.92
$CO_2 + C_2H_2$	0.91

Taken from Bett. K. E. Rowlinson, J. S., and Saville. G. (1975). *Thermodynamics for chemical engineers*, p. 477. Athlone Press, London.

7.7.2. Solutions of solids in non-aqueous liquids

The simplest approach to the solubility of solids in liquids uses the concept of ideal solubility. The equilibrium between a solid solute and the solution is analysed in terms of a two-stage dissolution process. In the first step, the melting of the solute to give a supercooled liquid is considered. This supercooled liquid is then assumed to form an ideal mixture with the solvent, with the accompanying changes in thermodynamic properties given in eqns (7.13). Not surprisingly, it is found that this approach is reasonably satisfactory only in cases where the non-ideality of the solution would be expected to be small. In principle, the ideal solubility of a given solute is independent of the solvent. In practice, the success of the model for solutions of naphthalene in benzene and its failure for naphthalene in n-hexane alerts us to the considerable differences in the intermolecular interactions between the unlike molecules in these two examples. Naively, an observed solubility which is less than the ideal solubility is an indication of relatively weak unlike interactions between solute and solvent, and vice versa. Hildebrand proposed that in many non-electrolyte solutions the non-ideality could be associated with a non-zero enthalpy change, $\Delta_{mix}H$, while the corresponding entropy change was approximately ideal. He was able to develop this concept of the 'regular solution' and to propose a number of rules for the prediction of the solubility and related properties of non-electrolytes, which have been found to be remarkably successful.

7.7.3. Electrolyte solutions

The solubility of solid electrolytes may be analysed in the same general terms as those used for non-electrolytes, but the interactions found with ionic species are rather different and the often complex nature of the solvents also introduces other factors, which have generally led to these two classes of solution being considered separately.

The primary difference between a molecular solid such as naphthalene and an ionic solid such as NaCl is found, of course, in the presence of the charges on the ions Na^+ and Cl^-. These lead to the formation of a very hard, high-melting crystal, in which charges of opposite sign are optimally arranged for maximum attractive energy. In consequence, the energy needed to break down the lattice, and to separate the oppositely charged ions, is very considerable. Only in solvents of high relative permittivity ('dielectric constant'), which are able to mute the strong electrostatic interactions, do we normally observe substantial solubility of ionic solids. Water is the classic solvent for such solids, and the majority of investigations have concentrated on aqueous solutions.

The large size of the lattice energy demands a compensating interaction between solute and solvent species, if there is to be significant solubility. This arises from the solvation of the ions—hydration in the case of aqueous solutions. Each ion becomes closely associated with a number of solvent molecules in a strongly exothermic process, resulting from the attractive charge–dipole, charge–quadrupole, and induction energies. The variation in solubility of series of ionic solids may generally be rationalized in terms of variations in the lattice energies and in the enthalpies of hydration. Large negative enthalpies of hydration will be generally favoured by small ionic size, which permits the close approach of solvent molecules. Doubly or triply charged ions will also be expected to have unusually large hydration enthalpies.

The simple physical concepts described above are incorporated into the widely used Born equation for the free energy of solvation of ions:

$$\Delta G_{solv} = \frac{Z^2 e^2}{8\pi\varepsilon_0 a}[1 - 1/K_r]$$ (7.19)

in which Z is the charge of the ion, regarded as a hard sphere of radius a, in a solvent treated as a uniform medium of dielectric constant K_r. Although this model has many deficiencies, it incorporates in a reasonable, simple and fairly realistic manner the primary factors that dominate the energetics of ionic solvation.

7.7.4. Aqueous solutions of non-electrolytes

This class of solutions shows a wide diversity of behaviour, and is far from completely understood. It is unrealistic in such systems to hope to account for the overall properties in terms of interaction effects alone, and both the enthalpic and entropic contributions to the free energy play important roles in determining the way in which these systems behave. However, we may observe naively that only substances that are readily able to form hydrogen bonds, such as the lower alcohols and ketones, are found to be substantially soluble in water or form completely miscible liquid mixtures. The general patterns of behaviour of such solutions may be roughly correlated with the number and strength of the hydrogen bonds formed. Nevertheless, even semi-quantitative prediction of the properties of aqueous solutions remains a distant target. Virtually all such solutions are formed with negative excess entropies, suggesting a loss of freedom on mixing. However the excess enthalpy is often found to have a complex composition dependence, and often changes sign as the composition is changed. Generally, exothermic mixing occurs for solutions very rich in water, but often mixing becomes endothermic at high solute concentrations. The excess free energy is most commonly positive (as it is for the majority of liquid mixtures), but in a few cases of systems that form especially strong and numerous hydrogen bonds between solute and water, the excess enthalpy, entropy, and free energy are all negative. In the latter cases H^E is necessarily negative at all compositions. Sugars, polyhydric alcohols, and urea provide examples of such behaviour.

Solutions of substances that are unable to form hydrogen bonds, though less common, have some characteristics that are both fascinating and puzzling. In very dilute solutions of solutes such as the simple aliphatic or aromatic hydrocarbons, the observed enthalpies of solution are found to be negative, contrary to the expectation that the introduction of solute would reduce the total number of hydrogen bonds, by disrupting the water structure. It appears instead that an increase in the extent of hydrogen bonding accompanies the introduction of a small amount of solute, and of the associated negative excess enthalpy and entropy it is the latter term that dominates the free energy change, and leads ultimately to the low solubility. The subject of these hydrophobic interactions is an extremely complex one, whose implications are remarkably widespread. It does, however, appear at present to be very far from being clearly explained in terms of molecular interactions and theories of the liquid state which have been thoroughly validated.

In conclusion, we observe that the enormous diversity of behaviour shown in liquids and solutions is a reflection of the effects of molecular interactions of many types. For simple liquids, quantitative calculations of most properties are now possible, largely through the use of computer simulation techniques. In more complex systems, the chief restriction on such calculations is now probably our ignorance of the details of the intermolecular forces, more than problems of statistical mechanics.

Suggested further reading

Maitland, G. C., Rigby, M., Smith, E. B., and Wakeham, W. A. (1981). *Intermolecular forces: their origin and determination.* Chapter 8. Clarendon Press, Oxford. (Referred to in text as MRSW.)

Barker, J. A. and Henderson, D. (1981), *Sci. Am.* Nov, 94.

Pryde, J. A. (1966). *The liquid state.* Hutchinson, London.

Murrell, J. N. and Boucher, E. A. (1982). *Properties of liquids and solutions.* Wiley, Chichester.

Rowlinson, J. S. and Swinton, F. L. (1982). *Liquids and liquid mixtures* (3rd edn). Butterworths, London.

Exercises

E7.1. The van der Waals equation of state

$$(P + a/\overline{V}^2)(\overline{V} - b) = RT$$

implies that the contribution to the internal energy from intermolecular interactions (the *configurational energy*) is given by

$$U_{conf} = -a/\overline{V},$$

where a is the characteristic attraction parameter of the substance. Using values of a from Table 4.1, calculate U_{conf} for argon near its triple point, $T = 84$ K, $V = 28.2$ cm^3 mol^{-1}, and for carbon dioxide at its critical point, $T = 304$ K, $V = 94.0$ cm^3 mol^{-1}. Compare these values with the corresponding molar translational energies, $3/2$ RT.

[1 cm^3 atm $\equiv$ 0.1013 J]

E7.2. Consider a model for a liquid whose intermolecular pair potential (a Sutherland potential) may be written

$$U(r) = \infty, r \leqslant \sigma; \quad U(r) = -\varepsilon\,\sigma^6/r^6, r > \sigma.$$

For such a liquid, $g(r) = 0$ for $r \leqslant \sigma$. Assuming that $g(r) = 1$ for $r > \sigma$, and using eqn (7.3), obtain an expression for the configurational energy of the liquid. Compare your result with that for the van der Waals equation in the previous question.

8
Potential functions—
the state of the art

In this chapter we summarize the present state of our knowledge of intermolecular forces, outline the problems that remain to be solved, and draw attention to the lessons that can be learnt from past successes and failures. In some cases full details of potential functions can be obtained by using the information contained in this chapter and Chapter 1. In general, however, the reader interested in the detailed form of functions used for particular systems is referred to Appendix 8A. This contains references to recent work giving typical potential functions for selected systems.

8.1. The development of intermolecular potentials

From about 1930 to the late sixties the subject of intermolecular forces was developed on the basis of two assumptions: first, that the pair potential could be adequately represented by simple functions such as the Lennard-Jones 12–6 potential, and second, that the intermolecular energy of a group of molecules could be taken as the sum of their pair interaction energies. However, as neither of these assumptions was in fact valid, little real progress was possible. This is illustrated by the uncertainties in the parameters proposed for the Ar–Ar interaction prior to 1970 compared with those for the intramolecular potential for I_2 given in Table 8.1. The maximum attractive energy for Ar_2 is roughly 100 times smaller than that for I_2, yet it was known to lower *absolute* accuracy. However, since 1970 a dramatic advance has taken place in our knowledge of intermolecular potential energy functions, particularly in the case of monatomic species. The reasons behind this rapid change are worth examining in a little detail, since within them lie a number of important lessons that should prove a useful guide in the assault on more complex molecules.

8.2. The basis of recent advances

The advances that led to the marked improvements in our knowledge of the potential functions of the inert gases may be summarized under seven

Table 8.1

Comparison of the spectroscopically-determined parameters for I_2 with the range of intermolecular parameters proposed for Ar_2 prior to 1970

	I–I	Ar–Ar
r_m(nm)	0.2666 ± 0.0002 (± 0.1 per cent)	0.383 ± 0.010 (± 2 per cent)
$10^{21}\varepsilon$(J)	246.99 ± 0.02 (± 0.01 per cent)	1.90 ± 0.30 (± 15 per cent)

headings. The benefits in each one of these areas are now being experienced in the study of more complex systems.

(a) *New accurate experimental measurements of bulk properties.* Measurements of low-temperature second virial coefficients were particularly useful in emphasizing the limitations of the Lennard–Jones 12–6 function. Redeterminations of high-temperature viscosities showed that earlier measurements were in error by up to 8 per cent. The new values did much to refute the apparent incompatibility of gas-transport data with other properties that had hindered the search for acceptable potential energy functions. Properties such as viscosity and thermal conductivity can now be measured routinely to better than ± 0.5 per cent over wide ranges of temperature. A class of measurements not available for the inert gases, involving the effects of magnetic fields on transport properties (Senftleben–Beenakker effect), should be valuable in aiding the determination of non-spherical interactions.

(b) *Improved calculation of intermolecular energy.* The most important achievement of calculation has been the estimation of the dispersion force coefficients that characterize the long-range forces. The use of experimental information such as refractive indices, polarizabilities, and photoionization cross-sections in conjunction with the oscillator strength sum rules has led to values of C_6 accurate to ± 3 per cent. For polyatomic molecules, the anisotropy of these coefficients is well-defined. Quantum mechanical calculations can also give information about the potential at small separations with reasonable accuracy. However, apart from the cases of very light systems like He_2, H_2–He and $(H_2)_2$, where significant progress has been made in calculating complete potential functions with high accuracy, there is no immediate prospect of accurately calculating potentials at intermediate separations by *ab initio* methods.

(c) *Spectroscopic measurements.* Spectroscopic measurements on van der Waals dimers of the inert gases have been of particular value in defining their potential functions with high precision. The vibrational fine structure of the vacuum ultra-violet absorption of the argon and krypton dimers was used to determine their vibrational energy levels, which can be utilized in the Rydberg–Klein–Rees (RKR) analysis to obtain the width of the potential energy well as a function of its depth (see Chapter 7). These spectroscopic data were also used to estimate the depth of the potential energy wells for the inert gases. Three different analyses gave values for argon in close accord: 142.1, 142.5, and 140.0 K. More recently the rotational fine structure of the Ar_2 molecule has been observed and used to refine the potential energy function for argon. The observation of microwave and infra-red spectra for polyatomic van der Waals dimers, especially those generated in rarefied molecular beams, provide a similar sensitive probe for the attractive region of the anisotropic potential energy surfaces of more complex molecules.

(d) *Molecular beams*. Technical advances in the design and construction of apparatus have greatly increased the importance of this technique. The information obtained from supersonic nozzle molecular beams has been of great value (Chapter 5). High-resolution experiments have enabled oscillations in the differential cross-section arising from quantum mechanical effects to be observed. Potential energy functions for the inert gases that were determined using these data were in good agreement with what are now known to be the correct functions.

In the case of polyatomic molecules, the use of state selectors for the incident and scattered beams enables rotational and vibrational state-to-state differential cross-sections to be measured with high resolution, in addition to state-averaged (total) cross-sections. The occurrence of inelastic collisions also brings new scattering features which are sensitive probes of potential function anisotropy.

(e) *Non-pairwise additivity*. For atoms, it is now generally agreed that the Axilrod–Teller triple-dipole term represents the dominant contribution to the long-range non-additive energy. Considerable success has been achieved in interpreting the properties of both solid and liquid inert gases using this single correction term alone, though it is possible that this success is due to the cancellation of higher terms.

The orientation dependence of the potential for polyatomic systems makes the evaluation of many-body effects more complex than for atoms. Nevertheless, crystal structure data in particular should yield considerable information about potential function anisotropy, in view of the preferred alignments adopted by molecules in the solid state.

(f) *Data inversion methods*. Methods have recently been developed for spherical molecules whereby the specific information about $U(r)$ contained in experimental measurements is determined directly without assuming a form for the potential energy function. They eliminate the need for the unsatisfactory trial-and-error methods that have been traditionally employed.

Of particular value is the development of inversion techniques for bulk properties, which are readily available for a wide variety of substances. For monatomic systems, these procedures can give the full potential function. When the methods are applied to the experimental data for polyatomic systems, we obtain *effective* spherical potentials, whose value is assessed later in the Chapter.

(*g*) *Computer calculation of properties.* The availability of electronic computers has enabled thermophysical and other properties to be readily and routinely evaluated for gases using any given potential energy function. The calculations are not restricted to analytical functions and their speed has done much to promote the multi-property approach to potential function evaluation, which it is now widely accepted is essential. More sophisticated use of computers using Monte Carlo or molecular dynamics techniques has also enabled liquid and solid phases to be simulated.

The angular dependence of the potential for polyatomic molecules, and the possibility of inelastic collisions, means that the evaluation of bulk properties for polyatomic fluids generally involves more complex integrations. The availability of fast, high storage computers is therefore particularly important for the evaluation of the properties of polyatomic gases and condensed phases. Nevertheless, the full evaluation of some properties, (e.g. thermal conductivity) from a complex anisotropic potential surface is still far from routine.

8.3. Potential functions for monatomic systems

8.3.1. The inert gases

The first potential function to be accurately defined was that of argon. A most important step towards its elucidation was due to Barker and Pompe in 1968. They utilized a very flexible functional form, assumed that the Axilrod–Teller term correctly represented non-additive contributions, and neglected the available gas transport coefficient data. These assumptions proved to be both judicious and effective, since the data they neglected were subsequently found to be erroneous.

The next significant advances came in 1971 when the problem of the intermolecular potential energy function of argon could be said to have been 'solved'. Barker, Fisher, and Watts produced a refined version of the early Barker functions by the careful fitting of a wide variety of gaseous and condensed phase properties. In the same year Maitland and Smith also introduced an improved version of the early Barker functions using quite different arguments. They inverted the spectroscopic data of Tanaka and Yoshino using the RKR analysis to obtain the precise shape of the potential bowl. The correspondence of the two functions drawn from quite different sources suggested that the problem of the interaction of argon was solved. In the following year Lee and co-workers introduced a potential function of yet another functional form based on scattering data, second virial coefficients, and the spectroscopic data, which was again in good agreement with the 1971 functions. The form of these functions is illustrated in Fig. 8.1.

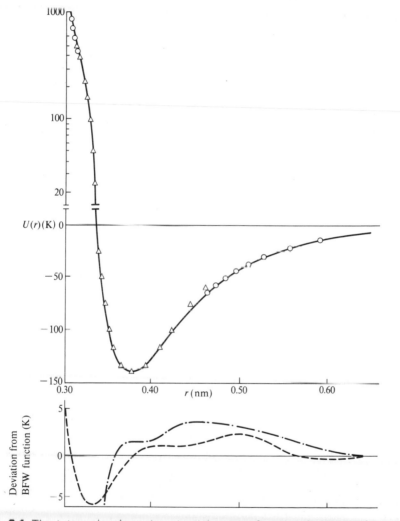

Fig. 8.1 The intermolecular pair potential energy function for argon: (———) accurate functions; (△) inversion of gas viscosities (○) inversion of second virial coefficients. Deviations from Barker–Fisher–Watts function: (– – – –), Maitland–Smith: (–·–·–·) Lee *et al*. (Maitland, G. C. and Smith, E. B., (1973) *Chem. Soc. Rev.* **2,** 181.)

Subsequently the work has taken two distinct directions. First, some workers have tried to refine the earlier functions further using a wide range of experimental information. However, changes to the original functions have been small and any further improvements probably require more accurate experimental data.

The other direction in which effort has been concentrated is in the prediction of the inert gas functions entirely from *theoretical* information. By recognizing that the potential for the triplet H_2 interaction (see Chapter 1, Section 1.6) is essentially conformal with the inert gas potentials, it has been possible to scale calculations for this system to determine potentials for other spherical systems. For instance, theoretical functions for argon of the HFD form have been obtained that are consistent with the best 'experimental' potentials described above. The potentials for other inert gas systems have also been elucidated. The pure interactions and the unlike interactions He–Ar and Ar–Kr are now known to high accuracy (probably better than $\pm 1\%$ in r for a given energy). For other mixed interactions experimental data is lacking, and the theoretically based potentials may be superior to those obtained from experiment. Although a wide variety of functions have been used for the inert gas interactions, they can all be represented with reasonable accuracy by the three-parameter $n(\bar{r}) - 6$ function, the parameters for which are given in Table 8.2. This indicates that the potentials are substantially conformal (i.e. identical when expressed in reduced form, U/ε vs r/r_{m}), both to each other and to the triplet H_2 potential. Such conformality suggests that the law of corresponding states should be of considerable predictive value for these systems (Appendix 3). This is found to be true even though small differences in the potentials have been noted outside the range $0.8 \leqslant r/r_{\mathrm{m}} \leqslant 1.2$.

Though conformal, the parameters for the mixed interactions are not in accord with the traditional Lorentz–Berthelot combining rules (see Chapter 1, Section 1.8). The geometric mean rule, in particular, is known to overestimate the magnitude of ε_{12} and the discrepancy is often expressed in terms of a parameter k_{12} where

$$\varepsilon_{12} = (1 - k_{12})(\varepsilon_{11} \cdot \varepsilon_{22})^{1/2}$$

The greater the size difference between the atoms, the larger is the observed value of k_{12}. The simplest rule to predict the surprisingly small increases in ε_{12} observed for the series He + Ne–Xe and Ne + Ar–Xe (see Table 8.2) is the harmonic mean rule, but even here the agreement is not quantitative. More complex rules have been developed that are consistent with theoretical predictions at long and short range, but the uncertainties in the data do not allow truly critical tests of these new rules at the present time.

8.3.2. Open-shell atoms

Atoms containing a single electron in the outer shell can interact according to two potential energy functions depending on the spins of the valence electrons:

Table 8.2
Parameters for the $n(\bar{r}) - 6$ *potential model for inert-gas pairs*

	m	γ	r_m(nm)	ε/k(K)	σ(nm)	Ref.
He–He	12	6	0.2967	10.9	0.2633	2
He–Ne	13	8	0.3005	20	0.2690	9
He–Ar	13	4	0.343	29.4	0.3065	8
He–Kr	13	4	0.364	30.4	0.3253	8
He–Xe	13	5	0.398	27.4	0.3554	8
Ne–Ne	13	5	0.30739	41.186	0.2745	3
Ne–Ar	13	9	0.343	66.9	0.3056	6
	13	4	0.3516	60	0.3142	9
	13	4	0.348	62.0	0.3110	10
Ne–Kr	13	9	0.358	71.8	0.3190	6
	13	5	0.3656	67.1	0.3265	10
Ne–Xe	13	9	0.374	74.5	0.3332	6
	13	5	0.3924	65.42	0.3504	10
Ar–Ar	13	7.5	0.3756	141.55	0.3350	4
Ar–Kr	13	9	0.3902	165	0.3477	7
	13	9	0.388	165	0.3457	6
Ar–Xe	13	10	0.406	187.4	0.3615	6
Kr–Kr	13	10	0.402	199.2	0.3580	5
Kr–Xe	13	10	0.418	231.1	0.3720	6
	13	8	0.4230	220	0.3771	9
Xe–Xe	13	11	0.436	275.3	0.3880	6
	13	11	0.426	281	0.3790	11

Potential energy function[4] $n = m + \gamma(r/r_m - 1)$.

References:
1. Maitland, G. C. and Smith, E. B. (1973). *Chem. Phys. Lett.* **22**, 483.
2. Aziz, R. A., Nain, V. P. S., Carley, J. S., Taylor, W. L., and McConville, G. T., (1979). *J. chem. Phys.* **70**, 4330.
3. Aziz, R. A. (1976). *Chem. Phys. Lett.* **40**, 57.
4. Aziz, R. A. (1976). *J. chem. Phys.* **64**, 490.
5. Aziz, R. A. Private communication.
6. van den Biesen, J. J. H., Stokvis, F. A., van Veen, E. H., and van den Meijdenberg, C. J. N. (1980). *Physica* **100A**, 375.
7. Gough, D. W., Matthews, G. P., Smith, E. B., and Maitland, G. C., (1975). *Mol. Phys.* **29**, 1759.
8. Smith, K. M., Rulis, A. M., Scoles, G., Aziz, R. A., and Nain, V. (1977). *J. chem. Phys.* **67**, 152.
9. Maitland, G. C. and Wakecham, W. A. (1977). *Mol. Phys.* **35**, 1443.
10. Aziz, R. A. Private communication.
11. Maitland, G. C. and Smith, E. B. (1977). In *Seventh Symposium on thermophysical Properties* (ed. A. Cezairlian), p. 412. Am. Soc. Mech. Eng.

a singlet potential corresponding to paired spins and a strong, covalent-type interaction, and a triplet potential that arises from parallel spins and is weakly bound, similar to the closed shell atoms. For the simplest of such systems, triplet H–H, accurate *ab initio* quantum calculations exist; indeed, as seen above, the system has been used as the prototype for inert gas interactions in the development of HFD-type theoretical potentials. This apart, among the best characterized interactions of this type are those of the alkali metal–mercury systems.

8.3.3. Group II closed-shell atoms

The potential for Mg_2 is particularly well-characterized in the well region, being obtained by RKR inversion of spectroscopic data supplemented by theoretical calculations at long and short range. Ca_2 has also been studied spectroscopically. There is a significant amount of thermophysical property data available for mercury; potentials based on these are available, although they are restricted to the simpler forms given in Section 1.8.

8.3.4. Ion–atom interactions

By measuring ion mobilities in alkali ion–inert gas mixtures over a wide range of electric field gradients, it is possible to systematically probe the entire separation range of the ion–atom potential function. These data may be inverted, using techniques similar to those developed for neutral gas transport coefficients, to give highly accurate numerical potential functions. They differ from those for neutral interactions in having a long-range maximum and can be approximated by an n–6–4 potential:

$$U(r) = \frac{n\varepsilon}{n(3+\gamma) - 12(1+\gamma)} \left\{ \frac{12}{n} (1+\gamma) \left(\frac{r_m}{r} \right)^n - 4\gamma \left(\frac{r_m}{r} \right)^6 \right.$$
$$\left. - 3(1-\gamma) \left(\frac{r_m}{r} \right)^4 \right\}$$

8.4. Potential functions for simple polyatomic systems

8.4.1. Review

Although highly accurate potential functions have been determined for only a few polyatomic molecules, there is a distinct difference in the current state of potentials for relatively simple molecules, containing just a few atoms, compared with larger, mainly organic-type molecules. For the smaller systems, there is already a reasonable body of experimental and theoretical data available.

However, even here there is an enormous range in the extent to which the potentials are known. For the lightest systems, H_2–H_2 and H_2–He, accurate theoretical potential surfaces exist. There is little hope of extending such calculations to heavier systems in the immediate future and so progress elsewhere must rely on a combined experimental/theoretical approach similar to that adopted for the inert gases. Most attention has been focused on the simplest 'polyatomic' system, the interaction of an atom with a diatomic molecule. The best characterized systems are the relatively low anisotropy H_2–inert gas pairs for which spectroscopic, molecular beam, bulk property, and theoretical data are all available. The potentials for some of these H_2–X systems are undoubtedly extremely accurate, especially in the attractive region. For more anisotropic systems like N_2–X or HCl–X, the major features of the potential surfaces have been determined, but the present generation of potentials will probably undergo significant modifications before they are capable of reconciling all the available data.

Of the diatomic molecules, N_2–N_2 is probably the most widely studied system. Even in this case, no potential has so far been proposed that can reconcile the available theoretical and bulk property data. It is not surprising that for more complex molecules than this, where the complexity of the potential increases and fewer data exist to use in its characterization, the existing functions can at best be described as semi-quantitative. They may be useful over limited ranges but must be used with caution. Perhaps the largest molecule for which a reasonably respectable potential has been developed is benzene.

For the larger systems, e.g. alkanes, substituted benzenes, polymers, and proteins, there is a paucity of data and the topology of the potential surfaces is exceedingly complex. Consequently, most of the potentials have to be based on empirical extensions from simpler systems or at best semi-quantitative model calculations. The degree of confidence one can have in any quantitative predictions made by these potentials is significantly less than for the small-molecule systems.

In the remainder of this section we will look in more detail at the procedures used and the potentials proposed for a number of representative systems of increasing complexity.

8.4.2. H_2–He and H_2–H_2

These two systems represent the simplest atom–diatom and diatom–diatom interactions, respectively, and contain sufficiently few electrons to make accurate quantum mechanical calculations feasible. The He–H_2 potential has been represented using a POTEX-type function (see Section 1.8). At long and intermediate range the potential is essentially spherical and only two terms are needed in the Legendre polynomial expansion, but at short range the anisotropy is greater so that U_2 is some 30 per cent of U_0 and an additional term, U_4, is necessary. The surface is claimed to be highly accurate but this has yet to be confirmed by extensive tests against experimental data.

   The results of a similar calculation of the potential function for H_2–H_2 by Meyer, Schaefer, and Liu have been represented by a spherical harmonic expansion of the POTEX-type, which includes the vibrational motion of the hydrogen molecules. The potential is dominated by the isotropic term U_{000} for which $\sigma = 0.311$ nm and $\varepsilon/k = 31.6$ K (see Fig. 8.2). Most of the anisotropy arises from second-order terms, which are weakly attractive at long range (U_{202} and U_{022}) and amount to about 1 per cent of U_{000}, although there is also a significant positive contribution from the long-range quadrupole–quadrupole interaction (U_{224}). This surface has been exhaustively tested against a wide range of experimental data, including those most sensitive to the anisotropy of the potential such as inelastic scattering cross-sections and Senftleben–Beenakker effects. These comparisons indicate that the surface describes the H_2–H_2 interaction well, particularly its anisotropy, although small modifications need to be made to reconcile all the data. This example illustrates the need to supplement theory with as much experimental information as possible in the refinement of a potential surface.

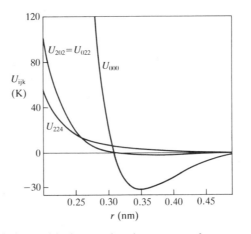

Fig. 8.2 The variation with intermolecular centre-of-mass separation of the coefficients of the expansion of the H_2–H_2 interaction potential of Meyer and Schaefer, and Schaefer and Liu.

8.4.3. H_2–inert gas systems

The infra-red spectra of the H_2–inert gas mixtures have been extensively studied experimentally. Since the weak anisotropy of the potential surface for these systems makes the calculation of such spectra relatively straightforward, they have been particularly useful in determining the potentials for these gases. LeRoy and his co-workers have employed a POTEX-type function, including bond vibration, in the form

$$U(r,\xi,\theta) = \sum_{n=0}^{\infty} \sum_{k=0}^{\infty} \xi^k P_n(\cos\theta) U_{nk}(r)$$

to investigate the potential well region for all the H_2–inert gas systems. Here ξ represents the extension of the H_2 bond relative to its vibrational ground state level, and U_{nk} is a radial function similar in form to the HFD model. A comparison between calculated and observed spectra was used to determine the parameters in the various terms U_{nk}. The most detailed surface for H_2–Ar included terms up to $n = 2$ and $k = 3$.

The dimer spectrum is not particularly sensitive to the repulsive part of the potential. However, the total differential scattering cross-section is sensitive to $U_0(r)$ in the repulsive region and the inelastic state-to-state cross-sections are determined by U_2/U_0 in the same region. When information of this type, widely available from molecular beam experiments, has been combined with that from the dimer spectrum, pair potentials for H_2–Ne and H_2–Ar have been obtained which are also consistent with transport property and second virial coefficient data. The potentials for these systems are therefore now known with an accuracy which is close to that of the inert gas functions.

A number of interesting generalizations can be made about the relative shapes of the surfaces for H_2–Ne, Ar, Kr, and Xe:

(a) The repulsive part of the $U_2(r)$ function always lies at smaller separations (for a given energy) than the corresponding part of $U_0(r)$, whereas the position of the well minimum of $U_2(r)$ lies at slightly greater separations than that of $U_0(r)$, i.e. the two contributions to the potential essentially cross over at σ (see Fig. 8.3).

(b) $U_2(r)$ is displaced to smaller distances relative to $U_0(r)$ as the inert gas atom becomes heavier, i.e. σ_2/σ_0 decreases Ne → Xe.

(c) For H_2–Ne and H_2–Ar, the $U_0(r)$ components are conformal, as are the $U_2(r)$ components. However, $U_0(r)$ and $U_2(r)$ do not have the same shape (i.e. $U_0^*(r^*) \neq U_2^*(r^*)$, $U_2^*(r^*)$ being slightly steeper in the repulsive region and less attractive at long-range (see Fig. 8.4)).

(d) The dependence of the potential on diatom bond length (through the parameter ξ) decreases as the inert gas atom increases in size. This implies that the order of efficiency of vibrational excitation of hydrogen is Ar > Kr > Xe.

The theoretical hybrid models that have proved so successful for spherical systems have also been extended to polyatomic molecules and, in particular, to H_2–inert gas systems. The anisotropic potential is expressed in the POTEX form

$$U(r,\theta) = \sum_n U_n(r) P_n(\cos\theta)$$

and the radial strength functions represented by HFD-type functions (see Section 1.8). The short-range and long-range attractive dispersion contri-

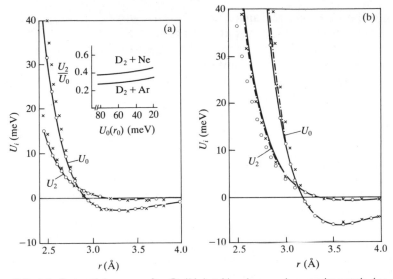

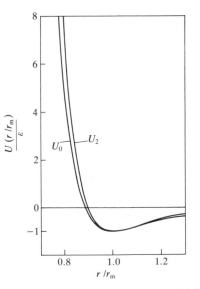

Fig. 8.3 (a) Potential curves for $D_2(H_2) + Ne$: (———) experimental; ($\times$, $\bigcirc$) theoretical. Inset: ratio of U_2/U_0 for the best experimental potentials as a function of the classical turning point $r_0(U_0)$ expressed by the values U_0 of the isotropic potential. (Buck, U. (1982). *Faraday Discuss. chem. Soc.* **73**, 187).

(b) Potential curves for $D_2(H_2) + Ar$: (———) experimental (beams + spectra); —·—·— experimental (spectra alone); $\bigcirc$, $\times$ theoretical. (Buck, U. (1982). *Faraday Discuss. chem. Soc.* **73**, 187).

Fig. 8.4 Reduced potential surfaces for the isotropic (U_0) and the anisotropic (U_2) potential term for both H_2–Ne and H_2–Ar. (Buck, U. (1982). *Faraday Discuss. chem. Soc.* **73**, 281).

butions to each $U_n(r)$ are evaluated by well-established quantum mechanical procedures. Damping functions are then used to interpolate between these components for each radial function $U_n(r)$ as in the spherical case. For the H_2–inert gas pairs, the potential surfaces generated in this way are not identical to those obtained from an analysis of experimental data, although the differences are not large (see Fig. 8.3). The models are therefore undoubtedly very useful in the absence of extensive experimental data and yield a basic surface that can gradually be refined as more information becomes available.

8.4.4. Atom–linear molecule systems

Many of the heavier atom–diatom systems have been extensively studied using various combinations of experimental and theoretical data. Although many reasonable potentials have been proposed, none of these pairs is as well characterized as the H_2–X systems described above. Nevertheless the general approach for this class of molecules is well established and the refinement of their potentials rests mainly on the production of the relevant experimental data to probe different components of the potential. For the more anisotropic systems, further refinement of the functional form beyond the two-term Legendre POTEX form may be necessary. Among the systems particularly well-studied experimentally are those involving the interaction of inert gases with N_2, O_2, CO_2 and the hydrogen halides. Also the theoretically based POTEX functions have been applied to some of the systems in a similar fashion to the H_2–inert gas cases. This approach is reasonably successful and is particularly useful in those cases where limited or no experimental data are available.

8.4.5. Diatomic molecules

Of the interactions between diatomic molecules heavier than H_2, the most widely studied system is N_2–N_2. A recent comprehensive approach to the determination of the pair potential for this system has been described by Ling and Rigby. In their approach the potential was broken down into three regions. At long range, a spherical harmonic expansion of the dispersion and electrostatic contributions was employed, making use of accurate theoretical calculations of the coefficients in the multipole expansion of the energy. At short range, quantum mechanical calculations of the energy for eight relative orientations of the molecules were fitted to a repulsive exponential four-centre site–site model with the sites located on the four nuclei. At intermediate range the functions for the two extremes were joined by damping functions containing several adjustable parameters. The parameters in the damping functions were determined by optimizing the fit to several types of experimental data, including second virial coefficients, gas viscosities, the heat of sublimation of solid α-N_2 at $0\,\text{K}(\Delta H_{sub})$, and the nearest neighbour distance, a_{eq}, in solid α-N_2 at $0\,\text{K}$. For the solid state calculations it was assumed that the non-additivity of many-body forces could be accounted for using the triple-dipole, three-body term. However, no surface was found that could reproduce all the experimental data to within their estimated errors. The surface giving the best fit hence serves as a prototype function for N_2–N_2, which can be refined in due course, although it cannot be said to provide an accurate representation of the full potential. It can be represented by a 14-term function of the POTEX-type. Its major features are illustrated in the energy contour diagram of Fig. 8.5, in which the four quadrants represent systematic changes in the relative orientation of the two molecules. In general, those orientations where the zero-crossing is at large separations have a shallow well, e.g. the linear configuration ($\theta_A = \theta_B = \phi = 0°$) has $\varepsilon/k = 23$ K, whereas for the crossed configuration ($\theta_A = \theta_B = 90°$) $\varepsilon/k = 155$ K. The potential energy is rather insensitive to ϕ for $\theta_A = \theta_B = 90°$ so that the radial dependence of the energy is very similar for the parallel (P) and crossed (X) configurations.

Although this approach to the potential surface of nitrogen has not yet proved completely successful, it illustrates the power of a method using many different properties, and also some of the problems that are still to be overcome.

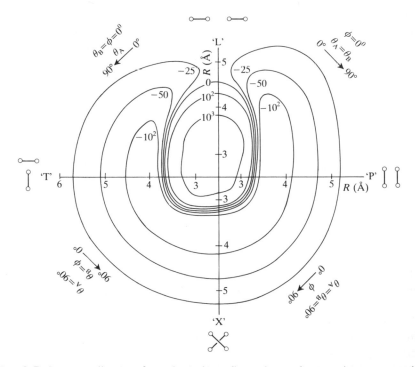

Fig. 8.5 Contour diagram for selected configurations of approximate potential surface for N_2–N_2. Contours are labelled as energy/K. (Ling, M. S. H. and Rigby, M. (1984). *Mol. Phys.* **51,** 855).

First, it is a difficult task to find a functional form sufficiently flexible to represent all points of the potentials adequately. Second, the analysis of solid-state data is subject to some doubt, owing to the influence of non-additive effects, which may not be sufficiently well represented by the three-body triple-dipole term. Finally, until rigorous calculations of transport properties can be carried out routinely for polyatomic systems, this extensive body of data cannot be fully exploited.

8.4.6. Polar molecules

When a molecule possesses a dipole moment, the characterization of the potential function tends to be more complex. This is not because any additional types of term appear in principle, compared with cases like N_2 where only higher multipoles exist, but because the effects due to dipoles are usually much greater. This means that in addition to permanent electrostatic effects, terms describing the induction and other polarization effects of dipole moments have to be included and cannot be neglected as they often can for higher moments. The simplest case is that of a dipolar diatomic molecule, and we use hydrogen fluoride, HF, as an example. The interaction between these molecules is particularly strong, falling into the category of a 'hydrogen bond', described qualitatively in Chapter 1, Section 1.7. However, the approach used to characterize it, and the types of functional forms used, are not restricted to hydrogen-bonding molecules and should be applicable to dipolar molecules in general.

The earliest functions used to represent polar interactions were based on the addition of long-range forms for electrostatic terms to the simplest functions used to represent a spherical interaction. The best known of these for dipolar molecules is the Stockmayer potential:

$$U(r, \theta_A, \theta_B, \phi) =$$
$$4\varepsilon \left[\left(\frac{\sigma}{r} \right)^{12} - \left(\frac{\sigma}{r} \right)^6 \right] \frac{\mu^2}{4\pi\varepsilon_0 r^3} (2\cos\theta_A \cos\theta_B - \sin\theta_A \sin\theta_B \cos\phi)$$

where μ is the dipole moment and the orientation angles θ_A, θ_B and ϕ are defined in Fig. 1.3. Simple functions of this type, whilst useful as model potentials for characterizing the general properties of polar molecules and observing the gross effects of polarity on measurable properties, are unable to represent accurately the potential functions for any real system. Not only is an $n - 6$ function too inflexible, as for monatomic systems, but the anisotropy of all contributions to the energy is neglected, apart from the long-range dipole–dipole term. In addition, not all relevant electrostatic or induction terms are included and no account is taken of modifications to the long-range energies that occur as the molecules approach each other and rearrangements of electron density occur.

For our representative system $(HF)_2$ Brobjer and Murrell have adopted an approach similar to that described for $(N_2)_2$, except that the total potential for polar polyatomic molecules must be divided into four contributions: exchange, electrostatic, polarization, and dispersion energies.

The *electrostatic contributions*, may be conveniently represented by means of a series of point charges whose magnitudes and positions are chosen to reproduce the known non-zero multipole moments of the molecule. The electrostatic energy is then evaluated from the coulombic interaction of the point charges (the multipole-fitted point charge model). An alternative approach, in which point multipoles are used (the distributed multipole method) has been successfully applied by Price and Stone. Either of these procedures is entirely general and may be applied to any molecule, although the effects of electron cloud distortions at short range must be included separately. In the analysis of $(HF)_2$ performed by Brobjer and Murrell, this 'charge penetration' effect was included in the *repulsive energy* along with the overlap energy. A quantum mechanical calculation was carried out for eight relative configurations of the HF molecules and the results represented by the single exponential

$$U_{rep} = \exp\{\alpha(\theta_A, \theta_B, \phi) + \beta(\theta_A, \theta_B, \phi)r\}$$

where r is the separation of the centres of mass of the two molecules. The anisotropic coefficients α and β were represented by expansions in spherical harmonics.

The *polarization energy* can be obtained from similar quantum mechanical calculations. It consists of the induction energies described in Section 1.3 and additional terms arising from the charge overlap. The most important of these additional terms is the exchange-polarization (or *charge-transfer* energy). It can be thought of as a polarization effect that takes place when charge cloud distortions occur as a result of overlap. It is an effect of major importance when a molecule with a low ionization potential interacts with one having a high electron affinity. For $(HF)_2$ the effect is relatively small, and the polarization energy was adequately represented by the combination of an isotropic exponential repulsion term and an angle-dependent inverse sixth-power attraction arising from the dipole-induced dipole energy.

For the *long-range dispersion energy*, the anisotropic dispersion coefficients are often not available for polyatomic molecules, and different methods must be employed. For $(HF)_2$, Brobjer and Murrell employed values of the isotropic C_n for the isoelectronic system $(Ne)_2$ and an isotropic damping function of the HFD-type to represent the correlation energy.

The combination of all of these terms yields a potential exclusively based on theory; there are only a few items of experimental information available against which to test it. An analysis of molecular beam microwave and radiofrequency spectra of the $(HF)_2$ dimer shows a planar equilibrium structure having $\theta_A = -12°$, $\theta_B = 68°$, $\phi = 0$, with $r_e \approx 0.268$ nm. The preferred potentials based on the theoretical construction yield reasonably good agreement with this configuration. Judged on experience of the HFD-type approaches for simpler systems, the $(HF)_2$ function proposed by Brobjer and Murrell may well prove to be a good initial approximation to the actual potential and provide a suitable functional form, but its parameters will probably need to be refined by comparison with new experimental data.

At the same time, the procedure adopted for $(HF)_2$ provides a useful guideline for other polyatomic systems and the results provide some useful physical insight. For example, if we examine the relative contributions to the equilibrium dimer dissociation energy $(-D_e = -18.0 \text{ kJ mol}^{-1})$, which are set out in Table 8.3, we see that the repulsive energy is partially cancelled by the polarization and dispersion terms, so that the strength of the hydrogen bond in $(HF)_2$ is dominated by the electrostatic energy. This turns out to be true for most hydrogen bonds, as we shall see in Section 8.6.2.

Table 8.3

Relative contributions to the equilibrium dimer energy of $(HF)_2$.

	kJ mol^{-1}
Electrostatic	−22.4
Repulsion	14.2
Polarization	−4.2
Dispersion	−5.6
Total Energy	−18.0

8.4.7. Water

Because of its obvious importance in both chemical and biological systems, a great deal of work has been carried out on the molecular interactions of water. Most of the interest arises from a desire to understand its properties as a liquid—the potentials proposed have often been used in computer simulations of the liquid state. This means that the non-additivity of the pair interactions must be given some attention, particularly since the failure of the assumption of pairwise additivity is known to be more marked than for simpler non-polar molecules.

The major sources of information about the pair energy of water have been quantum mechanical calculations, second virial coefficients, and molecular beam spectroscopic studies. At first sight the availability of reasonably accurate calculations for the relatively complicated system $(H_2O)_2$ may seem surprising in view of their absence for some simpler systems. However, when two water molecules approach each other the interaction is characterized by gross electronic changes. These large effects can be handled by present-day computers, whereas the smaller, more subtle, effects that give rise to, say, the dispersion energy cannot yet be calculated with accuracy for large systems. The quantum mechanical calculations yield an equilibrium dimer structure for water, shown in Fig. 8.6., which is consistent with that observed spectroscopically. There is a preference for the hydrogen atoms to be arranged tetrahedrally about the oxygen atoms; the hydrogen bond is linear ($\alpha \sim 0°$) and the angle θ is about 58°. The bond length $\langle r_{0-0} \rangle$ is 0.298 nm.

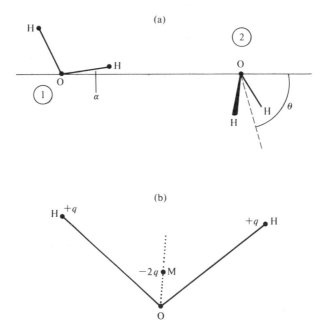

Fig. 8.6 (a) The structure of the water dimer. Molecule 1 lies in the plane of the paper. (b) The centres of force for the interaction of water molecules in the model proposed by Clementi *et al.* .

Early attempts to represent the pair potential by Rowlinson, and by Rahman and Stillinger, used a central Lennard-Jones 12–6 function and a number of point charges arranged within each water molecule. Generally the positions of the charges were chosen so that the resultant coulombic interaction favoured the known dimer geometry. Because explicit many-body forces were often neglected in the comparisons with liquid and solid-phase properties, these pair potentials are really *effective* pair potentials. Thus, whereas such potentials predict some of the anomalies characteristic of water, comparisons with neutron and X-ray scattering data are not totally convincing.

More modern potential functions, such as those due to Clementi and his co-workers, have been based more on theory and upon the representation of the isolated dimer. Many-body forces are then included explicitly in treating the condensed phase. Some features of one recent potential obtained by Clementi and Habitz are shown in Figs 8.6 and 8.7. In formulating this surface, a fit to calculations of 165 dimer configurations was employed using a point charge distribution and a site–site function of the exp–exp form between pairs of sites located on different molecules, as indicated in Fig. 8.6(b). Figure 8.7 gives both three-dimensional surfaces and contour diagrams for two orientations of a reference water molecule as a second molecule is moved in the $x-y$ plane and its orientation adjusted to give the minimum energy at each position. These diagrams illustrate the approximately spherical locus of the overall minimum centred on the oxygen atom, the strong minimum along the O–H bond direction, and the weaker interaction associated with the lone pair of electrons on the oxygen atom. The agreement of the predictions of this pair potential and the experimental dimer structure is excellent, but the predicted values of the second virial coefficient are a factor of two larger than experiment. Thus the representation of all the experimental data for water dimers by a single pair potential remains an outstanding problem.

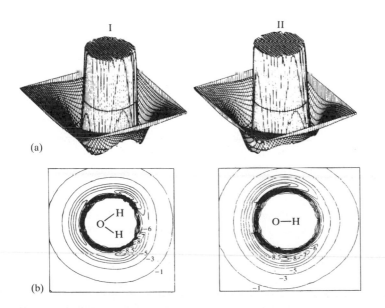

Fig. 8.7 Isoenergy maps (b) and their three-dimensional representation (a) for two cross-sections of the water interaction energy hypersurface. The interactions are computed for given oxygen positions, with relative orientation of second molecule optimized for minimum energy. Units in millihartree. (Based on Clementi, E. and Habitz, P. (1983). *J. phys. Chem.* **87,** 2815.)

Using a somewhat simpler representation of the pair potential, Barnes, Finney, and their collaborators have introduced the major (inductive) non-pairwise additive effects by incorporating the dipole polarizability. For a chosen molecule the total electric field used is that arising from all the sourrounding molecules. Calculations on small clusters of molecules suggest that only the three-body interactions are significant in practice, amounting to as much as 20 per cent of the total energy. This approach appears to be a promising one for calculating many-body energies for polar systems generally.

8.4.8. Ionic systems

Closed shell atomic ion–diatomic molecule systems bear some resemblance to the atom–diatom cases considered earlier. The most extensively studied systems of this kind are of the type $Li^+–X_2$. Here the overlap, electrostatic, and induction energies are the dominant contributions, and reasonably accurate quantum mechanical calculations are available for some systems, e.g. $X_2 = H_2$, N_2, CO. These give the major features of the potential but only a semi-quantitative description of the absolute energies, e.g. the uncertainty in the maximum well depth is probably 10 per cent for H_2 and up to 30 per cent for the heavier systems. The theoretical potential surfaces have been represented analytically using functions of the POTEX Legendre polynomial form whose strength functions have the correct long-range behaviour of the various charge–multipole interactions. There are considerable molecular beam inelastic scattering and ionic mobility data for these systems, which have been used in some limited refinement of the potentials and should prove a rich source of information in the future.

There are a number of interesting features of the $Li^+–X_2$ surfaces that illustrate the different behaviour of the systems. For $Li^+–H_2$, the minimum energy occurs for the broadside, T-shaped, configuration, whereas for $X_2 = N_2$ and CO it is the colinear geometry that is favoured. This can be understood on electrostatic grounds, since N_2 and CO have negative quadrupole moments, whereas that of H_2 is positive. On similar grounds the small positive dipole moment of CO in the dimer (corresponding to $C^{\delta+}O^{\delta-}$) means that the $Li^+–CO$ surface is slightly deeper as the ion approaches the O atom than when it approaches the C atom, whereas for the $Li^+–N_2$ system the surface is symmetrical. For more complex molecules interacting with atomic ions, a similar approach to that used for neutral interactions has been adopted. For example, the potentials of water with Li^+, Na^+, K^+, and Cl^- have been represented using a charge distribution for water similar to that of Fig. 8.6(b), which accurately reproduces the experimental dipole and quadrupole moments and gives a very good description of the next six moments predicted by quantum mechanical calculation. A site–site function has been used for the other terms of the potential.

In considering interactions between molecular ions, a very similar approach has been adopted. Klein and McDonald have modelled the potential for potassium cyanide by representing the charge distribution of the CN^- ion using seven charge centres. Their magnitudes and positions were chosen to fit the dipole, quadrupole, octopole, and hexadecapole moments given by theoretical calculations. The non-electrostatic contributions to the potential energy were represented by a site–site function of the exp–6 type. This function has been used as an effective pair potential in molecular dynamics simulations of solid KCN and is able to account semi-quantitatively for a wide range of properties. Our understanding of many-body effects for such systems is very limited at the moment. Nevertheless, this is a promising approach for formulating the potentials of a wide range of systems. The absence of extensive experimental data on the multipole moments of molecular ions (and even for most molecules) means that semi-quantitative estimates from quantum mechanical calculations can be very useful in giving an initial approximation to the potentials of more complex polar and ionic systems.

8.4.9. Benzene

We include benzene as an example of one of the most complex molecules for which a serious attempt has been made to determine its pair potential using a combination of theoretical calculations and experimental measurements. Evans and Watts represented the molecule by six sites located at the vertices of a regular hexagon and used a site–site representation of the potential. The site–site function included an exponential repulsion term and a long-range term in which the known dispersion energy was partitioned equally between the sites. The parameters were optimized by comparison with second virial coefficients, gas transport coefficients, and solid-state data, which were reproduced to within 15 per cent. We can regard this as a semi-realistic potential for benzene, which will no doubt be refined as more experimental data and greater theoretical insight become available.

8.4.10. Potentials for atomic and molecular systems

Appendix 8A contains references to potential functions currently available for a wide range of atomic and molecular systems. For each case a typical study has been chosen. Whilst in most cases we have attempted to choose the 'best' function available, such a judgement is not always straightforward and often subjective, particularly for molecular systems. The purpose of Appendix 8A is merely to provide the reader with a reasonably realistic potential function and an entry into the relevant literature.

8.5. Potential energy functions for large polyatomic molecules

For most molecules containing more than four or five atoms it has not been possible to characterize the intermolecular potentials to the extent discussed in the preceding sections. In order to develop reasonable descriptions of these interactions we must select a suitable functional form and determine values of scale and shape parameters that are as realistic as possible, though often based on very limited experimental and theoretical results. Many assumptions and gross simplifications must clearly be made, but in favourable cases the existing schemes can yield potential functions that give qualitative or even semi-quantitative descriptions of structure and properties. The most useful approach seems to be that based on site–site functions combined with point-charge distributions, though other approaches have also been widely studied.

8.5.1. Site–site point charge models

These potential functions resemble in form those used for small polyatomic systems, though the parameter determination now relies heavily on a mixture of simple model calculations and empiricism. Theoretical studies indicate how the total energy may be decomposed into components, and suggest suitable functional forms for each component. The usual split is

$$U = U_{\text{overlap}} + U_{\text{electrostatic}} + U_{\text{induction}} + U_{\text{dispersion}}.$$

Some attempts have been made to include charge transfer and polarization terms also, but we shall neglect these here. We shall consider the functions used to model each of these energy contributions in turn.

$U_{\text{overlap}} + U_{\text{dispersion}}$: These two contributions are usually combined together, and for non-polar molecules are the only ones that need be considered. The site–site energies U_{ij} are represented using a simple spherical potential, most commonly

$$U_{ij}(r_{ij}) = A_{ij} \exp\left(-\gamma_{ij} r_{ij}\right) - \frac{C_{ij}}{r_{ij}^6}$$

where r_{ij} is the separation between site i on one molecule and site j on the other.

The attractive coefficients C_{ij} can be estimated using the Slater–Kirkwood equation for the dispersion coefficients:

$$C_{ij} = \frac{3}{2} \frac{(e\hbar/m^{1/2})}{(4\pi\varepsilon_0)^{3/2}} \frac{\alpha_i \alpha_j}{\{(\alpha_i/N_i^{\text{eff}} + \alpha_j/N_j^{\text{eff}}\}}$$

Here $\alpha_{i,j}$ are the atomic polarizabilities and $N_{i,j}^{\text{eff}}$ is the number of effective electrons surrounding the nucleus when the atom is bound in the molecule; m is the electronic mass and e its charge.

The parameter γ_{ii} has been empirically related to atomic number, Z, by Scott and Scheraga. For light atoms it is a weak function of Z and lies between 4.5 and 4.6. For mixed interactions the geometric mean rule has usually been used:

$$\gamma_{ij} = (\gamma_{ii}\gamma_{jj})^{1/2}.$$

Values of A_{ij} are usually selected to make the potential minimum occur at the sum of the van der Waals' radii, R^v. The latter is generally based on separations found in crystal structures. Alternatively, for hydrocarbons Flory has suggested that A_{ij} can be estimated from the experimental value of the energy difference between the *trans* and *gauche* conformational isomers of the chain. Values of A_{ij}, C_{ij} and γ_{ij} used for particular atom pairs are listed in Table 8.4.

Table 8.4
Values of parameters for use in site–site potential functions

Interaction	A_{ij} (kJ mol^{-1})	γ_{ij} (nm^{-1})	$10^6 C_{ij}$ (kJ mol^{-1} nm^6)	r_m (nm)
H ... H	41.6	45.4	188.9	0.260
C ... H	359.9	45.7	530.9	0.310
C ... C	3798.0	45.9	1517.3	0.360
O ... O	564.3	45.9	907.1	0.304
C=O ... O=C	877.8	45.9	1546.6	0.300
H ... O	112.0	45.7	377.9	0.272
H ... O=C	144.6	45.7	510.0	0.270
H ... F	70.6	45.7	262.1	0.267
H ... Cl	163.0	41.5	1341.8	0.295
H ... Br	91.1	36.6	2202.9	0.305
F ... F	251.6	46.0	493.2	0.294
Cl ... Cl	1312.5	37.5	10533.6	0.350
Br ... Br	144.6	27.8	21652.4	0.370
F ... Cl	614.5	41.8	2202.9	0.322

$$U = \sum_{i<j} \{A_{ij} \exp(-\gamma_{ij} r_{ij}) - C_{ij}/r_{ij}^6\}$$

Scott, R. A. and Scheraga, H. A. (1965). *J. chem. Phys.* **42**, 2209.
Abe, A., Jernigan, R. L., and Flory, P. J. (1966) *J. Am. chem. Soc.* **88**, 631.

$U_{\text{electrostatic}}$: In the simplest representations the charge distribution is represented by multipole moments located at some centre of force (usually the centre of mass) within the molecule. Frequently the overall dipole and quadrupole moments are known. Recommended values for a range of molecules, based on both theory and experiment, are listed in Table 8.5. The relevant expressions for the interaction energy are given in Section 1.2. If no values for dipole moments exist, they can often be approximated by summing typical bond contributions, such as those listed in Table 8.6.

A more generally successful approach has been to represent the molecular charge distribution by a series of point charges located either on the atoms or at arbitrary points within the molecule. Their magnitudes, δ_k, and positions

Table 8.5
Molecular dipole and quadrupole moments

Molecule	Dipole moment, μ(Debye) (1 Debye $\equiv 3.3 \times 10^{-30}$ C m)	Quadrupole moment, $\Theta(10^{-40}$ C m^2)
H_2	0	+2.1
HD	9×10^{-4}	+2.12
D_2	0	+2.14
Li_2	0	+45.5
N_2	0	−4.90
O_2	0	−1.33
F_2	0	+2.90
Cl_2	0	+10.8
Br_2	0	+15.9
I_2	0	+18.7
CO	0.112	−8.2
NO	0.158	−4.1
HF	1.93	+7.8
HCl	1.07	+12.3
HBr	0.828	+13.6
HI	0.448	+20.0
LiH	5.882	−16.0
LiF	6.33	+19.2
BeO	—	+21.7
BF	—	−14.9
NaF	8.15	−6.5
KF	8.59	−30.7
CsF	7.88	−59.4
TlF	4.23	−43.2
CO_2	0	−14.9
CS_2	0	11.6
H_2O	1.855	$\Theta_{xx} = +8.7, \Theta_{yy} = -8.3, \Theta_{zz} = -0.4$
N_2O	0.161	−11.2
SO_2	1.59	$\Theta_{xx} = -16.2, \Theta_{yy} = +12.7, \Theta_{zz} = +3.4$
OCS	0.715	−2.8
HCN	2.984	10.9
ClCN	2.80	21.8
BrCN	2.94	22.4
NH_3	1.47	−7.7
C_2H_2	0	25.1
CH_2Cl_2	1.62	13.5
C_2H_4	0	$\Theta_{xx} = -10.7, \Theta_{yy} = +5.3, \Theta_{zz} = +5.3$
C_2H_6	0	−3.34
C_6H_6	0	−29.7

(Updated version of original survey of Stogryn, D. E. and Stogryn, A. P. (1966). *Mol. Phys.* **11**, 371.

Table 8.6
Bond dipole moments

Bond	Dipole moment μ(Debye)
O–H	1.53
N–H	1.31
C–H	0.35
C–F	1.50
C–Cl	1.56
C–O	0.86
C=O	2.48
C≡N	3.65
O–CH$_3$	0.65

Hopfinger, A. J. (1973). *Conformational properties of macromolecules*, Academic Press, London.

can be determined by ensuring that they reproduce all the known multipole moments—the multipole fitted point charge model. The total electrostatic energy is then given by summing the Coulomb energies of all pairs of charges on different molecules.

$U_{\text{induction}}$: Though generally smaller than the electrostatic energy, this term cannot usually be neglected, and its estimation can cause problems. Theoretical considerations suggest that the natural representation of the induction energy, if molecular polarizabilities are not available, is in terms of bond contributions. However, as most of the other contributions to the energy are expressed as sums over site–site interactions, it is more convenient to express the induction term in this way also. Caillet and Claverie have accordingly devised a scheme for calculating effective atomic polarizabilities by redistributing bond polarizabilities according to the number of electrons associated with each atom.

The calculation of induction contributions may also be complicated by many-body non-additive corrections when dense systems are being studied. An approach often adopted is similar to that used by Barnes and Finney for water (see Section 8.4.7):

$$U_{\text{ind}} = -\tfrac{1}{2}\Sigma\alpha_i\varepsilon_i^2$$

where α_i is the effective polarizability of atom i and ε_i is the electric field created at atom i of a particular molecule by all the other molecules in the system.

8.5.2. Applications of site–site functions

Functions of the type described in the previous section have been applied to an extremely wide range of systems. Although the predictions using such potentials cannot be taken as quantitatively accurate, they have in many cases given physical insight into molecular behaviour that was not intuitively obvious beforehand due to the shear complexity of the system. There have been several calculations of the properties of n-alkanes using site–site potentials, taking account of the fact that the C–C bonds in n-alkanes are not freely rotating but show a conformational preference for the positions *trans* (rotational angle $\phi \sim 0°$), *gauche*$^+$ ($\phi \sim 120°$) and *gauche*$^-$ ($\phi \sim 240°$). This exchange interaction between adjacent bonds may be most simply represented by

$$U_{rot}(\phi) = \tfrac{1}{2} U_0 (1 - \cos 3\phi)$$

where the height of the rotational barrier U_0 is about 12 kJ mol^{-1}.

These n-alkane studies are really prototypes for calculations on polymer molecules. Site–site potentials have been used extensively by Flory and by Scheraga to characterize the conformations of such long-chain molecules. This involves the mapping out of the *intra*molecular energy of a molecule for the many possible conformations that correspond to rotation about each bond in the chain. The objective has been to identify the minimum energy structures and to characterize the barrier heights between the many rotational isomers arising from occupation of the various *trans–gauche* type states along a chain.

The study of chain conformations and molecular shape has been carried out for a large number of synthetic macromolecules and also for biological polymers, such as nucleic acids and proteins. Here the objective has been to gain insight into the stability of helical molecules like DNA and how they are modified by interaction with various substrates. A number of calculations have been carried out on the interactions between the purine and pyrimidine base pairs in DNA in order to elucidate how the subtle balance of forces determines the unique double helical structure of this molecule, and how small changes might lead to perturbations of the genetic code. In addition, semi-realistic potentials for polymers have been extensively used in computer simulation studies of the thermodynamic and transport properties of polymers in solution or in the molten state.

As a final example, we turn to the study of the structure and energies of molecular crystals. Caillet and Claverie applied these atom–atom potentials to the crystal properties of CH_4, CO_2, C_6H_6, and $C_6H_5NO_2$. They found that the energies calculated for the experimental configurations of the molecules on the lattice were close to the observed sublimation energies. When the configurations corresponding to the minimum energy were calculated, these were found to be close to the observed structures, although in some cases several other local minima close to this energy were also located.

8.5.3. Potential functions based on convex cores

An alternative approach to the potentials of polyatomic molecules has been explored by Kihara. In his model, the shape of a molecule is associated with a suitable hard convex core and the potential energy is based on the shortest distance, ρ, between the surfaces of the two interacting molecules (see Fig. 8.8). In its simplest form, the dependence of U on ρ is represented by a Lennard–Jones 12–6 function:

$$U(\rho) = \infty \qquad \rho \leqslant 0$$

$$U(\rho) = \varepsilon \left\{ \left(\frac{\rho_m}{\rho}\right)^{12} - \left(\frac{\rho_m}{\rho}\right)^6 \right\} \qquad \rho > 0$$

$$U(\rho_m) = -\varepsilon$$

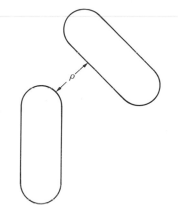

Fig. 8.8 The Kihara core model. ρ is the shortest distance between the surfaces of the cores.

It differs qualitatively from the other functions we have considered in representing the anisotropy of the interaction by concentrating the interaction centres on a single, movable site for each molecule. One particular advantage of the function is that, by making use of certain mathematical relationships for convex surfaces, second virial coefficients may be evaluated analytically. It has been used to describe a range of molecules of varying complexity, from argon to tetramethylsilane $Si(CH_3)_4$, and is able to reproduce experimental values of $B(T)$ for many systems. However, this must be taken as an indication of the general insensitivity of $B(T)$ to the detailed form of the potential function, rather than as evidence of the accuracy of the Kihara potential.

The main value of this formulation is that it is a particularly convenient way of modelling molecular shape and obtaining a function of the correct symmetry on the basis of relatively little information. For instance, a suitable core for CF_4 would be a regular tetrahedron, for C_6H_6 a thin hexagonal plate, or for C_6H_{12} a truncated double core. Although the model assumes that the molecule is undeformable, it has been successfully used to describe the second virial coefficients of the highly flexible n-alkanes using a rectangular planar core. In general, however, the functional form is not sufficiently realistic to describe quantitatively the detailed features of the potential surfaces for polyatomic molecules. In the most favourable cases it probably gives a semiquantitative description of both the short-range and the long-range anisotropies of polar molecules. Even this can, of course, be very useful for molecules as complex as tetracyanoethylene or silicon tetrafluoride, for which very little other information is available. The crystal structures of these and other complex molecules have been simulated using physical models that incorporate these two major features of the anisotropy.

8.6. Interactions in the liquid phase

The quantitative calculation of liquid and solution properties from the fundamental interactions is severely restricted at present by our poor knowledge of both the pair potentials for molecules of typical interest (e.g. water, methanol) and the nature of the many-body interactions between such complex molecules. Nevertheless, it is possible to say something about the general effects of a solvent and about the form of the interaction potential for particular cases.

8.6.1. General solvent effects

The major effects that must be considered when an isolated pair of molecules become surrounded by solvent molecules in a liquid are as follows:

(a) The electromagnetic interaction energy of the molecules is modified by the intervening medium; for instance electrostatic interactions are reduced by a factor ε_s, where ε_s is the dielectric constant of the solvent.

(b) The liquid structure is disturbed by the presence of the dissolved molecules. There is thus a net change in energy due to the replacement of one set of interactions by a new one. This is sometimes referred to as a 'solvation force'; a particular example is considered in Section 8.7.4.

(c) These local rearrangements often result in a significant entropy change; a consideration of interactions in condensed media should strictly consider the free energy, $E (= U(r) - TS(r))$, averaged over all the configurations of the solvent molecules.

(d) The electronic distributions of the dissolved molecules are distorted from their free space values due to interactions with those of the solvent. This in turn will modify the solute molecule interactions.

As an example of the changes that can take place in going from the gas to the liquid phase, consider the interaction free energy arising from dispersion forces of two molecules in a medium of dielectric constant ε_s. This is given by a similar expression to that in a vacuum:

$$E = -C_6^{(s)}/r^6$$

However, the coefficient C_6 now depends not only on the properties of the two molecules, but also on the difference between the molecular polarizabilities (or the local dielectric constants) of the solute and solvent. This quantity is sometimes called the *effective* or *excess polarizability* α^*. This reflects the fact that the change in free energy on immersion in a solvent depends on the loss of energy by the displaced molecules as well as the interaction of the dissolved molecules. By analogy with expression (1.13) for C_6 *in vacuo* ($C_6 \propto \alpha_1\alpha_2$), for two solute molecules immersed in a solvent $C_6^{(s)} \propto \alpha_1^*\alpha_2^*/\varepsilon_s$. For like solute molecules, α_1^* and α_2^* are identical and the dispersion energy is always negative, as it is in free space. However, for unlike molecules, α_1^* and α_2^* can be of opposite sign and the net interaction is then repulsive.

8.6.2. The hydrogen bond and related interactions

In considering specific types of interaction that occur in the liquid phase, by far the most important is the hydrogen bond. We have described the main physical features and origins of hydrogen bonds in Chapter 1, Section 1.7. They arise principally from the small size of the hydrogen atom and the electron redistributions that take place when it is bonded to an electronegative atom. We have also looked in some detail at the form of the potential energy function for an isolated hydrogen bond, as exemplified by the gas phase dimers $(H_2O)_2$ and $(HF)_2$. However, it is in the liquid state that the hydrogen bond really comes into its own. Here the interactions are highly cooperative because many hydrogen bonds, both solute–solvent and solvent–solvent, can be associated with a single solute molecule. It is the large energy decreases brought about by these cooperative interactions that result in the high solvency power of liquids such as water and alcohols. The structure and function of biological macromolecules are particularly dependent on hydrogen-bonded interactions.

We saw in Section 8.4.6 that it is convenient to partition the total potential energy into electrostatic, repulsion, polarization, and dispersion contributions, i.e.

$$U = U_{rep} + U_{elec} + U_{pol} + U_{disp}.$$

Although the precise meaning of each term and its magnitude will vary slightly according to the particular quantum mechanical method used, it is a useful division for understanding the physical origins of the stability of particular complexes. For instance, we have seen (Section 8.4.6) that for $(HF)_2$ at its equilibrium separation the energy is dominated by the electrostatic term; U_{pol} and U_{disp} are essentially compensated for by U_{rep}. This is a common feature of most hydrogen bonds; the interaction is predominantly electrostatic at long range and determined to a large extent by U_{elec} at $r = r_m$, although the balance between the other terms can sometimes play a crucial role in determining the precise strength of the interaction.

Although the hydrogen bond is unique amongst specific interactions in terms of its strength, many molecular complexes are formed through interactions of the same type that contribute to hydrogen bonding. Of particular note are the strong interactions that can occur between a molecule that has a low ionization potential (an electron donor) and one that has a high electron affinity (an electron acceptor). The distortion that occurs when the electron clouds of the approaching molecules overlap gives rise to a movement of charge from the donor to the unoccupied orbitals of the acceptor molecule. This attractive charge transfer interaction, in conjunction with the electrostatic and dispersion contributions, can outweigh the repulsive terms to give strong interactions and even stable complex formation. Benzene and iodine form such *donor–acceptor or charge-transfer* complexes, which are characterized by a broad absorption spectrum. Even where stable complex formation does not result, many interactions between polar molecules have charge-transfer energy contributions that are comparable with or exceed the dispersion, electrostatic, and normal induction terms.

In looking further into the details of hydrogen-bonded interactions, it is convenient to distinguish between weak and strong complexes. *Weak hydrogen bonds* are the normal interactions between neutral molecules that we have concentrated on so far. The magnitude of the contributing energies is normally:

$$U_{elec} > U_{rep} > U_{disp} > U_{chtr} > U_{ind}.$$

The interaction is highly directional, but little change occurs in the bond lengths of the participating molecules and the hydrogen atom is asymmetrically located between its neighbouring atoms X and Y: X–H .... Y–Z. Some ion–molecule complexes, such as $Na^+–H_2O$, behave in a similar fashion although the energies are now much bigger, and U_{elec} is even more dominant.

Strong hydrogen bonds are formed if the hydrogen atom can approach Y closely and interacts with it almost as strongly as with X. The most common situations of this type are when X = Y, e.g. $(F ... H ... F)^-$, $(H_2O ... H ... H_2O)^+$, although some mixed complexes such as $H_3N–HCl$ also have very large binding energies. Here, the hydrogen atom is essentially symmetrically placed between X and Y and large changes in bond length occur as the molecules approach to form the complex. A characteristic of the potential energy surfaces for these strong interactions is that the energy well within which the central proton moves is rather flat for the equilibrium separation (X ... H ... X), in contrast to smaller or larger values of r_{xx} where it is constrained in either a single or double minimum. Consequently, the hydrogen atom is highly mobile and this type of hydrogen bond is highly polarizable. This characteristic gives rise to distinctly different infra-red and n.m.r. spectra, for instance, than the normal weak bond.

The electrostatic interaction between two species HX and YZ that form a hydrogen bond can be thought of crudely as arising from the attraction between a polar bond (HX) and a lone-pair of electrons on atom Y. Allen has used this idea and the results of quantum mechanical calculations to develop an approximate formula for estimating the binding energy of hydrogen-bonded complexes:

$$\frac{D_e}{kJ\, mol^{-1}} - \frac{6.86\mu_{XH}\Delta I_Y}{r_m^{XY}}$$

where μ_{XH} (Debye) is the X–H bond dipole moment, ΔI_Y (eV) is the difference between the ionisation potential of Y and the inert gas atom of the same period, and r_m^{XY} (Å) is the equilibrium X ... Y separation. This equation may be used to estimate the strengths of hydrogen bonds in the absence of more detailed information on the potential energy surface.

8.6.3. *Liquid crystals*

We have seen in Section 7.6 that some molecules can exist as liquid crystalline, or mesomorphic, phases, which exhibit properties intermediate to those of liquids and solids. Structurally these phases are characterized by a high degree of orientational order combined with relatively little spatial order. Such behaviour implies a high degree of anisotropy in the intermolecular potential, so that certain relative orientations have a very much lower potential than the rest. Most liquid crystals consist of either elongated (rod-like) or flat (plate-like) molecules; increasing the length of a rod-like molecule or the diameter of a plate-like system results in systematic changes in the transition temperature, T_{NI}, between the nematic liquid crystalline phase and the isotropic liquid (i.e. transition (c) → (d) in Fig. 7.8). This is illustrated for typical systems in Fig. 8.9. Hence molecular shape, or repulsive anisotropy, is at least one factor that determines the nature of liquid crystalline materials.

However, 'shape' is not the only important factor. Consider the composition of a typical rod-like nematic liquid crystal:

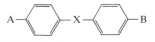

The effect of the linking group X on T_{NI} is typically

$$\bigcirc > \bigcirc > \underset{H}{\overset{H}{C}}=\overset{/}{C} > -N=N-> -CH=N-> -C\equiv C-$$
$$\qquad\qquad\qquad\qquad\qquad\qquad\qquad\downarrow\qquad\qquad\downarrow$$
$$\qquad\qquad\qquad\qquad\qquad\qquad\qquad O\qquad\qquad O$$

$$> -N=N-> -CH=N-> -\underset{\parallel}{\overset{}{C}}-O-> -C-C-$$
$$\qquad\qquad\qquad\qquad\qquad\qquad O$$

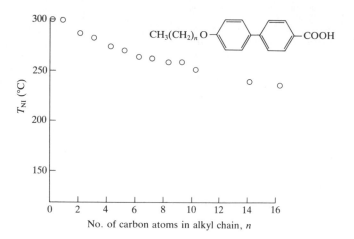

Fig. 8.9 Effect of chain length on nematic–isotropic transition temperature, T_{NI}, for typical rod-like liquid crystals (4–4′ n-alkoxybiphenyl carboxylic acids).

Here we see the effects of polarizability anisotropy. For instance, replacing the phenyl group by the bridged cyclohexyl group alters neither the shape nor the rigidity of the overall molecule significantly, but it does remove the highly polarizable delocalized π-electron system from the chain and so reduces the anisotropy of the dispersion interaction considerably. Another function of group X is to maintain chain rigidity; the more flexible group X allows the molecule to become, the more internal rotations within the molecule can damp out the anisotropy of the interaction energy.

There is evidence, therefore, that anisotropy in both the short- and long-range regions of the potential need to be considered in any complete description of liquid crystal behaviour. Most studies, however, have adopted the simpler approach of considering just one type of anisotropy. One view has been to consider only the anisotropy of the dispersion energy. Maier and Saupe used the simple potential

$$U(\mathbf{r}_{ij}, \mathbf{n}_i, \mathbf{n}_j) = -\varepsilon P_2 (\cos \gamma_{ij})$$

where r_{ij} is the centre of mass separation of molecules i and j, γ_{ij} is the angle between the unit vectors $\mathbf{n}_i$ and $\mathbf{n}_j$ characterizing the orientations of the molecules, and $P_2(\cos \gamma) \equiv (3 \cos^2 \gamma - 1)/2$. The alternative type of simple model used has neglected entirely the attractive forces and represented the anisotropic repulsion by a hard convex core of the type used in the Kihara potential (Section 8.5.3). The most common core shapes used have been a cylinder or a spherocylinder. However, to reconcile the properties of liquid crystalline phases quantitatively, more sophisticated potential functions and structural models must be used.

The simple potentials have been improved in two ways: by including both attractive and repulsive anisotropy, and by using more complicated functional forms for both these contributions, e.g. PAREX-type functions similar to those described in Chapter 1, Section 1.8, usually based on a 12–6 form. Although these more complex functions are better able to describe the local structure and thermodynamic properties of real liquid crystals like 4,4'-dimethoxyazoxybenzene (p-azoxyanisole), they must still be regarded as model functions. To date little effort has been directed at optimizing the functional form and parameters of the potentials for real systems. This will undoubtedly involve replacing the n–6 function by some of the more realistic functions described in Section 1.8. In addition, at least two other factors need to be taken into account. First, all the above functions assume that the molecules possess cylindrical symmetry. In practice, 'rod-type' molecules are far from cylindrical, being typically long and flat or 'lath-like'. Some work has been done with rectangular parallelopiped-type hard cores to simulate this effect. More generally, POTEX-type potentials for molecules of arbitrary shape have been used. Both these types of study show that this lowering of the symmetry of the intermolecular potential has significant effects on the structure and properties of nematic liquid crystals.

A second assumption implicit in all the potentials described is that the molecules are perfectly rigid. Yet all real liquid crystal-forming molecules possess some degree of flexibility, both in the tail groups A and in the linkage groups X, for instance. A full description of liquid crystalline behaviour will probably therefore also require the inclusion of intramolecular potential energy functions governing the internal rotations within the molecule itself. The site–site type potentials, developed for polymer chains and described in Section 8.5.1, should be suitable for this purpose.

A final note of caution should be registered regarding all the potentials described for liquid crystals, and indeed for most condensed phase studies of complex molecules: pairwise additivity is almost universally assumed. Although our current state of ignorance about the exact nature of many-body forces means that such an assumption is difficult to avoid, it should be recognized that the potentials that are being used are at best *effective* pair potentials, whose utility is likely to be restricted to a particular density range. The only viable alternatives at present appear to be either to assume that all non-pairwise energies are accounted for by the Axilrod–Teller triple dipole term (an assumption whose universality for different types of molecules is as yet unclear) or, in the case of highly polarizable molecules, to use a mean field electrostatic approach as in Section 8.4.7.

8.7. Interactions involving solid surfaces

So far we have been concerned mainly with the interaction between pairs of molecules, or relatively small groups of molecules. Situations involving condensed phases require a consideration of the cooperative interaction of large numbers of molecules. There are two general approaches to this problem. The first—the discrete approach—starts from the premise that the dominant contribution to the total energy arises from the various pair interactions, and sums such energies over all combinations of molecular pairs in the system. Corrections for higher-body effects are made where possible but as we have seen the precise form of such terms is not well established, even for three-body interactions. The second approach treats the condensed phase(s) as a continuum and evaluates the interactions in terms of bulk electromagnetic properties. In this way, many-body interactions are included implicitly in the calculation. We consider here two types of interaction involving solid surfaces: gas–solid interaction potentials, relevant to problems of adsorption, in which the former approach is generally used; and surface–surface interactions, which dominate the behaviour of colloidal systems, where continuum methods are the norm.

8.7.1. Molecule–surface (gas–solid) interactions

A discrete model that is frequently used for molecule–surface interactions considers the surface to consist of a rigid planar array of atoms, ions or molecules having the same characteristics (spacing, symmetry, composition) as the bulk solid. The interaction energy between a gas-phase molecule and the surface is then evaluated by summing all the interactions of the gas molecule and the individual solid molecules for all relative positions of the molecule and the surface. Hence, if z is the perpendicular distance of the gas molecule from the surface, the total interaction energy (assuming pairwise additivity) is given by

$$U_s(z) = \sum_i U_{gs}(r_i)$$

where $U_{gs}(r_i)$ is the interaction energy between the gas-phase molecule and the ith molecule in the solid, separated by a distance r_i (see Fig. 8.10).

Various devices have been used for simplifying the above infinite discrete sum for $U_s(z)$ into analytic expressions, especially where $U_{gs}(r_i)$ is taken to have

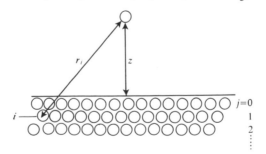

Fig. 8.10 Coordinates for gas–surface interactions.

a simple form like a Lennard–Jones (12–6) function. The discrete interaction sites in the solid, i, can be replaced by a continuous distribution and the sum replaced by an integral. Two procedures may be adopted. In the first, the integration takes place over the positions of solid molecules in each plane parallel to the surface, and summation over the layers is retained. In the second, integration is also carried out over these layers. If a 12–6 function is assumed for $U_{gs}(r)$, the resulting potentials, $U_s(z)$, are found to have 10–4 and 9–3 dependence respectively. The first procedure is found to give more satisfactory results, though it fails to describe the variation in the energy of an adsorbed molecule as it crosses the solid surface at fixed z. Potential curves corresponding to three positions A, B, C are shown in Fig. 8.11, and it is seen that these may have different shapes and will certainly vary in the depth and position of their attractive wells:

$$\varepsilon^A > \varepsilon^B > \varepsilon^C \quad \text{and} \quad \sigma^A < \sigma^B < \sigma^C$$

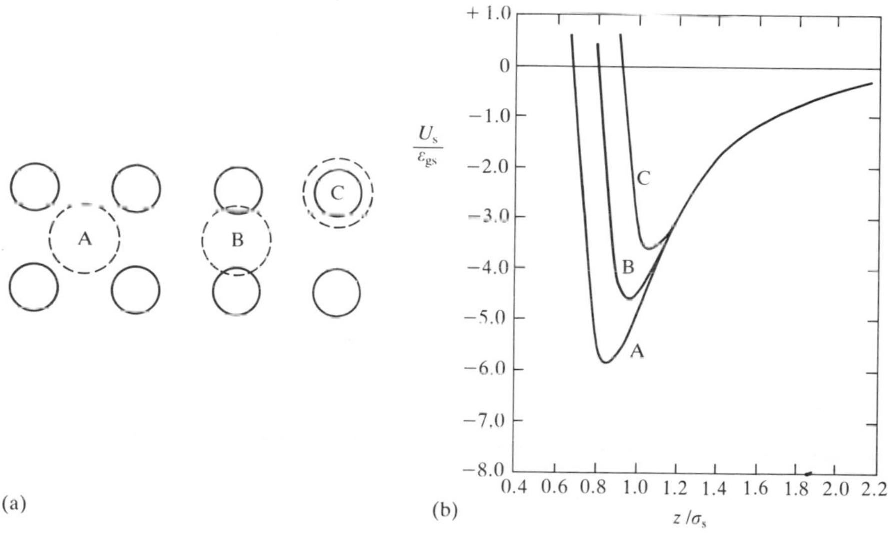

(a)

(b)

Fig. 8.11 (a) Selected positions for adsorbed molecules (dotted circles) on the 100 surface of a simple cubic solid (solid circles). (b) Gas–solid potential functions corresponding to positions A, B, and C. Solid curves are direct sums of a Lennard–Jones 12–6 pairwise energy, U_{gs}, for the case where $\sigma_s = \sigma_g$.

These complex 'corrugation' effects reflect the periodicity of the solid surface, and determine the detailed behaviour of molecules that are adsorbed on a surface and migrating over it, or simply collide with it and return to the gas phase. They may be incorporated into the gas–surface interaction potential, which then becomes a function of a vector $\mathbf{r}$ that locates the gas molecule relative to a reference point on the surface:

$$U_s(\mathbf{r}) = \sum_j U_s(z_j, \tau)$$

where τ is a surface vector which locates the positions of solid molecules in the jth layer.

Until relatively recently, most representations of gas–surface potentials were based on fairly crude model potentials for U_{gs}, such as n–6 or Morse functions. These gave a wealth of information on the qualitative features of surface scattering and adsorption phenomena, but were not accurate representations of the true potential. As with bulk phases, the emergence of new, more selective experimental techniques together with more sophisticated theoretical analyses has led to a significant improvement in the characterization of surface potentials in recent years.

Thus, when a gas is in contact with a surface, its PVT characteristics are influenced by the gas–surface interaction. By analogy with a bulk gas, one can define a second virial coefficient that is related to the gas–surface potential by:

$$B_s(T) = \int [\exp(-U_s/kT) - 1] \, dV$$

where dV is a differential volume element in the solid. Measurements of $B_s(t)$ can be used to screen proposed potentials and, if available over a wide enough temperature range, may be inverted to give the surface potential directly using methods similar to those described in Chapter 4.

Scattering of molecular beams from surfaces is another direct source of information about surface potentials. At high energies, the diffractive scattering pattern that is observed gives information about the repulsive forces between the molecule and the surface, particularly about the corrugation features described earlier. At lower energies, the molecules can become trapped in the bound vibrational levels supported by the surface potential, and selective absorption resonances are observed in the angular dependence of the scattering. Such data are very sensitive to the shape of the attractive well, the corrugation terms, and the effects of long-range multi-body energies. They provide a sensitive probe of the detail of molecule–surface potentials.

Relatively few gas–solid systems have been characterized in any detail. Gas-phase pair potentials of the HFD and $n(\bar{r})$-6 types have been shown to successfully describe the scattering characteristics of He from a monolayer of Xe adsorbed on graphite. The interactions between the inert gases and graphite itself have been described by 10–4 potentials of the type described earlier, and display relatively small corrugation effects. For molecules, more complex forms (Site–Site and POTEX) have been used. The interaction energy between gas molecules and metal surfaces is dominated by the presence of the high charge-density of mobile electrons in the metal. Potential functions have been constructed based on theoretical expressions for the overlap, dispersion and polarization energies, and experimental heats of adsorption used to optimize some of the parameters.

8.7.2. Surface–surface interactions

In a number of areas of science and technology, such as the physics and chemistry of colloids, adhesion, cleaning operations, and many biological processes, the interactions between large groups of molecules in the form of particles, biological cells or even larger macroscopic bodies are extremely important. Although the range of the forces between individual molecules is quite short, of the order of a few nanometres, the forces between aggregates of molecules have a much larger range, extending up to 50 nm from the surface of the aggregate. Within the aggregate itself the molecules contributing to this force lie within a narrow zone near its surface, so that these forces are often thought of as surface forces.

The origin of the forces between two large assemblies of molecules suggests that the simplest method of evaluation of the corresponding potential would be the addition of the potentials between each pair of molecules. This approach was indeed followed by Hamaker and others in evaluating the force between two macroscopic bodies. Assuming, for simplicity, that the molecular interaction consists solely of the leading London dispersion term, the energy of interaction between two bodies a and b composed of N_a molecules of species 1 and N_b molecules of species 2 is

$$U_{att} = -\int_{V_a}\int_{V_b} N_a N_b \frac{(C_6)_{12}}{r^6}\, d\tau_a d\tau_b$$

In this expression $(C_6)_{12}$ represents the dispersion energy coefficient for a pair of molecules, r their separation, and the integrals extend over the volumes V_a and V_b of the bodies. For bodies of a relatively simple shape, the integrals above may be evaluated analytically. For example, the attractive interaction energy between two semi-infinite slabs of molecules, separated by a distance d, is given by:

$$U_{att} = -A/12\pi d^2$$

and for two spheres of radii R, whose surfaces are separated by a distance d, the result is:

$$U_{att} = -\frac{A}{12}\left\{\frac{R+d}{d} + 2\ln (d/R)\right\} \simeq -\frac{AR}{12d}$$

when $R \gg d$, and for larger separations

$$U_{att} = -\frac{2AR^2}{3d^2}.$$

At very long range, the finite time taken for radiation to pass between the two particles results in a further weakening of the interaction, the so-called retardation effect, and $U_{att} \propto d^{-3}$.

In these formulae A is the 'Hamaker constant', defined by

$$A = \pi^2 N_a N_b (C_6)_{12}.$$

Its value depends on the nature of the particles and on the medium that separates the two bodies; typically it is 10^{-19}–10^{-21} J, i.e. 0.25–25 kT at 25°C.

The two examples quoted above, and others, are of considerable interest in surface chemistry, because the dispersion interaction between two spheres contributes significantly to the process of flocculation in colloids. If the attractive forces so far considered were the only interactions between colloidal particles, they would always flocculate and form large aggregates. Since many sols containing unaggregated particles are stable, it is clear that repulsive forces are also present. These are not the electromagnetic exchange interactions which operate between molecules, since these are too short-ranged. The repulsive forces responsible for colloid stability are of two main types— *electrostatic*, due to surface charges on the particles, and *steric*, due to polymer chains that are attached to the particle surface.

The surface charge of a colloidal particle causes it to be surrounded by an atmosphere of counter ions (see Fig. 8.12(a)), consisting of a thin, tightly bound layer (the Stern layer) and a longer-ranged, more diffuse layer (the Gouy–Chapman layer). This double layer can be quite extensive, and its thickness is expressed in terms of the Debye–Huckel reciprocal length, κ^{-1}, whose value is largely determined by the electrolyte concentration in the solution.† The repulsive potential energy of two spherical particles of radius R carrying such double layers may be approximated by

$$U_{rep} = 2\pi \varepsilon_r \varepsilon_0 R \psi^2 \exp(-\kappa d)$$

where ε_r is the relative permittivity of the solution, ε_0 the permittivity of a vacuum, d is the shortest distance between the spheres, and ψ is the potential at the position of the Stern layer.

An approximation to the pair potential between two spherical particles can be obtained by adding the electrostatic repulsive and the attractive dispersion terms. This was first done by Deryagin, Landau, Verwey, and Overbeek, and is often referred to as the DLVO theory. The resulting potential has the form shown in Fig. 8.12(b). The attractive forces dominate at long and very short range, but at intermediate separations a repulsive energy barrier occurs of

†

$$\kappa = \left\{ \frac{N_A e^2 \sum_i c_i z_i^2}{\varepsilon_r \varepsilon_0 kT} \right\}^{\frac{1}{2}}$$

where e is the electronic charge, ε_r the dielectric constant of the solution, ε_0 the permittivity of a vacuum, c_i the concentration of ions of type i, and z_i their charge.

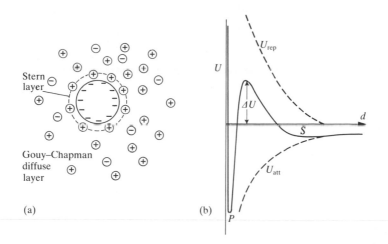

Fig. 8.12 (a) The electrical double-layer—schematic representation of the ion distribution. (b) Pair potential energy function (schematic) for electrostatically stabilized colloid particles.

height ΔU, typically several times kT. This keeps the particles apart and stabilizes the colloidal suspension, though weak association can result from the shallow minimum, S. This weak, reversible association is usually called *flocculation*. The situation shown in Fig. 8.12(b) is typical of low electrolyte concentrations. As the concentration (ionic strength) is increased, the range and height of the stabilizing repulsive barrier are reduced, until $\Delta U \simeq kT$. The particles will then associate irreversibly in the primary attractive minimum, P, in a process called *coagulation*.

The second type of repulsive interaction that can occur between colloid particles, *steric repulsion*, arises when long chain molecules protrude from the surface, as in Fig. 8.13. These chain molecules may arise naturally in the colloid surface layer, be grafted on chemically, or may simply be adsorbed. Their presence is of particular importance in stabilizing colloids in non-aqueous, non-polar media. The repulsive energy arises from two sources: a mixing term, U_{mix}, due to the interpenetration of the chains as two particles approach, and an entropic term, U_{ent}, due to the reduction in the number of possible conformations the chains can adopt as d decreases. This steric repulsion begins to rise dramatically for $d \gtrsim 2\delta$, where δ is the thickness of the surface layer. The overall potential function, combining the attractive and repulsive contributions, has a single attractive minimum (Fig. 8.13(b)), and so resembles a simple potential for atoms. Typically, for coverages of $\sim 10^{-7}\,\mathrm{kg\,m^{-2}}$ using terminally anchored polymer chains of r.m.s. length $\sim 8\,\mathrm{nm}$ for particles having $A \sim 10^{-20}\,\mathrm{J}$, σ is about 15 nm and ε about $10^{-6}\,\mathrm{J\,m^{-2}}$. Reducing the chain molecular weight, or adsorption as loops, both lower the thickness of the

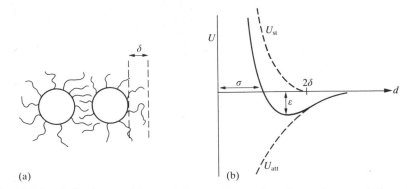

Fig. 8.13 (a) Steric repulsions: chain overlap and conformation restriction. (b) Pair potential energy function.

adsorbed layer and hence reduce the separation at which the steric repulsion term becomes significant. Hence σ is reduced and ε increased. Similarly increasing the chain length increases δ and displaces the potential to larger separations with a diminished well depth, until for very long chains the interaction becomes essentially purely repulsive, and $U(d) \simeq U_{st}$.

Another important parameter in determining the pair potential is the solvency power of the intervening medium towards the adsorbed chains. In a good solvent, U_{mix} is a repulsive energy. However, in a poor solvent the polymer–polymer interactions become more favoured and U_{mix} becomes attractive, reinforcing the dispersion attraction. In this case, U_{ent} is the sole source of repulsive interactions and consequently the well depth ε increases. This situation can be brought about by either changing the temperature or adding a non-solvent to the system. When $\varepsilon \gtrsim kT$, the particles can flocculate, forming doublets and higher clusters by virtue of the attractive well, with $\delta < d < 2\delta$. These effects are usually reversible and the strong temperature dependence of the stability of sterically stabilized colloids is a characteristic that distinguishes them from electrostatically stabilized dispersions.

The approach outlined above for the evaluation of attractive surface forces is incomplete for a number of reasons. First, a more complete treatment from the microscopic point of view requires an analysis of many-body interactions, which is generally not available. For this reason an alternative approach to the interaction of two bodies, termed the macroscopic or Lifshitz theory, has also been employed. The essential step of the macroscopic theory is analogous to that of the theory of molecular dispersion forces, namely the recognition that the attractive energy arises from the correlation of electronic motion in the two interacting entities. Whereas in the microscopic theory the dispersion coefficient C_6 is related to the molecular polarizability, Lifshitz theory relates the Hamaker constant A to the macroscopic analogue of polarizability, the dielectric constant, whose experimental values include the effects of many-body interactions. Generally, energy calculations carried out by the micro-scopic and macroscopic methods give the same functional dependence on d but the Hamaker constants differ by some 10–25 per cent because of many-body effects in condensed media.

A second complicating factor is that the surface forces are very long range. Consequently the time taken for radiation to pass between the two bodies is significant and leads to a decrease in the correlation between the motions of the electrons in the two bodies. These so-called *retardation effects* contribute significantly to surface forces at long range and have been evaluated for several geometric arrangements. In general they weaken the dependence of U_{att} on separation from d^{-n} to $d^{-(n+1)}$.

Finally, it must be recognized that in many situations of interest, the two interacting bodies may be separated, not by a vacuum as we have assumed so far, but by a fluid. In such cases the presence of the fluid can significantly modify the interaction of the two bodies and can even change it from an attractive interaction to a repulsive one. Effects of this type are obviously of great importance in studies of the stability of colloids, and may be readily treated by the Lifshitz approach. For instance, the interaction energy per unit area between two planar surfaces (1 and 3), separated by a fluid (2), is given by:

$$E = -\frac{A_{123}}{12\pi d^2}$$

where A_{123} depends on the product $\Delta_{12}\Delta_{32}$, where $\Delta_{ij} = (\varepsilon_i - \varepsilon_j)/(\varepsilon_i + \varepsilon_j)$, where ε is the dielectric constant. This expression for the energy has the same form as that given earlier in this section; now, however, the Hamaker constant A depends on the dielectric properties of all three phases. We see that if $\varepsilon_1 = \varepsilon_3$, E is negative; hence two bubbles or two similar colloidal particles always attract one another, but have an energy that is modified (usually reduced) by the medium. However, where $\varepsilon_1 > \varepsilon_2 > \varepsilon_3$, A_{123} is negative and the net interaction becomes repulsive. In this case the attractive forces between the molecules of the fluid and both surfaces outweigh the attraction between the surfaces themselves.

Table 8.7 gives Hamaker constants A_{ijk} for a range of systems involving liquid hydrocarbon and solid substances separated by air or water. These are estimated to be accurate to within a few per cent. The strong influence of replacing air by a water film between two surfaces is particularly noticeable. The multi-phase Hamaker constants A_{ijk} may be estimated from the free space values A_{i0i} of the single components by using the approximate combining rules

$$A_{i0j} \simeq (A_{i0i}A_{j0j})^{1/2}$$
$$A_{iji} \simeq (A_{i0i}^{1/2} - A_{j0j}^{1/2})^2$$
$$A_{ijk} \simeq (A_{i0i}^{1/2} - A_{j0j}^{1/2})(A_{k0k}^{1/2} - A_{j0j}^{1/2}).$$

Table 8.7

Hamaker constants A_{ijk} *for selected solid–fluid combinations*

A. Saturated alkane–water–air systems.

$A_{ijk}(10^{-20}J)$

Liquid, L	L–air–L	L–H₂O–L	L–H₂O–air	H₂O–L–air
n-alkanes				
$n = 5$	3.75	0.336	0.153	0.108
6	4.07	0.360	−0.004	0.285
7	4.32	0.386	−0.118	0.423
8	4.50	0.410	−0.200	0.527
9	4.66	0.435	−0.275	0.624
10	4.82	0.462	−0.344	0.719
11	4.88	0.471	−0.368	0.751
12	5.04	0.502	−0.436	0.848
13	5.05	0.504	−0.442	0.855
14	5.10	0.514	−0.464	0.886
15	5.16	0.526	−0.490	0.923
16	5.23	0.540	−0.518	0.964
Water	3.70			

Data taken from: Hough, D. B. and White, L. R. (1980). *Adv. Colloid Interface Sci.* **14**, 3.

B. Solid–air–water–systems.

$A_{ijk}(10^{-20}J)$

Solid, S	S–air–S	S–H₂O–S	S–H₂O–air	S–air–H₂O
Crystalline quartz	8.83	1.70	−1.83	5.59
Fused silica	6.55	0.849	−1.03	4.83
Calcite	10.1	2.23	−2.26	6.00
Calcium fluoride	7.20	1.04	−1.23	5.06
Sapphire	15.6	5.32	−3.78	7.40
Poly(methyl methacrylate)	7.11	1.05	−1.25	5.03
Poly(vinyl chloride)	7.78	1.30	−1.50	5.25
Poly(styrene)	6.4	0.93	−1.0	4.8
Poly(isoprene)	5.99	0.743	−0.836	4.59
Poly(tetrafluoroethylene)	3.80	0.333	−0.128	3.67

Some caution should be exercised in using these rules, especially where the intervening medium is a highly polar liquid like water.

Information about the variation of dielectric constant of materials with frequency is relatively common and estimates of dispersion interactions have been made for a wide range of physical, chemical, and biological systems. For instance, this method has been applied to the interactions between dissolved macromolecules and proteins, sufficiently large ($\sim$ 10 nm) to be regarded as macroscopic bodies. The interactions between biological cells have been simulated by calculating the long-range energies across hydrocarbon–water–hydrocarbon systems, modified by sugar-type adsorbed layers. The inclusion of electrical double-layer energies has enabled cell specificity to be studied. A large number of surface phenomena, such as wetting and film stability, which are usually dominated by dispersion interactions, can also be characterized in this way.

This theoretical work has been supported by a considerable amount of experimental activity in the direct measurement of forces between surfaces. Such experiments are very difficult and require extreme care, but it has been possible to measure directly the forces between two macroscopic bodies both *in vacuo* and in the presence of fluids and adsorbed layers. Direct measurement of surface charge can be made for electrostatically stabilized systems and the double layer can be further characterized using such techniques as electrophoresis. Other less direct measurements involving the stability of colloids have also been performed for both kinds of system, but their interpretation in terms of potential energy functions is inevitably more difficult.

8.7.3. *The hydrophobic interaction*

It has been widely observed that hydrocarbons and other organic non-polar molecules appear to attract one another in water significantly more than one would expect on the basis of the dispersion energies. This *hydrophobic interaction,* as it is called, has been used to explain the very low solubility of hydrophobic molecules in water and is claimed to be important in determining the conformations of proteins, the structure of biological membranes and the way surfactant molecules interact to form micelles. It arises from the net changes in energy and entropy that take place due to the rearrangement of the local water structure as the two hydrophobic species approach one another. A comparison of the measured repulsive force between two mica surfaces coated with a hydrocarbon layer submerged in various electrolytes with that expected from electrical double layer and dispersion interactions indicates that the pair interaction free energy arising from this effect has the form

$$E_h = -B\left(\frac{R_1 R_2}{R_1 + R_2}\right)e^{-d/d_0}\text{ kJ mol}^{-1}$$

where R_1, R_2 are the radii in nm of the spherical interacting particles or molecules, separated by a distance d. The experiments give a value for B of 84 kJ mol^{-1} nm^{-1} with the decay length $d_0 = 1.0 \pm 0.1$ nm. The hydrophobic interaction is about an order of magnitude larger than the dispersion energy for these systems, and operates over a similar long range (up to 10 nm).

8.7.4. Hydration forces

In contrast to hydrophobic surfaces, hydrophilic surfaces in water exhibit anomalous behaviour at small separations. The short-range repulsive forces between such surfaces are called *hydration* or *structural forces*. They arise because of the energy required to remove water molecules bound to ionic or polar groups on the surfaces as they approach one another. Fig. 8.14 shows the repulsive force measured between two curved mica surfaces immersed in

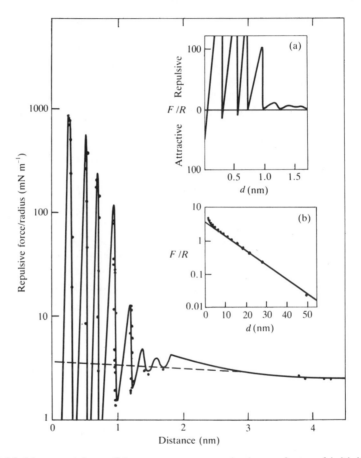

Fig. 8.14 Measured force F between two curved mica surfaces of initial radius $R \approx 1$ cm as a function of distance d in 10^{-3} M KCl solution (the plotted normalized force F/R is equivalent to $2\pi E$, where E is the interaction energy per unit area of two flat surfaces at the same separation d). Inset (a), force law at small separations (below 2 nm) plotted on a linear scale. Inset (b), force law at large separations (beyond 2 nm) where the solid line (and dashed line in main figure) is the theoretical electrostatic double-layer force for a surface potential of -78 mV. (Israelachvili, J. and Pashley, R. (1982). *Nature* **306,** 249).

10^{-3} M KCl solution at pH 5.5. At separations greater than 3 nm, the interaction is just that expected due to the diffuse double layer repulsion. At shorter separations the repulsion increases more steeply, but below $d = 1.5$ nm it exhibits rapid oscillations of increasing amplitude and periodicity ~ 0.25 nm. This is essentially the diameter of a water molecule and it is believed that the oscillations reflect the local ordered layering of the water molecules interacting with the hydrophilic surface groups. Such effects have also been observed in organic fluids, both polar and non-polar, and appear to be a general phenomenon if the surfaces involved are rigid.

8.8. Summary

In this chapter we have ranged from the interaction of two isolated atoms to the forces between large assemblies of molecules in the solid state acting through a highly structured polar fluid medium. The accuracy with which these energies can be characterized decreases sharply as the complexity of the molecules increases, and as the number of interacting molecules increases, although we are still able to make reasonable estimates of pair energies and three-body non-additive terms and the relative shapes of potential energy surfaces for quite complex systems. Yet when the system becomes sufficiently complex that the many interacting molecules essentially form a continuous medium, the quantitative calculation of the interaction energies again becomes feasible through the use of methods based on the macroscopic properties of the substance. The judicious combination of molecular and macroscopic approaches shows encouraging signs of being able to characterize the role of molecular interactions in systems of practical interest containing molecules of a wide range of complexity.

Suggested further reading

Monatomic Systems

Maitland, G. C., Rigby, M., Smith, E. B., and Wakeham, W. A. (1981). *Intermolecular forces: their origin and determination*. Clarendon Press, Oxford. Chapter 9. (Referred to in text as MRSW.)

Scoles, G. (1980). Two-body, spherical atom–atom and atom–molecule interaction energies. *Ann. Rev. phys. Chem.* **31**, 81.

Huxley, P. and Murrell, J. N. (1983). Ground-state diatomic potentials. *J. chem. Soc. Faraday Trans. II*. **79**, 323.

Viehland, L. A. (1984). Interaction potentials for the alkali ion—rare gas systems. *Chem. Phys.* **85**, 291.

Simple polyatomic molecules

Gray, C. G. and Gubbins, K. E. (1984). *Theory of molecular fluids*, Vol. 1, *Fundamentals*, Chapter 2. Clarendon Press, Oxford.

LeRoy, R. J. and Carley, J. S. (1980). Spectroscopy and potential energy surfaces of van der Waals molecules. *Adv. Chem. Phys.* **42**, 353.

Maitland, G. C., Rigby, M., Smith, E. B., and Wakeham, W. A. (1981). *Intermolecular forces: their origin and determination.* Clarendon Press, Oxford. Chapter 9.

Rodwell, W. R. and Scoles, G. (1982). Intermolecular forces via hybrid Hartee–Fock plus damped dispersion (HFD) energy calculations. *J. phys. Chem.* **86**, 1053.

Van der Waals molecules (1982). *Faraday Dis. chem. Soc.* **73**.

Large polyatomic molecules

Abe, A., Jernigan, R. L., and Flory, P. J. (1966). Conformational energies of n-alkanes and the random configuration of higher homologues, including polymethylene. *J. Am. chem. Soc.* **88**, 631.

Caillet, J. and Claverie, P. (1975). Theoretical evaluation of the intermolecular interaction energy of crystals. *Acta crystallogr.* **A31**, 448.

Flory, P. J. (1969). *Statistical mechanics of chain molecules.* Interscience, New York.

Helfand, E., Wasserman, Z. R., and Weber, T. A. (1980) Brownian dynamics study of polymer conformational transitions. *Macromolecules* **13**, 526.

Hopfinger, A. J. (1973). *Conformational properties of macromolecules.* Academic Press, New York.

Pullman, B., ed. (1978). *Intermolecular interactions: from diatomics to biopolymers.* Wiley, New York.

Scott, R. A. and Scheraga, H. A. (1965). Conformational analysis of macromolecules. *J. chem. Phys.* **42**, 2209.

Shipman, L. L., Burgess, A. W., and Scheraga, H. A. (1975). A new approach to empirical intermolecular and conformational potential energy functions. *Proc. nat. Acad. Sci. USA* **72**, 543.

Interactions in the liquid phase

Hildebrand, J. H., Prausnitz, J. M., and Scott, R. L. (1970). *Regular and related solutions.* Van Nostrand, New York.

Luckhurst, G. R. and Gray, G. W., ed. (1979). *The molecular physics of liquid crystals.* Academic Press, London.

Rowlinson, J. S. and Swinton, F. L. (1982). *Liquids and liquid mixtures.* (3rd edn). Butterworths, London.

Schuster, P., Zundel, G., and Sandorfy, C., ed. (1976). *The hydrogen bond.* North Holland, Amsterdam.

Tsykalo, A. L. and Bagmet, A. D. (1978). Molecular dynamics simulation of nematic liquid crystals. *Mol. Cryst. Liq. Cryst.,* **46**, 111.

Interactions involving solid surfaces

Ben-Naim, A. (1980). *Hydrophobic interactions.* Plenum, New York.

Hough, D. B. and White, L. R. (1980). The calculations of Hamaker constants from Lifshitz theory with applications to wetting phenomena. *Adv. Colloid. Interface. Sci.* **14**, 3.

Hutson, J. M. and Schwartz, C. (1983). Selective adsorption resonances in the scattering of helium atoms from xenon-coated graphite: close-coupling calculations and potential dependence. *J. chem. Phys.* **79**, 5179.

Israelachvili, J. N. and Pashley, R. M. (1983). Molecular layering of water at surfaces and origin of repulsive hydration forces. *Nature* **306**, 249.

Nicholson, D. and Parsonage, N. G. (1982). *Computer simulation and the statistical mechanics of adsorption.* Academic Press, London.

Ninham, B. W., Overbeek, J. T. G., and Zettlemoyer, A. C., ed. (1982). Interactions of particles in colloidal suspensions. *Adv. Colloid. Interface. Sci.* **17**.

Richmond, P. (1975). Theory and calculation of Van der Waals forces. In *Specialist periodical reports: Colloid Science 2*, (ed. D. H. Everett). Chemistry Society, London.

Appendix 8A. References to potential functions for selected systems

For the systems listed, reference is given to a *typical* study. In the case of atoms and some atom–molecule interactions, these will describe functions close to the true potential. However for more complex cases, the potential energy surfaces are far from being quantitatively characterized. Here we have attempted to give the 'best' function available, although it must be recognized that this usually involves some subjective judgement.

8A.1. Spherically symmetrical systems

$H-H$ ($^3H_2$). Kolos, W. and Wolniewicz, L. (1974). *Chem. Phys. Lett.* **24**, 457.

Inert gases and their mixtures. Chapter 8, section 8.3.1. MRSW, Chapter 9.

Group I and group II metal dimers. Huxley, P. and Murrell, J. N. (1983). *J. chem. Soc. Faraday Trans. II* **79**, 323.

Varandras, A. J. C. and Brandão, J. (1982). *Mol. Phys.* **49**, 857.

Buck, U. (1975). *Adv. chem. Phys.* **30**, 313.

Alkali ion–rare gas systems. Viehland, L. A. (1984). *Chem. Phys.* **85**, 291.

8A.2. Atom–molecule systems

$H-H_2$. Varandras, A. J. C. (1979). *J. chem. Phys.* **70**, 3786.

$H-O_2, CO, CO_2, CH_4, C_nH_{2n+2}$. Este, G. O., Knight, D. G., Scoles, G., Valbusa, U., and Grein, F., (1983). *J. phys. Chem.* **87**, 2772.

$He-H_2$. Mayer, W., Hariharan, P. C., and Kutzelnigg, W. (1980). *J. chem. Phys.* **73**, 1880.

Inert gas–H_2. Buck, U. (1982). *Faraday Dis. chem. Soc.* **73**, 187.

LeRoy, R. J. and Carley, J. S. (1980). *Adv. chem. Phys.* **42**, 353.

Inert gas–N_2. Fuchs, R. R., McCourt, F. R. W., Thakkar, A. J. and Grein, F. (1984). *J. phys. Chem.* **88**, 2036.

Inert gas–O_2. Corey, G. S. and McCourt, F. R., (1984). *J. chem. Phys.* **81**, 3892.

He–CO, NO. Keil, M., Slankas, J. T., and Kuppermann, A. (1979). *J. chem. Phys.* **70**, 541.

He–CO$_2$, N$_2$O, C$_2$N$_2$. Parker, G. A., Keil, M., and Kuppermann, A. (1983). *J. chem. Phys.* **78**, 1145.

Inert gas–HF, HCl. Hutson, J. M. and Howard, B. J. (1982). *Mol. Phys.*, **45**, 769, 791.

Inert gas–SF$_6$. Pack, R. T., Valentini, J. J., and Cross, J. B. (1982). *J. chem. Phys.* **77**, 5486.
Pack, R. T., Piper, E., Pfeffer, G. A., and Toennies, J. P. (1984). *J. chem. Phys.* **80**, 4940.

Inert gas–alkali halides. Meyer, G. and Toennies, J. P. (1982). *J. chem. Phys.* **77**, 798.

Na–alkyl halides. Buck, U., Gestermann, F., and Pauly, H. (1980). *Chem. Phys.* **50**, 217.

Li$^+$–N$_2$, CO. Staemmler, V. (1975, 76) *Chem. Phys.* **7**, 17; **17**, 187.

8A.3. Molecule–molecule systems

H$_2$–H$_2$(D$_2$). Schaefer, J. and Meyer, W. (1979). *J. chem. Phys.* **70**, 344.
Buck, U., Huisken, F., Kohlhase, A., Otten, D., and Schaefer, J. (1983). *J. chem. Phys.* **78**, 4439.

H$_2$–CO. Andres, J., Buck, U., Meyer, H., and Launay, J. M. (1982). *J. chem. Phys.* **76**, 1417.

O$_2$–O$_2$. Brunetti, B., Luiti, G., Luzzatti, F., Pirani, F. and Vecchiocattivi, F. (1981). *J. chem. Phys.* **74**, 6734.

N$_2$–N$_2$. Ling, M. S. H. and Rigby, M. (1984). *Mol. Phys.* **51**, 855.

HF–HF. Barton, A. E. and Howard, B. J. (1982). *Faraday Dis. chem. Soc.* **73**, 45.
Brobjer, J. T. and Murrell, J. N. (1983). *Mol. Phys.* **50**, 885.

H$_2$O–H$_2$O. Clementi, E. and Habitz, P. (1983). *J. phys. Chem.* **87**, 2815.
Gellatly, B. J., Quinn, J. E., Barnes, P., and Finney, J. L. (1983). *Mol. Phys.* **59**, 949.

CO$_2$–CO$_2$. Turfa, A. F. and Knaap, H. F. P. (1981). *Chem. Phys.* **62**, 57.

NH$_3$–NH$_3$. Duquette, G., Ellis, T. H., Scoles, G., Watts, R. O., and Klein, M. L. (1978). *J. chem. Phys.* **68**, 2544.

CH$_4$–CH$_4$. Righini, R., Maki, K., and Klein, M. L., (1981). *Chem. Phys. Lett.*, **80**, 301.

SF$_6$–SF$_6$. Powles, J. G., Dore, J. C., Deraman, M. B., and Osae, E. K. (1980). *Mol. Phys.* **50**, 1089.

F$_2$–F$_2$. Murthy, C. S., Singer, K., and McDonald, I. R. (1983). *A.C.S. Adv. in Chem. Ser.* **204**, 189.

Cl_2–Cl_2. Price, S. L. and Stone, A. J. (1982). *Mol. Phys.* **47**, 1457.

Br_2–Br_2. Singer, K., Taylor, A., and Singer, J. V. L., (1976) *Mol. Phys.* **33**, 1757.

C_6H_6–C_6H_6. Evans, D. J. and Watts, R. O. (1975, '76) *Mol. Phys.* **29**, 277; **31**, 83; **32**, 93.

$C_5H_5N_5$ *and other azabenzenes.* Price, S. L. and Stone, A. J. (1984). *Mol. Phys.* **51**, 569.

CN^-–CN^-. Klein, M. L. and McDonald, I. R. (1983). *J. chem. Phys.* **79**, 2333.

Cl^-–H_2O. Bounds, D. G., and Bounds, P. J., (1983). *Mol. Phys.* **50**, 1125.

8A.4. Large polyatomic molecules

Site–site functions. Chapter 8, sections 8.5.1 and 8.5.2, and suggested further reading.

Convex core functions. Kihara, T. (1978). *Intermolecular forces*, Wiley, New York.

8A.5. Interactions involving condensed phases

See Chapter 8, suggested further reading. Examples for specific systems:

Solvation of Li^+, F^-, NH_3 . . . HF. Noell, J. O., and Morokuma, K. (1975). *Chem. Phys. Lett.* **36**, 465.

Strength of hydrogen bonds. Allen, L. C. (1975). *J. Am. chem. Soc.* **97**, 6921.

H_2–tungsten (001) *surface.* Elkowitz, A. B., McCreery, J. H., and Wolken, G. (1976). *Chem. Phys.* **17**, 423.

N_2–graphite surface. Talbot, J., Tildesley, D. J., and Steele, W. A. (1984). *Mol. Phys.* **51**, 1331.

He–Xe coated graphite. Hutson, J. M. and Schwartz, C. (1983). *J. chem. Phys.* **79**, 5179.

Colloidal systems. See Chapter 8, Section 8.7.2.

Appendix 1
Characteristic properties of some simple substances

	T_c(K)	V_c(cm^3 mol^{-1})	P_c(bar)	T_B(K)	B_0(cm^3 mol^{-1})	$\omega^\dagger$
^{4}He	5.19	57.3	2.27			
Ne	44.40	41.7	27.6	127	9.0	
Ar	150.8	74.9	48.7	410	18.3	−0.002
Kr	209.4	91.2	55.0	577	22.3	−0.002
Xe	289.7	118	58.4	755	29.7	0.002
CH_4	190.5	99	46.1	509.3	25.2	0.013
CF_4	227.6	140	37.4	518.1	48.3	0.173
SF_6	318.7	198	37.6	693	72.0	0.209
$C(CH_3)_4$	433.7	303	32.0			0.195
N_2	126.2	89.5	33.9	327	22.8	0.040
O_2	154.6	73.4	50.4	405	18.7	0.021
N_2O	309.6	97.4	72.5			0.145
CO_2	304.2	94.0	73.8	713	30.2	0.225
C_2H_6	305.4	148	48.8			0.105
C_3H_8	369.8	203	42.5			0.152
C_2H_4	282.4	129	50.3			0.085

The critical parameters are taken from: (1) Mathews, J. F. (1972) *Chem. Rev.* **72,** 71 (inorganic substances); (2) Kudchadker, A. P., Alani, G. H., and Zwolinski, B. J. (1968) *Chem. Rev.* **68,** 659 (organic compounds).

$\dagger$ In the extended principle of corresponding stages the reduced properties of a fluid are taken to be functions of three variables:(Pitzer, K. S. and Curl, R. F., Jr. (1957) *J. Am. chem. Soc.* **79,** 2369) the reduced temperature, $T_R(= T/T_c)$, reduced pressure $P_R(= P/P_c)$ and the acentric factor ω, defined in Chapter 4. For second virial coefficients the analytical expressions given below were developed and were found to reproduce the results for many substances quite accurately. It should be noted however that the recent low-temperature (below 0.6 T_c) measurements for the rare gases are not well reproduced.

$$\frac{BP_c}{RT_c} = (0.1445 + 0.073\omega) - (0.330 - 0.46\omega)T_R^{-1} - (0.1385 + 0.50\omega)T_R^{-2}$$

$$- (0.0121 + 0.097\omega)T_R^{-3} - 0.0073\omega T_R^{-8}.$$

Appendix 2
Molecular parameters

Approximate values of the maximum well depth, ε/k, and the collision diameter σ. These may be used in conjunction with the corresponding states functions of Appendix 3 or the reduced properties given in Appendix 4 to calculate thermophysical properties.

Substance	$\varepsilon/k(K)$	$\sigma(nm)$
He	10.41	0.2602
Ne	42.0	0.2755
Ar	141.6	0.3350
Kr	199.8	0.3581
Xe	281	0.3790
N_2	104.2	0.3632
O_2	126.3	0.3382
CO_2	245.3	0.3762
CH_4	161.3	0.3721
CF_4	156.5	0.4478
SF_6	207.7	0.5252
C_2H_6	241.9	0.4371
C_3H_8	268.5	0.4992
nC_4H_{10}	285.6	0.5526
iC_4H_{10}	260.9	0.5629
C_2H_4	244.3	0.4070
N_2O	266.8	0.3703
CCl_3F	267.4	0.5757
$CHClF_2$	288.3	0.4647

The values of ε/k and σ given in this table are not necessarily those that secure the *optimum* representation of the properties of the gases by means of the correlations given in Appendix 3. For some species small adjustments have been made to the parameters so that they coincide with the best estimates of the true well depth and collision diameter of the species.

Appendix 3
Corresponding states correlation of thermophysical properties

The correlation is based upon the hypothesis that, to a good degree of accuracy, the intermolecular potentials for a number of pair interactions can be rendered conformal by the choice of two scaling factors ε and σ characteristic of each interaction, which are given in Appendix 2. From this hypothesis it follows that all the collision integrals for this universal potential are universal functions of a reduced temperature $T^* = kT/\varepsilon_c$. The combinations of these universal collision integrals necessary for the evaluation of the viscosity, diffusion coefficient, and thermal conductivity of monatomic gases and gas mixtures at low density and the viscosity and diffusion coefficient of polyatomic gas mixtures have been correlated empirically.

For the viscosity, to a first approximation,

$$\eta = \frac{2.6696 \times 10^{-2}\,(MT)^{1/2}}{\sigma^2 \Omega^{(2,2)*}(T^*)}$$

where

$$T^* = kT/\varepsilon$$

and the viscosity is measured in μPa s $(= \mu$N s m$^{-2} = 10\,\mu$poise), the temperature T in K and the length parameter of the potential σ in nm. M is the relative molecular mass.

For the thermal conductivity of a *monatomic gas*, to a first approximation

$$\lambda = \frac{0.83236(T/M)^{1/2}}{\sigma^2 \Omega^{(2,2)*}(T^*)}$$

where the thermal conductivity is measured in mW m^{-1} K^{-1}. For the self-diffusion coefficient

$$D = \frac{2.6636 \times 10^{-5}(T^3/M)^{1/2}}{P\sigma^2 \Omega^{(1,1)*}T^*}$$

where the diffusion coefficient is measured in 10^{-5} m^2 s^{-1}, and the pressure, P, in MPa $(= 10^6$ N m$^{-2} - 10$ bar).

The reduced second virial coefficient, B^*, is also a functional of the pair potential function (Chapter 4) and for the monatomic gases can be included in the correlation scheme. $B(T) = b_0 B(T^*)$, where $b_0 = 1261.3\,\sigma^3$ for σ in nm and b_0 in cm^3 mol^{-1}. The correlations of these quantities as functions of the reduced temperature are given below.

$$\Omega^{(2,2)*} = \exp\{0.46649 - 0.57015\ln T^* + 0.19164(\ln T^*)^2 - 0.03708(\ln T^*)^3$$
$$+ 0.00241(\ln T^*)^4\} \qquad 1 < T^* < 90$$

$$\Omega^{(1,1)*} = \exp\{0.348 - 0.459 \ln T^* + 0.095(\ln T^*)^2 - 0.010(\ln T^*)^3\}$$
$$1 < T^* < 25$$

$$\mathbf{B}^* = (T^*)^{-1/2}\{-0.7175 + 0.2377 \ln T^* + 0.50172\,(\ln T^*)^2 - 0.1026\,(\ln T^*)^3$$
$$+ 0.0068\,(\ln T^*)^4\}\exp\left(\frac{1.0582}{T^*}\right) \qquad 0.5 < T^* < 130$$

The accuracy of the correlation scheme is estimated as ± 1.0 per cent for viscosity, ± 2 per cent for the diffusion coefficient, and ± 1.0 per cent for the thermal conductivity of monatomic gases and gas mixtures. The correlation cannot be directly applied to the thermal conductivity of polyatomic gases or mixtures containing polyatomic components.

References

Kestin, J., Ro, S. T., and Wakeham, W. A. (1972). *Physica* **58**, 165.
Kestin, J., and Mason, E. A., (1973). *AIP Conf. Proc.* **11**, 137.

Appendix 4
Collision integrals and second virial coefficients for a realistic potential

The table contains a listing of the reduced collision integrals $\Omega^{(1,s)*}$ and the reduced second virial coefficients B^* as functions of $T^* = kT/\varepsilon$, for the $n(r)$–6 potential

$$U^*(r^*) = \left\{ \left(\frac{6}{n-6}\right) r^{*-n} - \left(\frac{n}{n-6}\right) r^{*-6} \right\}$$

where $n = 13 + 8(r/r_m - 1)$, $r_m = 1.1217\sigma$, $U^* = U(r)/\varepsilon$ and $r^* = r/r_m$. This function gives a good representation of the interactions of the inert gases and may also be used to estimate the properties of other substances (Maitland and Smith 1978).

The relationships between the transport coefficients and the collision integrals are given in Appendix 3, as is the relation of B^* to $B(T)$.

The zero-pressure Joule–Thomson coefficient $\mu^0 = (\partial T/\partial P)_H$ can be obtained from the expression

$$(\mu^0 C_p^0)^* = \frac{\mu^0 C_p^0}{b_0} = T^* \frac{dB^*}{dT^*} - B^*.$$

C_p is the low pressure molar heat capacity of the gas measured at constant pressure.

Reference

Maitland, G. C. and Smith, E. B. (1973). *Chem. Phys. Lett.* **22**, 443.

T^*	$\Omega^{(1,1)*}$	$\Omega^{(1,2)*}$	$\Omega^{(2,2)*}$	B^*	$T^*(\mathrm{d}B^*/\mathrm{d}T^*)$
0.1	3.5781	3.1989	3.7244	—	—
0.2	2.8540	2.5273	3.0143	—	—
0.3	2.4597	2.1359	2.6585	$-0.25216694E+2$	$0.707356E+2$
0.4	2.1807	1.8596	2.3987	$-0.12276094E+2$	$0.276316E+2$
0.5	1.9689	1.6591	2.1871	$-0.76580332E+1$	$0.153160E+2$
0.6	1.8038	1.5110	2.0125	$-0.53825969E+1$	$0.101123E+2$
0.7	1.6727	1.3993	1.8683	$-0.40483892E+1$	$0.738371E+1$
0.8	1.5669	1.3128	1.7491	$-0.31776046E+1$	$0.574676E+1$
0.9	1.4803	1.2445	1.6500	$-0.25668660E+1$	$0.467115E+1$
1.0	1.4085	1.1895	1.5672	$-0.21159163E+1$	$0.391684E+1$
1.2	1.2966	1.1066	1.4377	$-0.14963839E+1$	$0.293710E+1$
1.4	1.2142	1.0473	1.3425	$-0.10922939E+1$	$0.233342E+1$
1.6	1.1511	1.0026	1.2702	$-0.80890754E+0$	$0.192624E+1$
1.8	1.1013	0.9676	1.2138	$-0.59978781E+0$	$0.163380E+1$
2.0	1.0610	0.9393	1.1587	$-0.43954250E+0$	$0.141391E+1$
2.5	0.9871	0.8871	1.0875	$-0.16716947E+0$	$0.104685E+1$
3.0	0.9363	0.8504	1.0331	$0.22536871E-2$	$0.820869E+0$
3.5	0.8989	0.8225	0.9937	$0.11660378E+0$	$0.667786E+0$
4.0	0.8697	0.8001	0.9634	$0.19818863E+0$	$0.557218E+0$
4.5	0.8460	0.7816	0.9392	$0.25877860E+0$	$0.473601E+0$
5.0	0.8263	0.7657	0.9191	$0.30515749E+0$	$0.408141E+0$
6.0	0.7947	0.7396	0.8872	$0.37052137E+0$	$0.312237E+0$
7.0	0.7701	0.7187	0.8652	$0.42334833E+0$	$0.245351E+0$
8.0	0.7500	0.7011	0.8423	$0.44273711E+0$	$0.196046E+0$
9.0	0.7331	0.6861	0.8252	$0.46355129E+0$	$0.158204E+0$
10.0	0.7185	0.6729	0.8105	$0.47861170E+0$	$0.128254E+0$
12.0	0.6941	0.6506	0.7859	$0.49781803E+0$	$0.838965E-1$
14.0	0.6743	0.6321	0.7658	$0.50827688E+0$	$0.526796E-1$
16.0	0.6576	0.6165	0.7488	$0.51372859E+0$	$0.295443E-1$
18.0	0.6432	0.6029	0.7340	$0.51613887E+0$	$0.117658E-1$
20.0	0.6306	0.5908	0.7209	$0.51662328E+0$	$-0.229756E-2$
25.0	0.6044	0.5658	0.6938	$0.51322273E+0$	$-0.271416E-1$
30.0	0.5835	0.5457	0.6719	$0.50675589E+0$	$-0.432292E-1$
35.0	0.5662	0.5290	0.6537	$0.49920674E+0$	$-0.543707E-1$
40.0	0.5514	0.5148	0.6380	$0.49139170E+0$	$-0.624553E-1$
50.0	0.5272	0.4914	0.6121	$0.47619686E+0$	$-0.732004E-1$
60.0	0.5078	0.4727	0.5913	$0.46222162E+0$	$-0.798083E-1$
80.0	0.4780	0.4439	0.5589	$0.43812895E+0$	$-0.870267E-1$
100.0	0.4554	0.4222	0.5343	$0.41830745E+0$	$-0.904392E-1$

Appendix 5
Inversion functions for gas phase properties

The inversion methods that utilize the functions tabulated here are based on the use of the thermophysical property, P, to define a characteristic temperature-dependent cross-section $\pi \tilde{r}_P^2$ and hence a characteristic length $\tilde{r}_P$. The potential energy at this separation $U(\tilde{r}_P)$ is given by the equation

$$U(\tilde{r}_P) = G_P(T^*)kT$$

where $G_P(T^*)$ is the appropriate inversion function. The success of the method is due to the fact that the functions $G_P(T^*)$ are not very sensitive to the nature of the potential energy function and thus may be estimated using only approximate potential functions. A knowledge of T^* ($= kT/\varepsilon$) and so an estimate of the well depth ε (or in practice any characteristic feature of the potential function) may be required. Accounts of the inversion techniques are given in Sections 4.6 and 5.7.

Viscosity

From Chapter 5,

$$\eta = \frac{5}{16} \frac{(m\pi kT)^{1/2}}{\bar{\Omega}^{(2,2)}(T)} f_\eta. \tag{A5.1}$$

From the definition $\tilde{r}_\eta = [\bar{\Omega}^{(2,2)}/\pi]^{1/2}$, $\tilde{r}_\eta$ may be related to the coefficient of viscosity. Evaluating the various constants involved gives the simple equation

$$\tilde{r}_\eta = 0.16339 \left[\frac{(MT)^{1/2} f_\eta}{\eta} \right]^{\frac{1}{2}}$$

where $\tilde{r}_\eta$ is in nanometres, M is the relative molecular mass, T the absolute temperature in K, η is in units of μPa s (μN s m^{-2}), and f_η is a factor in the range 1.000–1.008, which may be calculated using an approximate potential function. Then $U(\tilde{r}_\eta) = G_\eta(T^*) . kT$. The values of G_η calculated using the Lennard–Jones 12–6 function and the BBMS potential, a realistic function devised for argon, are given in Table A5.1. The corresponding values of f_η are given in Table A5.2.

Self-diffusion.

The coefficient of self-diffusion is related to the collision integral, $\bar{\Omega}^{(1,1)}$ as shown in the equation

$$D = \frac{3}{8P} \left[\frac{k^3 T^3}{m} \right]^{1/2} \frac{f_D}{\bar{\Omega}^{(1,1)}}. \tag{A5.2}$$

Table A5.1
Inversion functions

T^*	BBMS				Lennard–Jones(12–6)			
	G_η	G_D	G_α	G_B	G_η	G_D	G_α	G_B
0.3	-0.561	-0.691	-1.062	-0.00373	-0.549	-0.679	-1.063	-0.0056
0.4	-0.566	-0.746	-1.212	-0.0254	-0.573	-0.743	-1.196	-0.0367
0.5	-0.599	-0.817	-1.293	-0.0979	-0.611	-0.806	-1.287	-0.117
0.6	-0.644	-0.874	-1.328	-0.239	-0.652	-0.858	-1.320	-0.251
0.7	-0.684	-0.908	-1.301	-0.402	-0.689	-0.893	-1.294	-0.418
0.8	-0.714	-0.923	-1.225	-0.595	-0.718	-0.910	-1.220	-0.585
0.9	-0.732	-0.920	-1.111	-0.744	-0.736	-0.908	-1.111	-0.720
1.0	-0.739	-0.902	-0.969	-0.833	-0.743	-0.892	-0.979	-0.806
1.1	-0.737	-0.869	-0.810	-0.861	-0.741	-0.861	-0.833	-0.839
1.2	-0.727	-0.824	-0.644	-0.831	-0.730	-0.819	-0.682	-0.823
1.3	-0.709	-0.770	-0.477	-0.756	-0.711	-0.768	-0.530	-0.767
1.4	-0.686	-0.706	-0.313	-0.650	-0.686	-0.711	-0.382	-0.683
1.5	-0.657	-0.635	-0.156	-0.525	-0.657	-0.649	-0.238	-0.581
1.6	-0.624	-0.566	-0.007	-0.390	-0.623	-0.548	-0.101	-0.468
1.7	-0.558	-0.490	$+0.134$	-0.254	-0.588	-0.517	$+0.0281$	-0.350
1.8	-0.550	-0.417	0.267	-0.121	-0.551	-0.450	0.150	-0.233
1.9	-0.511	-0.340	0.388	$+0.0063$	-0.512	-0.382	0.264	-0.118
2.0	-0.471	-0.267	0.502	0.127	-0.474	-0.315	0.371	-0.008
2.4	-0.316	$+0.013$	0.882	0.518	-0.324	-0.0626	0.733	$+0.367$
2.8	-0.175	0.254	1.165	0.790	-0.190	$+0.159$	1.009	0.643
3.0	-0.114	0.360	1.278	0.893	-0.130	0.257	1.121	0.750
3.4	-0.005	0.544	1.465	1.050	-0.025	0.430	1.310	0.918
4.0	$+0.127$	0.762	1.670	1.205	$+0.103$	0.640	1.523	1.088
4.5	0.212	0.910	1.795	1.288	0.189	0.779	1.656	1.183
5.0	0.281	1.017	1.893	1.346	0.255	0.893	1.761	1.250
6.0	0.384	1.186	2.032	1.419	0.358	1.066	1.916	1.336
8.0	0.510	1.388	2.190	1.483	0.485	1.284	2.103	1.415
10.0	0.582	1.500	2.278	1.508	0.558	1.410	2.209	1.447
12.0	0.629	1.570	2.328	1.518	0.605	1.492	2.278	1.461
15.0	0.674	1.632	2.372	1.524	0.651	1.571	2.345	1.469
20.0	0.720	1.687	2.407	1.523	0.694	1.646	2.410	1.471

Again defining the distance $\tilde{r}_D = [\bar{\Omega}^{(1,1)}/\pi]^{1/2}$ we obtain an expression for $\tilde{r}_D$ in terms of D, giving

$$\tilde{r}_D = 5.161 \times 10^{-3} \left[\frac{f_D}{PD} \left(\frac{T^3}{M} \right)^{1/2} \right]^{1/2}$$

where P is the pressure in MPa and D is the coefficient of self-diffusion in 10^{-5} m^2 s^{-1}.

Table A5.2

Second-order Kihara correction factors for the calculation of transport properties

	12–6				BBMS			
T^*	f_η	f_D	f_λ	f_α	f_η	f_D	f_λ	f_α
0.3	1.00098	1.00020	1.00153	1.04683	1.00163	1.00077	1.00184	1.03349
0.5	1.00001	1.00003	1.00001	1.00521	1.00027	1.00006	1.00042	1.02659
0.7	1.00006	1.00006	1.00010	0.99350	1.00002	1.00001	1.00003	0.99930
1.0	1.00000	1.00001	1.00001	1.00036	1.00003	1.00009	1.00005	0.98551
1.5	1.00033	1.00058	1.00051	0.97203	1.00051	1.00072	1.00079	0.97574
2.0	1.00133	1.00106	1.00207	0.97277	1.00149	1.00169	1.00232	0.97680
2.4	1.00224	1.00256	1.00348	0.97621	1.00234	1.00245	1.00364	0.98017
3.0	1.00345	1.00371	1.00537	0.98181	1.00344	1.00341	1.00536	0.98576
5.0	1.00581	1.00601	1.00903	0.99433	1.00546	1.00511	1.00850	0.99878
10.0	1.00732	1.00765	1.01139	1.00394	1.00636	1.00577	1.00990	1.00996
20.0	1.00774	1.00817	1.01204	1.00689	1.00587	1.00508	1.00912	1.01493

The potential energy at the separation $\tilde{r}_D$ is given by the equation

$$U(\tilde{r}_D) = kT. G_D(T^*),$$

where G_D is a function similar to G_η and is tabulated in Table A5.1. The correction factor f_D is given in Table A5.2.

Thermal conductivity.

Like viscosity, the coefficient of thermal conductivity, λ, of a substance with no internal degrees of freedom, is related to the collision integral, $\overline{\Omega}^{(2,2)}$. The equation is

$$\lambda = \frac{25c_v}{32\overline{\Omega}^{(2,2)}} \left\{ \frac{kT\pi}{m} \right\}^{1/2} f_\lambda = \frac{15}{4} \eta . \frac{k}{M} . \frac{f_\lambda}{f_\eta}. \tag{A5.3}$$

Since $\overline{\Omega}^{(2,2)}$ is equal to $\pi \tilde{r}_\lambda^2$, then

$$\tilde{r}_\lambda = 0.9123 \left\{ \left(\frac{T}{M} \right)^{1/2} \frac{f_\lambda}{\lambda} \right\}^{1/2}$$

where λ is the coefficient of thermal conductivity in units of $mW\,m^{-1}\,K^{-1}$.

The potential energy may be obtained using the equation

$$U(\tilde{r}_\lambda) = kT. G_\eta(T^*).$$

The function G_η is involved, since both viscosity and thermal conductivity are related to the same collision integral. However, f_λ differs slightly from f_η and is tabulated in Table A5.2.

Thermal diffusion.

One inversion method uses $\Omega^{(1,2)}$ determined from the isotopic thermal diffusion factor for monatomic species, $[\alpha_0]_1^\kappa$. This is related to collision integrals by

$$C^* = \frac{8[\alpha_0]_1^\kappa A^*}{45} + \frac{5}{6}$$

and since

$$C^* = \Omega^{(1,2)*}/\Omega^{(1,1)*} = \bar{\Omega}^{(1,2)}/\bar{\Omega}^{(1,1)}$$

$$A^* = \Omega^{(2,2)*}/\Omega^{(1,1)*} = \bar{\Omega}^{(2,2)}/\bar{\Omega}^{(1,1)}$$

$$\bar{\Omega}^{(1,2)} = \frac{8[\alpha_0]_1^\kappa}{45} + \frac{5}{6A^*}\bar{\Omega}^{(2,2)}$$

$[\alpha_0]_1^\kappa$ may be obtained from the experimental values $[\alpha_0]_{\text{expt}}$ by the relation

$$[\alpha_0]_1^\kappa = [\alpha_0]_{\text{expt}}/f_\alpha$$

where f_α is a correction factor that is insensitive to the potential energy function. In general $\bar{\Omega}^{(2,2)}$ is well known from viscosity measurements. Hence $\bar{\Omega}^{(1,2)}$ can be determined and

$$\tilde{r}_\alpha = [\bar{\Omega}^{(1,2)}/\pi]^{1/2}$$

$$U(\tilde{r}_\alpha) = G_\alpha kT.$$

Again G_α and f_α are tabulated in Tables A5.1 and A5.2. [Strictly G_α should be labelled $G_{\Omega(1,2)}$].

Second virial coefficients.

We define

$$\tilde{r}_{\text{B}} = \left[\frac{B + T\left(\dfrac{dB}{dT}\right)}{2/3\pi N_{\text{A}}}\right]^{1/3}$$

$$= 9.256\left[B + T\left(\frac{dB}{dT}\right)\right]^{1/3}$$

where B is the second virial coefficient in $\text{m}^3\,\text{mol}^{-1}$ and $\tilde{r}_{\text{B}}$ is in nm.
   Again

$$U(\tilde{r}_B) = G_B kT.$$

Answers to exercises

Chapter 1

E 1.1.

	$\rightarrow\rightarrow$	$\rightarrow\uparrow$
U	-8.3×10^{-22} J	0
U	-7.0×10^{-23} J	-4.4×10^{-23} J

E 1.2.

	$1.5r_m$	$4r_m$
U_8/U_6	22%	3.1%
U_{10}/U_6	6.1%	0.1%

E 1.3. $A = 3\sqrt{3}/2 = 2.5981$.

Chapter 2

E 2.1. $E = 3 \times 10^{-23}$ J.

E 2.2. Differentiating eqn (2.2) gives

$$\frac{d\mathbf{c}_c}{dt} = \frac{m_a(d\mathbf{c}_a/dt) + m_b(d\mathbf{c}_b/dt)}{m_a + m_b}$$

$$= \frac{F - F}{m_a + m_b} = 0$$

i.e. the centre of mass velocity $\mathbf{c}_c$ is constant.

E 2.3. $I/I_0 = 0.2$; $d = 0.26$ nm.

Chapter 3

E 3.1. There is a positive outer maximum in $V(L, r)$

E 3.2. The appropriate plot is well-width ($= 2(r - r_m) = 2(U/\kappa)^{1/2}$
where $\kappa = 2\pi\nu\mu^2$, $\nu = 6 \times 10^{11}$ Hz, and $\mu = 3 \times 10^{-26}$ kg) as a function of energy U
measured from the well minimum.

E 3.3. $U(r) = \varepsilon\{1 - e^{-\beta(r - r_m)}\}^2$
where $\varepsilon = 8.29 \times 10^{-22}$ J $= 60.0$ K, $\beta = 9.45 \times 10^9$ m^{-1} $= 9.45$ nm^{-1}.

Chapter 4

E 4.1. $\sigma = 0.341$ nm.

E 4.2. $(\partial T/\partial P)_H = 0.80$ K atm^{-1}.

E 4.3. $B = 98$ cm^3 mol^{-1}.

Chapter 5

E 5.1. $\eta = 12.30 \ \mu\mathrm{Pa\,s}$ (cf. experimental value of $12.35 \ \mu\mathrm{Pa\,s}$).

E 5.2. $D_{\mathrm{SF}_6}/D_{\mathrm{N}_2} = 0.300$.

E 5.3. $\alpha_{\mathrm{o}} = 0.338$.

Chapter 6

E 6.1. $a = 4.33 \times 10^{-10} \ \mathrm{m}$; $U(a) = -4.37 \times 10^{-21} \ \mathrm{J}$; $U(a)/k = -317 \ \mathrm{K}$.

E 6.2. $U(a) = -4.92 \times 10^{-21} \ \mathrm{J}$; $U(a)/k = -357 \ \mathrm{K}$.

Chapter 7

E 7.1.

	Ar	CO_2	
U_{conf}	-4.84	-3.87	$\mathrm{kJ\,mol}^{-1}$
$U_{\mathrm{trans}} \ (3/2 \ RT)$	1.05	3.79	

E 7.2. $U_{\mathrm{conf}} = (-2\pi N/3)\varepsilon\sigma^3 \ (N/V)$.

Index

ab initio calculations 16, 166
absorption spectra 64
  analysis for the inert gases 71
  anisotropic systems 72, 73, 76–80
  collision-induced 65
  hydrogen–argon 75
  interpretation 66
  measurement 64, 66
  Morse-potential 67
  nitrogen-argon 75
  of dimers 175
  of X_2–Y systems 72
  results for inert gases 70–2
  RKR analysis 67, 68, 167, 168, 172
  rotational fine structure 167
  semi-rigid systems 73
  simple harmonic oscillator 66
  strongly anisotropic systems 73, 78 80
  ultra-violet 167
  van der Waals molecules 29, 62
  weakly anisotropic systems 73, 76–78
acentric factor 98, 215
adhesion 201
adsorption 198
aggregates of molecules 201
alcohols 193
alkali ion-inert gas mixtures 172, 211
alkali metal–mercury systems 172
n-alkanes 190, 192, 206
ammonia–hydrogen chloride complex 194
anisotropic systems 21, 72–80, 119, 138, 174
argon
  absorption spectrum 71
  potential function 137, 168
  scattering 38
  (*see also inert gases*)
argon–hydrogen
  absorption spectrum 75
  potential 77, 79, 175, 176
argon–nitrogen, absorption spectrum 75
atom–molecule systems 177, 211
atoms
  Groups I and II 172
  open-shell 170–2

Axilrod–Teller energy 27, 30, 92, 167, 168, 197
p-azoxyanisole 156, 197

Barker–Pompe potential 168
BBMS potential 221
benzene 185, 190, 191
biological,
  cells 201, 207
  macromolecules 190, 193
  membranes 207
Boltzmann weighted energy 7
  dipole–dipole 8
  dipole–quadrupole 8
  quadrupole–quadrupole 8
bound states 63
Boyle temperature 81, 87, 97, 215

calcite 206
calcium 172
calcium fluoride 206
carbon dioxide 190
carbon dioxide–inert gases 177
carbon tetrafluoride 89, 191
charge
  distribution 30, 187
  penetration 180
charge-transfer 180, 194
classical turning point 42
coagulation 203
collision diameter 216
collision integral 116, 217, 219
collision rate 108
colloids 198, 201–7
combining rules 25, 101, 159, 160, 170, 186, 205
complexes 194
compression (compressibility) factor 81, 101, 103
computer simulation 141, 147, 190
condensed phases 127, 141, 198, 213
configurational integral 104

conformality 21, 170, 217
conformational isomers 187, 190
contour diagram 178, 183
corresponding states 21, 96–9, 170, 217
corrugation effects 199
critical properties 81, 85, 215
cross-section
  classical 48
  deflection angle and 55
  differential 38, 46, 50, 167
  for anisotropic interactions 57
  individual differential 57
  inelastic scattering 174
  integral 38, 47, 50
  inversion of 53
  oscillations in 52
  potential from 53
  rigid spheres 47
  state-to-state differential 167
crystal structure
  and intermolecular forces 128, 167
  determination of 129
cyclohexane 192

damping functions 21, 177
de Broglie wavelength 36
Debye–Huckel reciprocal length 202
Debye model 134
deflection
  angle 42, 117
  function 43, 49
  function and cross-section 55
deuterium–HD scattering 57
dielectric constant 192
diffraction 129, 145
diffusion coefficient 28, 107, 113–15, 117,
    124, 217, 221
dimers,
  bound 62, 63, 65
  hydrogen fluoride 180
  infra-red spectrum 175
  metal 211
  metastable 63
  water 182, 183
dipole moment 5, 31, 179, 188, 189
dispersion 4, 181
dispersion coefficients 186
dispersion energy 10–11, 180, 186
  Drude (harmonic oscillator) model 32–34
  expansion 34
  higher order contribution 11
  London 201
dispersion forces 166
  in liquids 192
distributed multipole method 180

distribution function,
  atom–atom 145
  radial 142, 144
  triplet 143
DLVO theory 202
DNA 190
donor–acceptor complexes 194
double layer 202, 203, 209
Drude model 10, 32–34

Einstein model 134
electrical double layer 202, 203, 209
electrolyte solutions 161–2
electron affinity 194
electrophoresis 207
electrostatic energy 4–8, 30–2, 180, 186
energy,
  charge-transfer 180
  dipole–dipole 6, 32
  dipole–induced dipole 9
  dipole–quadrupole 6
  dispersion 10–11, 180, 186, 201
  electrostatic 4–8, 30–2, 180, 186
  exchange 180
  induction 4, 8–10, 186, 189
  intermediate range 16
  intramolecular 190
  long-range 11
  overlap 186
  polarization 180
  quadrupole–quadrupole 6
  short-range 12–16
  zero point 137
equation of state
  perfect gas 81
  van der Waals 1, 84–6, 163
  virial 28, 86–7
Eucken factor 119
exchange
  energy 180
  forces 14
  –polarization 180
excluded volume 84
experimental methods,
  gas imperfection 28, 101–3
  spectroscopy 29, 64–6
  transport properties 28, 121–5

Fick's law 114
flocculation 202, 203
Fourier's law 112

gas imperfection 28
  experimental methods 101–103

glory effect 45, 47, 50, 51
Gouy–Chapman layer 202
graphite 200, 213

Hagen–Poiseuille equation 121
Hamaker constant 202, 204, 205, 206
hard sphere
  molecules 47, 108, 141, 151
  potential 90
harmonic oscillator model 32
Hartree–Fock dispersion (HFD) func-
    tion 21, 170, 175, 200
heat capacity 29, 130
Heitler–London model 12
helium (see also inert gases)
  second virial coefficient 89
  scattering 38
helium–hydrogen potential 173
Hellmann–Feynman theorem 14
hexadecapole moment 185
hydration forces 208–9
hydrocarbon 190, 192, 205
hydrogen 12
  potential 173
  scattering 57
  second virial coefficient 89
  triplet state 170, 172
hydrogen–argon
  absorption spectrum 75
  potential 77, 79, 175, 176
hydrogen bond 16–17, 154, 179, 181, 193,
    195, 213
hydrogen fluoride dimer 179, 180
hydrogen–helium potential 173
hydrogen–inert gas potentials 77, 79, 174–
    176
hydrophilic surfaces 208
hydrophobic interaction 207

impact parameter 42, 120
induction energy 4, 8–10, 26, 179, 186, 189
inert gas
  –alkali ion mixtures 172, 211
  –carbon dioxide potentials 177
  –hydrogen potentials 174
  –inert gas potentials 168–71
  –nitrogen potentials 177
  –oxygen potentials 177
  spectra 70–72
interactions
  atom–diatom 173
  charge–transfer 194
  diatom–diatom 173
  gas–surface 200

hydrogen atom 12
hydrophobic 207
in liquids 192–7, 210
many–body 192, 198, 204
molecule–surface 198–201
polymer–polymer 204
solute–molecule 192
surface–surface 198
triplet–hydrogen 170, 172
unlike 25, 170
intermediate range energy 16
internal rotations 197
intramolecular energy 190
inversion
  functions 94, 221–4
  methods 19, 167–8
  of ion mobilities 172
  of second virial coefficients 93–96, 200
  of transport properties 120
ionic systems 184–185
ionization potential 194
ion mobilities 172, 184
ion–molecule complexes 194
isomers,
  conformational 187, 190

Joule–Thomson effect 82–84, 102, 219

Kihara core model 191, 192, 196
krypton–hydrogen potential 175
krypton (see also inert gases)
  absorption spectrum 71
  scattering 38

lattice dynamics 135
lattice energy 29, 129
lattice vibrations 130, 132
  anharmonicity 136
Lennard–Jones 12–6 function 20, 139, 165,
    166, 199, 221
Lifshitz theory 204
liquid crystals 156–7, 195–7
liquid mixtures 157–63
liquids 29, 141–63
  hydrogen–bonded 154
  interactions in 192–7, 210
  molecular 154–6
  perturbation theories of 142, 150–3, 154
  structure 142–6
lithium ion
  –carbon monoxide potential 184

lithium ion (*contd.*)
—hydrogen potential 184
—hydrogen scattering 59, 184
—nitrogen potential 184
—X_2 potential 184
London dispersion energy 10, 180, 186, 201
long-range
energy 11
forces 166
Lorentz–Berthelot combining rules 25, 101,
159, 170

magnesium dimer potential 172
Maitland–Smith potential 21, 170, 171, 200,
219
many-body interactions 167, 177, 192, 197,
198, 204
Maxwell–Boltzmann distribution 108
Mayer f-function 87, 88, 105
mean free path 109, 111
melting points 128
membranes 207
mercury
—alkali metal systems 172
dimer potential 172
—sodium potential 56
mesomorphic phases 195
metal
dimers 211
surfaces 200
methane 190
mica surfaces 207, 208
micelles 207
molecular beams 29, 167, 200
crossed 39
detectors for 40
intensity 37
spectrometers 66
molecular collision 36
sudden approximations 60
interference 49, 52
one-body equivalent 42
orbiting 45
pairs 65
quantum mechanical theory 48
rainbow angle 45
reference frames 41, 46
molecular complexes 194
molecular crystals 128, 138, 190
molecular dynamics 147, 148, 168
molecular ions 184
molecular liquids 154–156
monatomic
solids 137
systems 19, 168–172, 209
Monte Carlo method 147, 168

Morse potential 67
multipole
expansion 31, 180
moments 5, 180, 187

nematic phase 195
neon (*see also inert gases*)
absorption spectrum 71
scattering 38
neon–hydrogen potential 175, 176
Newton's law 110
nitrobenzene 190
nitrogen
—argon absorption spectrum 75
—inert gas potential 177
—nitrogen potential 177
second virial coefficient 89
non-additivity (see also Axilrod–Teller
energy) 25–8, 91, 132, 167, 177, 184,
189
contributions to lattice energy 129, 137
nucleic acids 190

octopole 5, 185
overlap energy 4, 12, 186
oxygen-inert gas potential 177

parameter expansion (PAREX) 25
partition function 104
Pauli exclusion principle 12
perfect gas equation of state 81
perturbation theories 142, 150–3, 154
Barker and Henderson 152
Weeks, Chandler, and Anderson 152
phase shift 50
point charge model 180, 186–189
polarizability
anisotropy 196
atomic 186
bond 189
excess 193
molecular 189, 193
static 9
polarization 8, 181
effects 179
energy 180
polymer 190
biological 190
—liquid interactions 206
—polymer interactions 204
potassium cyanide potential 185
potential—*see under substance name(s)*
potential expansion (POTEX) 24

potential functions 19, 165
  Barker–Pompe 168
  BBMS 221
  development of 165
  18–6 35
  exp–6 20
  from spectroscopic measurements 166
  gas–solid 199
  Hartree Fock dispersion (HFD) 21, 170, 175, 200
  ion–atom 172
  Kihara 191, 196
  Lennard–Jones 12–6 20, 139, 165, 166, 199, 221
  Maier and Saupe 196
  Maitland–Smith, $n(\bar{r})$–6 21, 170, 171, 200, 219
  Morse 67
  multicentre 23
  n–m 35
  n–6–4 172
  site site 23, 185, 186, 189–90
  stockmayer 179
Principle of Corresponding States 21, 96–9, 170, 217
proteins 190, 207

quadrupole moment 5, 31, 185, 188
quantum mechanical calculations 12, 48–53, 166, 177, 182, 184, 185, 195
quartz 206

radial strength functions 175
rainbow
  rotational 59
  scattering 38, 45, 48, 51, 52
  supernumary 52
retardation effect 202, 205
rotational fine structure 167
Rydberg–Klein–Rees (RKR) analysis 67, 68, 167, 168, 172

sapphire 206
scale parameters 186
scattering 36, 37
  glory 45, 47, 50
  hydrogen 57
  inelastic 55, 174, 184
  inert gases 38
  lithium ion–hydrogen 59, 184
  polyatomic molecules 54
  rainbow 48
  surface 200

second virial coefficient of gases
  corresponding states 96–9
  definition 81
  inversion of 94
  gas–surface 200
  of mixtures 100
  non-spherical molecules 90
self-diffusion 221
Senftleben–Beenakker effects 191, 166, 174
shape
  molecular 191, 195
  parameters 186
short-range energies 12–16
silica 206
silicon tetrafluoride potential 192
site–site potential functions 23, 185, 186, 189–90
Slater–Kirkwood equation 186
sodium–mercury potential 56
solids 29–30, 127–40
  phase transitions in 138
solvation 213
solvent effects 192
spectroscopic measurements 166
  (see also absorption spectra)
spectrum
  infra-red 175
  microwave 180
  time-of-flight 59
  ultra-violet 167
Stark effect 65
steric repulsion 203
Stern layer 202
Stockmayer potential 179
sublimation, heat of 177, 190
supersonic nozzles 39, 65, 167
surfaces 197–210, 213
surfactant molecules 207

tetracyanoethylene potential 192
tetramethylsilane potential 191
thermal conductivity
  of gases 28, 107, 112–13, 117, 166, 217, 223
  experimental methods 124
  of hard sphere gases 113, 115
thermal diffusion 117, 125, 224
time–correlation functions 149
transport properties 28
  and intermolecular forces 119–21
  experimental methods 121–5
  hard-sphere gases 107–114, 115
  liquids 149
  polyatomic gases 118–119
  real gases 114–118
tungsten surfaces 213

valence bond model 12
van der Waals
  constants 86
  dimers 166
  equation 1, 84–86, 163
  molecules 29, 62
  one-fluid model 159
  radii 187
velocity auto-correlation function 149
vibration
  energy levels 167
  lattice 130, 132
  normal modes 133
  zero point 132
virial
  equation 28, 86–87
  theorem of Clausius 143
virial coefficients
  and intermolecular forces 87, 103–6
  gas mixtures 100
  quantum corrections 92
  second–see second virial coefficients
  third 91
  third cross coefficients 100
viscometers 122, 123

viscosity
  of gases 28, 107, 110–12, 117, 166, 177,
    217, 221
  experimental measurements 121–4
  hard-sphere gas 112, 115
  Newton's law 110

water
  dimer 182, 183
  energy contour diagrams 183
  on surfaces 208
  potential 181–184
  second virial coefficient 183
well-depth parameter 69, 216, 221
well-width 90

xenon–hydrogen potential 175
xenon (see also inert gases)
  absorption spectrum 71
  scattering 38

zero-point
  energy 137
  vibration 132